STATE POLICIES AND INTERNAL MIGRATION: STUDIES IN MARKET AND PLANNED ECONOMIES

The World Employment Programme (WEP) was launched by the International Labour Organisation in 1969, as the ILO's main contribution to the International Development Strategy for the Second United Nations Development Decade.

The means of action adopted by the WEP have included the following:
— short-term high-level advisory missions;
— longer-term national or regional employment teams; and
— a wide-ranging research programme.

Through these activities the ILO has been able to help national decision-makers to reshape their policies and plans with the aim of eradicating mass poverty and unemployment.

A landmark in the development of the WEP was the World Employment Conference of 1976, which proclaimed *inter alia* that 'strategies and national development plans should include as a priority objective the promotion of employment and the satisfaction of the basic needs of each country's population'. The Declaration of Principles and Programme of Action adopted by the Conference have become the cornerstone of WEP technical assistance and research activities during the closing years of the Second Development Decade.

This publication is the outcome of a WEP project.

State Policies and Internal Migration

STUDIES IN MARKET AND PLANNED ECONOMIES

Edited by A.S. Oberai

A study prepared for the International Labour Office within the framework of the World Employment Programme with the financial support of the United Nations Fund for Population Activities

CROOM HELM
London & Canberra
ST. MARTIN'S PRESS
New York

© 1983 International Labour Organisation
Croom Helm Ltd, Provident House, Burrell Row,
Beckenham, Kent BR3 1AT
Croom Helm Australia, PO Box 391, Manuka,
ACT 2603, Australia

British Library Cataloguing in Publication Data

State policies and internal migration.
   1. Migration, Internal—Social aspects
   2. Migration, Internal—Economic aspects
   I. Oberai, A.S.   II. International Labour Office
   304.8'1   HB1951
   ISBN 0-7099-1933-6

All rights reserved. For information write:
St. Martin's Press, Inc., 175 Fifth Avenue, New York, NY 10010
First published in the United States of America in 1983

Library of Congress Cataloging in Publication Data
Main entry under title:

State policies and internal migration studies in market
   and planned economies.

   Bibliography: p.
   Includes index.
   1. Migration, Internal—Government policy—Developing
countries—Addresses, essays, lectures. 2. Migration,
Internal—Government policy—Asia—Addresses, essays,
lectures. 3. Migration, Internal—Government policy—
Poland—Addresses, essays, lectures. I. Oberai, A.S.
HB1952.S72 1983   304.8   83-40097
ISBN 0-312-75630-5

Printed and bound in Great Britain

LIST OF CONTENTS

LIST OF TABLES

PREFACE

Population movements and the spatial distribution of population have become matters of vital concern in most developing countries. The major urban centres are already too large and growing too rapidly relative to the smaller cities, towns and rural areas, creating greater inequity between regions, increasing the management costs of overcongested large cities, and hampering the general goals of development. This was amply demonstrated in a survey carried out by the United Nations in 1978. Among the 116 developing countries covered by the UN survey, only 6 reported the over-all spatial distribution of their population as entirely acceptable (United Nations, 1980, p. 19). Of the remaining 110 countries, 42 regarded the spatial distribution as unacceptable to some extent and 68 found it to be highly unacceptable.

The UN survey also indicates that the majority of governments not only perceive the problems but have already adopted policies and programmes to slow down or reverse the flow of migration towards the metropolitan regions and other urban centres, relying either on incentives and disincentives or on coercive methods.

But, despite the considerable importance attached to the subject by many governments, there has been a general lack of emphasis on the study of migration-influencing policies as an issue in policy analysis and for their impact on migration. Most governments make little attempt to evaluate programmes and activities concerned with the distribution of population, or to examine their feasibility and consistency with other development objectives. Consequently, where specific policies such as direct controls on mobility, resettlement programmes, and urban dispersal schemes have been introduced, they have had little long-term effect on migration, or less effect than intended, and have proved both costly and administratively difficult to implement. One reason why population distribution policies have had limited success so far is that they have often been formulated without an adequate knowledge of the causes and consequences of migration, so that little is known as to whether the existing policies are in fact justified and appropriate.

It is to fill this gap that the ILO initiated a comprehensive research programme on migration at the beginning of 1976, under which several small-scale studies of migration-influencing policies, based largely on secondary data, were conducted in a number of developing countries in Asia, Africa, Latin America and Eastern Europe. The major objective of these studies was to identify the causes of success or failure of specific policies. The types of policies examined included not only those specifically introduced to influence migration, but also those which indirectly affect the rate, direction or composition of migration. Particular emphasis was given to rural development policies, including measures of land reform, promotion of rural industries, resettlement schemes, and land development programmes. Other policies studied included rural-urban price and incentive differentials, urban development schemes, and more generally state intervention in the promotion of capitalist or socialist development.

The present volume reports the findings of the studies carried out in Asia and in Eastern Europe. The country case studies included are those conducted in India, Indonesia, Malaysia, Nepal, Sri Lanka, and Poland. In addition, the policy experiences of China, Japan, the Republic of Korea, and the Philippines are also discussed. The volume therefore provides a comparative analysis of population distribution problems and policies in countries of varying levels of economic development and with different types of economy - planned, market and mixed. The collection of studies carried out in Latin America and Africa have been published separately (see, for example, Peek and Standing, 1982; Gaude, 1982. Other recent ILO studies on migration include Todaro, 1976; Birks and Sinclair, 1980; Böhning, 1981; Oberai and Singh, 1983).

Many people in addition to the authors of the chapters have contributed to this volume. A workshop organised in collaboration with the ILO Labour and Population Team for Asia and the Pacific was held in Bangkok in 1980 to discuss the preliminary results of the country case studies. The participants included both researchers and government officials. I am indebted to all of them, both for the papers and for the discussions.

I am also grateful to Richard Anker, Lionel Demery, Ghazi Farooq, Jacques Gaude, Cayetano Paderanga, Peter Peek, Gerry Rodgers, M.T.R. Sarma, Salem Sethuraman, Alan Simmons, Guy Standing, and René Wéry for their valuable comments on the earlier drafts of the chapters.

I also owe thanks to Kailas C. Doctor, Chief, Population and Labour Policies Branch, ILO, and to Gerry Rodgers, Head, Research Wing, for providing advice and encouragement in the preparation of this volume.

The work of typing the manuscript and the production of the camera-ready copy was handled by Mary Dominguez. I gratefully acknowledge her assistance.

And, finally, I wish to express my thanks to the United Nations Fund for Population Activities (UNFPA) for their support of this work.

Needless to say, the views and opinions expressed in this volume reflect those of the individual authors, and not, necessarily, those of the ILO or UNFPA.

A.S. Oberai

Geneva

⋅.

Chapter 1

INTRODUCTION

By A.S. Oberai

In many developing countries, the rate of growth of the urban population has assumed alarming proportions and has already had far-reaching economic and social consequences. The urban population in developing countries increased from 275 million in 1950 to 793 million in 1975. During the same period, whereas the over-all population in developing countries grew by 2.17 per cent per annum, the urban population increased by 4.27 per cent (United Nations, 1980, pp. 125-127). Nearly half of this growth in the urban population is due to rural-urban migration, and large and metropolitan cities are growing much faster than small and medium-sized towns. And in spite of the widespread unemployment and under-employment in almost all cities, rural-urban migration continues unabated.

Projections of the rural and urban population do not give rise to optimism about the future urbanisation situation in developing countries. It is estimated that the urban population will increase from 793 million in 1975 to 2,115 million in the year 2000, while the urban proportion of the total population will rise from 28 per cent to 43 per cent. Such an annual geometric growth rate – averaging 3.9 per cent over 25 years – will call for a massive increase in investment to cope with employment, housing, sanitation, and other associated problems of urban growth.

In recognition of these problems of spatial population distribution, the majority of developing countries have already taken measures to alter migration flows or rural and urban population configurations. But for many governments the development of national, humane, and cost-effective policies continues to be hindered by the absence of information on the causes and consequences of migration, and more particularly by the lack of knowledge of the likely impact of different types of policy.

The purpose of the studies in this volume is three-fold: first, to identify policies and programmes that are explicitly or implicitly designed to influence migration; second, to investigate why they were adopted and how far they have actually been implemented; and third, to assess their direct and indirect consequences.

The volume contains eight chapters. After examining the basic causes of rapid urbanisation and the growth of large cities, particularly in Asia, the rest of this chapter has been devoted to a brief review of the consequences of migration and the need for government intervention. Chapter 2 attempts to synthesise the main conclusions of the country case studies presented in the subsequent chapters and to bring out the implications for policy design. Chapter 3 critically evaluates the development strategies and their influence on migration in Peninsular Malaysia. Chapter 4 examines the impact of industrial decentralisation, rural resettlement, and rural industrialisation programmes on internal migration in India. Chapter 5 deals with land and industrial development policies in Sri Lanka. It also examines the extent to which rural development policies, including village expansion, land reform, and social welfare policies regarding housing, health and education, have enhanced the retentive capacity of the rural areas. Chapter 6 places the evolution of transmigration policies in Indonesia in an historical context, depicting their adoption as a response to the socio-economic pressures arising from the pattern of underdevelopment in that country. As such it presents an interesting and provocative alternative analysis to many other studies which have done little more than attribute the failure of the transmigration programme to lack of funds, administrative inefficiency or population growth. Chapter 7 presents a wide-ranging analysis of land settlement schemes as a means of population redistribution in Nepal. It also examines the causes of success or failure of such schemes from the point of view of the populations concerned, in relation to the original objectives of the policy-makers, and with respect to development objectives other than population redistribution. And, finally, Chapter 8 attempts to place migration in Poland in the context of the post-war socialist transformation of the Polish economy, and explores the interesting question of whether the lower level of urbanisation relative to the degree of industrialisation is a result of socialist development strategy or of historical legacies.

Basic Causes of Rural-urban Migration and the Growth of Large Cities

In many Asian countries, as in the Third World in general, rural poverty, manifested in low agricultural incomes, low productivity, and underemployment, is an important factor in pushing migrants out of rural areas towards areas with greater employment opportunities. A number of recent studies have noted the increasing

unemployment and declining incomes of the rural poor
(ILO, 1976). The pressure of population, resulting in
higher labour-land ratios, has been widely hypothesised
as one of the important causes of poverty and rural
out-migration in Asia. With a given level of technology,
there is a certain labour force which can be absorbed by
agriculture. As the population continues to grow,
unless the non-crop husbandry sectors (dairy, poultry,
forestry and fisheries) or cottage and small-scale industries in the rural areas expand so as to absorb the
surplus, increasing numbers of people must move to the
urban centres or other rural areas to obtain gainful
employment.

But the pressure of population is not the only or
even the principal cause of the increasing unemployment
and poverty of the rural population.[1] Equally important causes are the low rate of investment in agriculture,
fragmentation of land ownership, inequalities in the distribution of land and other productive assets, institutional
mechanisms which discriminate in favour of the owners of
wealth (e.g. in provision of credit), and a pattern of
relative prices, and therefore investment and technological
change, biased against labour (see, for example, Standing
and Sukdeo, 1977; Griffin, 1976). One of the main
reasons for this bias is the fact that much farm technology is imported from labour-scarce countries and
favours the use of capital relative to labour.

Most developing countries in Asia as well as in other
regions of the world have a highly unequal distribution of
land ownership.[2] Although land reform legislation
exists in many Asian and Latin American countries, redistribution of land has rarely been sufficient to contribute

---

[1] Population pressure is not always synonymous
with out-migration. Boserup, for instance, postulates
that the adoption of new labour-intensive methods of
cultivation might help alleviate the pressure of population
on available resources. She argues that an increase in
population density through population growth would
hasten the adoption of more intensive methods of farming.
If this were the case, high population densities would
have a positive impact on the introduction of new agricultural techniques which would reduce the outflow of
migrants (see Boserup, 1965; Bilsborrow, 1979).

[2] For example, the Gini concentration ratio for the
distribution of landholdings in India, Pakistan, and the
Philippines has been estimated at around 0.6 (ILO, 1976).
The ratios are even higher in most of Latin America and
parts of Africa.

to a significant reduction in inequality. Unequal land distribution has consequences for manpower absorption. Numerous farm management studies have shown that small farms absorb more labour than medium and large farms (see for example, Barraclough, 1970; Abercrombie, 1972). Further, unequal distribution of land has adverse effects on the distribution of rural income.

The structure of the capital and labour markets in many countries is also such that unequal distribution of income arising from an unequal distribution of productive assets is reinforced by the operations of the price mechanism. Those who have access to credit from institutions are able to meet their requirements for capital on relatively easy terms, which further encourages investment in capital-intensive technologies. Those with smaller farms usually have to borrow from moneylenders and others at usurious interest rates.

As a result of their greater access to new technology, the large landowners become richer, whereas the small farmers who find the new technology too expensive and risky are left behind. Because the subsequent increase in productivity and output brings down prices, the small farmers are doubly hurt: using traditional forms of production and receiving lower prices, their income drops. Many small farmers are forced to sell their land to the large landowners and seek wage labour in the area, to work as temporary or seasonal workers in other areas to supplement their reduced farm income, or to migrate permanently away from the area (Romero and Flinn, 1976; Peek, 1980).

The continuation of large inequalities in the ownership of land during a period of rapid demographic growth in Asia has resulted in increased landlessness and near-landlessness. Table 1 brings out the proportion of the rural labour force which falls into the categories of landless and near-landless in some selected Asian countries. As can be seen in the table, except in Malaysia and Thailand, the proportion of landless and near-landless has assumed alarming proportions. [1]

As the pool of landless and near-landless becomes enlarged, new forms of social relations in production emerge based on debt labour. The increasing commercialisation also affects the landless through changes in the modes of wage payment, particularly the increase of

---

1   The near-landless are the members of the rural labour force whose holdings are insufficient to provide them with a family livelihood and who must, therefore, spend a substantial proportion of their labour time working for others (see Esman, 1978).

Table 1: Incidence of landlessness and near-landlessness in selected Asian countries

Country	Rural labour force as % of the total labour force	Landless as % of the rural labour force	Near-landless as % of the rural labour force	Landless and near-landless as % of the rural labour force
Bangladesh (1977)	85	28	61	89
India (1971-72)	83	32	47	79
Indonesia (1971) (Java only)	63	60	29	89
Malaysia (1970)	68	12	39	51
Pakistan (1972)	58	43	45	88
Philippines (1971)	69	55	26	81
Sri Lanka (1971)	80	54	19	73
Thailand (1971)	78	10	40	50

Adapted from: Esman (1978), table 2.

monetary rather than share payments. This change speeds up the breakdown of traditional village social and economic relationships, and further encourages many of the landless to migrate to other rural areas (both more prosperous rural areas and frontier areas), while others abandon the countryside and move to the city in search of non-agricultural jobs.

While the forces listed above have led to rural-rural and rural-urban migration among the very poor, the opening of schools in rural areas has probably also done much to stimulate out-migration by providing education and increasing awareness of other opportunities among rural youth. Some migrate to further their education, while others migrate as they become dissatisfied with the prospects of rural life.

A few studies also seem to support the hypothesis that migrants are attracted to cities in search of better entertainment or "bright lights" (Findley, 1977), or better educational facilities for their children. In addition, a number of factors such as the presence of friends and relatives in urban areas to provide initial assistance, and the desire of migrants to break away from the traditional constraints of inhibiting rural social structures, have been cited as likely determinants of migration.

The policies of the state also exercise a powerful influence on the redistribution of population as between the rural and urban areas. The most significant among these are: policies which foster a concentrated growth of industrial infrastructure in the cities, import substitution programmes which are mainly oriented towards meeting the consumption needs of the well-to-do classes, and social service investments which are preponderantly urban. Of the utmost importance, however, is the weight assigned to the agricultural sector in the over-all development strategy. Evidence from many Asian countries suggests that the prime objective of supporting agriculture is often to extract the maximum agricultural output with the minimum amount of investment. Such policies invariably reinforce the position of the dominant farming groups, which make further gains through successful lobbying for input subsidies and higher procurement prices for their marketable surpluses. Fiscal policies with respect to agricultural incomes also tend to be regressive, in that it is often not easy to tax agricultural surpluses, as the Indian experience clearly shows. The cumulative effect of all this is to make the distribution of agricultural income and wealth less equal, and to create an environment for investment in capital-intensive technology.

Until recently, governments have also favoured public and social service investments in urban areas, particularly major urban areas (see, for example, Brigg, 1973). Similar investments in the rural areas have been neglected. At times, governments have engaged in deficit spending in order to provide jobs for the urban unemployed. This has had an inflationary impact on prices and wages in the urban areas. The minimum wage for unskilled labour has tended to rise much faster in urban areas because urban wage-earners have often succeeded in pressurising companies or the government into raising their wages. As a result, the income differential between urban and rural unskilled workers has been increasing, and this has encouraged further migration.

The above discussion is largely relevant for market and mixed economies, particularly in Asia. In socialist countries such as in Eastern Europe one may generally expect lower rates of internal migration. To the extent that the system in these countries implies a greater degree of equality of incomes, the maintenance of full employment, a more uniform development of regions, and a relatively equal distribution of social infrastructure and services throughout the country, there should be less incentive to move from one location to another.

In practice, however, this is not always the case. In many socialist countries, equality of incomes and opportunities is generally regarded as less important than fulfilment of the plan, particularly during the early phases of development. Moreover, agricultural policies that are accepted as an integral part of the development strategy create a strong "push effect" for migration from rural areas. This is largely because agricultural policies in many socialist countries, at some early stage, include the collectivisation of agriculture and a relative neglect of that sector of the economy in order to increase investment in industry (Fallenbuchl, 1977, p. 306). Even when a more balanced allocation of investment as between agriculture and other sectors is later introduced, agriculture remains a less important and less prestigious sector, with incomes lagging behind those in other sectors of the economy, particularly heavy industry. Moreover, during the early stages of socialist transformation, the emphasis on industrialisation prevents the narrowing of the gap between urban and rural infrastructures and facilities. This strengthens the "pull effect" of the towns and tends to increase the pace of rural-urban migration.

In most socialist countries, however, several measures are taken simultaneously to reduce the flow of internal migration. Administrative controls are used to limit movement into certain cities unless jobs in priority sectors have been secured in advance (see, for example, Chapter 8). Productive investment is often given priority over housing and urban living conditions and there is usually a shortage of amenities even in those cities that enjoy priority treatment.

The interaction of these forces, those that encourage and those that discourage migration, induces migration substitution, in the form of rural-to-urban commuting - a phenomenon linked with the expansion of the dual-occupational (farmer-worker) group, as in Poland. Rural-urban migration then tends to be replaced in this situation by rural-rural migration from villages in remote areas to those close to the industrial cities, in the same or in other regions, from which commuting is feasible.

Consequences of Migration and the Need for Government Intervention

Historically, the process of industrialisation and economic development has been associated with considerable migration to the growing urban centres of labour demand. But the extent of rural-urban migration in recent years has greatly exceeded the capacity of the urban sectors to absorb the influx. Fears have been expressed that migration is a major cause of rising urban unemployment, overcrowded housing, and relative shortage of public amenities. Migrants unable to find adequate employment or any employment at all are forced to live in squatter settlements or inner-city slums lacking even the most basic facilities. The resulting pressure on residential land and housing causes land speculation and excessive rents, and generally tends to depress living standards in the urban areas. Nor does migration to the cities leave the rural areas unaffected: not only does it tend to draw away their more dynamic members, but it may also divert national investment resources towards the towns (see Oberai, 1979).

Not all the consequences of migration are necessarily detrimental, however. Migration may yield substantial benefits to individual migrants and their families, and at the same time have a positive and significant impact on economic development. The influx of migrants seeking employment in the cities may stimulate industrial expansion and industrial investment by providing a cheap supply of unskilled and semi-skilled labour, and by filling certain labour bottlenecks. In the rural areas, out-migration may lead to a lowering of the labour-land ratio and thus provide a new environment conducive to changes in rural production techniques. In addition, the transfer of labour to the more productive, urban activity may eventually generate a growing demand for rural output and thus alter the rural-urban terms of trade, raising agricultural prices relative to those of urban goods.

The increase in agricultural prices is, in turn, likely to stimulate agricultural production and raise rural incomes. Remittances from the urban areas may also improve the distribution of income between the rural and urban populations, especially where such remittances are used for investment purposes (see, for example, Oberai and Singh, 1980).

Among specialist observers, therefore, opinion on the desirability of policies to restrain the growth of urban areas is sharply divided. Some studies have even suggested that many of the economic and other problems attributed to urban size and growth are really more closely related to failure in the planning and management of public urban facilities and services (see, for example, Townpore, 1979). While the debate continues, many planners now believe that steps need to be taken to curtail rural-urban migration and to reduce the flow of migrants to the large metropolitan areas.

But is government intervention necessary? Several observers have argued against government intervention to control migration (see Stohr, 1979). They give several reasons for this. First, it restricts the freedom of the individual to move and to choose his own residential and working location. Second, it is often very costly and administratively difficult to implement. Third, it is usually ineffective because of the complexity of the factors which govern population distribution. Fourth, it primarily serves the interest of certain dominant groups in society. And, finally, it throws out of gear an automatic equilibrium mechanism which on its own would have balanced the spatial distribution of population with economic opportunities.

But there are several reasons why the automatic equilibrium mechanism may not work as hypothesised. It is assumed, for example, that when labour moves from a less developed to a more developed area, wages will rise in the former and fall in the latter. This process is likely to continue until migration stops as a result of a substantial reduction in the wage differential between the two areas. This may not occur, however, since it is usually the young, economically active and better educated persons in the origin areas who dominate the migration flows. Their departure may adversely affect agricultural productivity and incomes, and thus encourage more migration.

Many observers, therefore, do believe that state intervention is necessary to regulate migration and to mitigate its adverse consequences (see Mabogunje, 1979). They argue that population movements left free and unguided lead to an inequitable, irrational and imbalanced distribution of population over the geographic space.

First, because clustering results in a wide variety of external economies for industrial and commercial firms as well as for households, pure market forces tend to concentrate economic activity in a few focal areas (see Hansen, 1979). Second, efficient utilisation of national resources is a legitimate concern in many developing countries and calls for government intervention. Even in Asia, where one is more conscious of extreme pressure of population on the land, there are still areas where underutilised land is available, and there are considerable opportunities for a fuller utilisation of the abundant labour resources if their mobilisation and productive organisation can be carefully planned. Third, in heterogeneous societies, marked by important cultural, political and linguistic differences, a major concern of governments is to maintain the cohesion of the state and national unity. But the growth of nativist movements in many countries in recent years conflicts with the objectives of ethnic integration and national unity and calls for solutions through appropriate spatial policies. And, finally, large concentrations of population and economic activity in a few cities entail numerous social costs and lead to a breakdown of urban services. But, despite these problems, urban growth may continue because external diseconomies are not internalised costs for private producers or for individual migrants - and this for many provides a strong justification for state intervention.

Chapter 2

AN OVERVIEW OF MIGRATION-INFLUENCING
POLICIES AND PROGRAMMES

By A.S. Oberai

Migration-influencing policies are generally classified
as direct policies, explicitly designed to alter migration
behaviour, or indirect policies, whose impact on migration
is secondary to the basic goals of the policy.
Direct policies are those that prescribe residence and
movement patterns. They include bans on urban in-
migration, travel restrictions, and resettlement programmes. Indirect policies are generally aimed at
improving conditions in the areas of origin or in alternative destinations such as frontier zones or intermediate
cities. The purpose is to reduce the relative attractiveness of large cities by making other areas more attractive.
Indirect policies are, therefore, likely to have a more
enduring and broader impact on migration, as they
operate on more crucial motivations among larger segments
of the population. Examples of indirect policies are:
provision of public services and amenities in the rural
areas, administrative and industrial decentralisation, land
reforms, rural development programmes, price support for
agricultural products to raise rural incomes, and income
policies to keep urban wage rates from rising. Similarly,
education and many other urban development policies
aimed at helping migrants and improving the "quality of
life" in the urban areas have indirect and unintended
effects on migration.
For the purposes of this overview chapter, however,
policies and programmes are classified according to
whether they prohibit or reverse migration, redirect or
channel it to specific rural or urban locations, reduce the
total volume of migration, or encourage or discourage
urban in-migration. The discussion of each type of
policy is accompanied by a description of its rationale and
implementation mechanism, examples of countries that have
had recourse to it, and its intended or actual effect on
migration.

Direct Controls on Mobility

Several countries in Asia as well as in other regions
have taken direct measures to reverse the flow of

migration and to stop or discourage migration to the urban areas. Such measures have included administrative and legal controls, police registration, and direct "rustication" programmes to remove urban inhabitants to the countryside.

In China, during the period 1969-73, between 10 and 15 million urban secondary school leavers were resettled in rural areas (Simmons, 1979, p. 90). At the same time administrative controls were introduced to prevent or limit the migration of rural inhabitants to the cities. Passes were required to leave a rural area and to enter and secure accommodation in an urban area. Police checks at entry points in the city, as well as periodic checks in urban areas, were used to enforce this regulation.

The major objective of the population redistribution programmes in China was to stimulate the development of the rural areas, increase agricultural production, and reduce or prevent unemployment in the cities. Unfortunately, lack of adequate data makes it difficult to estimate how many resettled students have stayed in rural areas and the extent to which this has contributed to rural development in China. However, many researchers have observed that the Chinese programmes were remarkably successful in transferring population to the rural areas (see, for example, Simmons, 1979). This may have helped the authorities to check problems of urban unemployment and poverty,[1] but if so it was largely accomplished by instituting laws and administrative procedures that restrict freedom of movement to a degree unknown in most other nations.

In Poland, after the Second World War, administrative restrictions were imposed on entry into the large cities, and there was obligatory registration of every change of residence. In order to be able to move to a city a person was first required to obtain a job of sufficiently high priority and to secure support from his future employer (the state or a firm or institution) for his application to the local authorities for accommodation. Manipulation of housing accommodation was resorted to as another method of diverting population to designated areas.

Frenkel's analysis presented in Chapter 8 suggests that internal migration, and particularly rural-urban migration, would have been substantially greater in Poland in the absence of an urban housing shortage and administrative restrictions. The existence of these obstacles

---

[1] As one observer noted, "in Chinese cities they have ... no teeming shantytowns, no one sleeping on the street, no beggars" (Munro, 1977, pp. 1-2).

appears to have induced some substitution in the form of commuting from rural residence to urban employment.

In Indonesia a slightly less strict system of statutory controls on migration to Jakarta is used as a method of dissuasion rather than of outright prohibition (see IRG, 1979, p. 120). In 1970 the Governor of Jakarta passed a decree limiting the entry of migrants, according to which a migrant to Jakarta must first apply for a "short visit" card and deposit a sum of money equivalent to twice the amount of the fare to Jakarta. Within six months of his arrival, if he can prove he has a job and accommodation, he is refunded his deposit and allowed to buy an identification card testifying to his "Jakarta citizenship". If he cannot prove he has a job and a home, the migrant is given a one-way ticket to his place of origin.

Over the past several years the Indonesian Government has also introduced other policies to limit the opportunities for employment of unskilled workers in Jakarta, including the removal of unlicensed sidewalk vendors, marginal workers, and beggars from the city streets.

These regulations have proved extremely difficult to administer and have incidentally led to a rise in petty corruption. There are simply too many people breaching them for effective control to be possible. In a single night, for example, city officials and police rounded up 13,000 persons who were without identification cards and sent them back to their villages of origin. However, it is believed that they returned to Jakarta almost immediately. The city authorities still periodically round up people whose papers are not in order, but the effort is acknowledged to be futile (Simmons, 1979, p. 93). Despite claims that migration to Jakarta has been drastically cut down, a number of studies suggest that the various administrative measures have had only a modest impact (see, for example, Sethuraman, 1976). The city is continuing to grow quickly, in large part through migration.

The Jakarta case shows that in the absence of tight control over the movement of people, as in China and Poland, it is almost impossible to reduce the flow of migration to large cities. It also shows the conflict inherent in attempting to guarantee freedom of movement on the one hand and to correct imbalances in population distribution through legal restrictions on the other.

Redirecting Migrants to Other Areas

(a) Land settlement schemes

The availability of public land has prompted many countries to adopt schemes bearing such labels as resettlement, transmigration, land colonisation or land development. These schemes have been designed to achieve one or more of the following aims: to provide land and income to the landless, increase agricultural production, correct spatial imbalances in the distribution of population or exploit frontier lands for reasons of national security. There have also been instances where extensive land settlement programmes have been used in place of more radical agrarian reform measures. Although they have the common aim of raising the incomes and standards of living of the rural landless, land settlement schemes in individual countries appear to differ in their approach and aims.

In Poland, during the period 1945-50, 2.7 million people moved from the south-eastern and central territories to the western and northern territories (Fallenbuchl, 1974, pp. 287-318). These population movements were largely organised by the state administration and were connected with alteration of the national frontiers and with wartime dislocations. The settlement operation – as the organisation of these transfers used to be called in Poland – was more or less completed by the end of the 1950s. It played an important role in the economic integration of the western and northern territories with the other parts of the country as well as constituting an example of active and direct state participation in the organisation of mass population movements.

In Indonesia the idea of population transfer is far from new. The Dutch tried it in 1905, but for economic reasons rather than to relieve population pressures, when they moved Javanese to Southern Sumatra where additional labour was needed (see Chapter 6).

Starting in the mid-1960s Indonesia pursued the idea much more vigorously and by the end of 1974 the transmigration programme had resettled about 790,000 people, while at least as many had moved independently without being officially recorded (MacAndrews, 1978). However, throughout the period there have been wide gaps between the targets set for the programme at various times and the actual numbers moved – due both to over-enthusiasm in setting the targets and to political and administrative problems (Oey and Astika, 1978). As regards the most often quoted objective – relieving population pressures – the programme has had only a minimal impact in Java. A recent study noted that the number of people who move from the outer provinces to Java is about two and a half times greater than that of people migrating from Java to the outer islands (Bahrin, 1979a, p. 300).

In Peninsular Malaysia the Federal Land Development Authority (FELDA), the oldest and largest organisation responsible for rural development and settlement schemes, was established in 1956. In 1966, the government created an additional organisation, the Federal Land Consolidation and Rehabilitation Authority (FELCRA). Whereas FELDA's programmes concentrated on the landless poor, FELCRA came into being in order to assist other poor rural groups such as those with small and fragmented landholdings. The available evidence suggests that the FELDA projects and other settlement schemes, combined with broader rural development programmes, have been rather successful in achieving their objectives (Bahrin, 1979b, pp. 34-44). A recent study observes that they appear to have increased rural production, raised rural incomes and lowered rural-urban migration. After adjusting urban population growth data for definitional and boundary changes, the study concludes that between 1957 and 1970 the urban population of Malaysia grew at the same rate as the rural population: 2.6 per cent a year. Since the natural population growth was somewhat lower in urban areas, some rural-urban migration obviously took place over the period, but the rate appears to have been low (Ying, 1977, p. 87).

Chan argues, however, that sole dependence on resettlement per se will not suffice, and that greater attention needs to be paid to employment, land tenure and income objectives (see Chapter 3). Unless this is done, second generation problems associated with a worsening labour-land ratio will reduce the area's retentive capacities.

In India rural resettlement projects have mainly been unsuccessful. In an evaluation of the Dandakaranya Project, for example, Bose observes that the project has failed to achieve its objectives (see Chapter 5). When it was set up in 1958, its aim was to resettle 20,000 displaced families by 1959. It was thought that it could eventually absorb as many as 2 million displaced persons. Bose's study indicates that by August 1979 only 31,007 families had been settled, and of these 11,364 (36.6 per cent) had already deserted. The number of deserters has been increasing in recent years: during 1978-79, 844 new families were settled while 2,504 families deserted.

In a recent review of planned resettlement in Nepal, Kansakar reaches similar conclusions:

"...the programme has not been able either to emerge as an example of agricultural development or to raise the standard of living of the resettlers. The apathy on the part of the resettlers in agricultural development and the discouraging environmental conditions of the resettlement projects indicate that the resettlers are just waiting to acquire land ownership certificates in order to sell the allotted land and go elsewhere" (Chapter 7, p. 244).

In one completed project in Nawalpur, where the land titles have been conferred, nearly 50 per cent of the original settlers have already disposed of their plots and left (ibid., p. 242).

By contrast, in Sri Lanka several studies point to the success of land settlement and irrigation schemes, which have resulted in increased food production and considerable relief of population pressures in the wet zone (see Chapter 4). About 75,000 families were resettled between 1946 and 1971. Taking account of the estimated average size of the resettled households, this means that nearly 4 per cent of the island's population was resettled within a period of 25 years. But a number of recent studies indicate that the major land settlement projects in Sri Lanka have not been profitable in terms of the returns on capital invested. The benefit-cost ratio of the Nagadeepa project, for example, is estimated to range from 0.42 to 0.82 according to the discount rates adopted, which vary between 6 and 15 per cent (see Kunasingham, 1972).

The above review of land settlement schemes suggests that they have so far made no more than a modest contribution to the solution of the problems of redistribution of population, unemployment and poverty, except in planned economies such as Poland. A major shortcoming has been the choice of sites that are unsuitable in respect of location, accessibility and soil conditions; this has led to slow development of the projects, and their abandonment or costly resurrection at a later stage. Lack of infrastructural facilities, such as housing, drinking water, approach roads and access to important market towns, and the scarcity of non-agricultural employment are among the important factors which have induced people to abandon the land resettlement projects. Other problems have been weak organisational structures, a lack of experienced personnel, and interdepartmental rivalry resulting in minimal co-operation and co-ordination. The success of FELDA in Malaysia can be attributed in part to its ability to obtain the assistance of other government departments when needed. Conversely, projects in Indonesia and elsewhere have been largely unsuccessful because such assistance has not been forthcoming.

(b) Growth pole and dispersed urbanisation strategy

One of the basic goals of decentralised industrialisation and regional development policies has been the reduction of inter-regional disparities and the redirection of migrants from large metropolitan areas to smaller, medium-sized towns. Initial infrastructure investments, tax benefits and other incentives have been provided to encourage industry to move to small urban locations. The conceptual basis for most of these efforts has been "growth pole" theory, which assumes that initial government expenditures in sparsely settled or previously economically disadvantaged regions will lead to self-sustaining economic growth with beneficial effects on their hinterland (Simmons, 1979, p. 98).

Japan provides an example of national attempts to reduce the overconcentration of population in principal cities, develop "counter-magnets", and improve the regional distribution of productivity and incomes. Poland seems to have encouraged the decentralisation of industry to exploit regional resources and to absorb the local labour force. India was one of the first Asian countries to experiment with industrial estates. The Government of the Republic of Korea, worried about the excessive concentration of population in Seoul, has adopted a policy of establishing heavy and semi-heavy industries outside the capital itself.

But have growth pole strategies been successful? The available evidence suggests that industrial and urban decentralisation programmes have in fact been fairly successful in the Republic of Korea, Poland and Japan.

In the Republic of Korea much of the industrial growth and migration of the early 1970s was directed to areas outside Seoul but still close to it so that the industries could take advantage of support services, supplies and markets in the capital. As a result the annual rate of growth of Seoul's population dropped from 9.8 per cent (during 1966-70) to 4.5 per cent, while smaller cities around Seoul grew at an impressive rate of 12.7 per cent (ibid., pp. 99-100).

In Poland, the basic socialist principle of uniform distribution of productive forces has led to the dispersal of industry and the creation of new towns in under-developed and rural zones. Secondly, the principle of uniform urbanisation has been followed to restrict overurbanisation of a limited number of cities and towns, and to spread urbanisation out to the countryside. Economic measures like wage differentials, tax reduction, and investment subsidies have been used to encourage industrial and urban decentralisation. Satellite towns have been developed around the large cities to facilitate dispersal of population, and new towns have been planted in selected locations to attract population towards new growth areas. In the process, commuting from the rural hinterland to the urban workplace has been encouraged by the opening up of a network of roads in different regions. Commuting in Poland has helped the process of occupational diversification without changing the place of residence (see Chapter 8).

In Japan growth centre policies have been an integral part of more comprehensive rural and regional development schemes; and, as many studies have noted, decentralisation objectives in Japan are being realised or soon will be (Hansen, 1979, pp. 30-32). With rapid industrial growth in the late 1950s Japan's regional structure underwent a significant change. Capital, technology, production, and labour force came to be concentrated in a few developed areas such as Tokyo, Osaka, Nagoya and Northern Kyushu. As a result, disparities in income and levels of living between the developed and underdeveloped areas widened considerably.

Faced with the problem of excessive concentration of population and economic activity, a comprehensive National Development Plan was formulated in 1962 with a view to achieving regionally balanced economic growth and a dispersal of industrial and urban development. The plan envisaged a nodal system of development focusing on growth pole and "local city" schemes.

The decentralisation of industry and other economic activities was further emphasised in the Development Plan of 1969. A major objective of this plan was to develop local cities and towns offering adequate employment opportunities and educational, social and cultural facilities so as to induce rural dwellers to look for jobs in their home towns and villages or within commuting distance, thereby obviating the need for them to migrate to the metropolitan areas. These policies were accompanied by several programmes specifically aimed at the improvement and development of the rural areas. All this resulted in a reduction in the disparities between the rich and poor regions, which slowed down migration flows and in some cases even reversed them.

In other countries industrial and urban decentralisation programmes have been fraught with problems such as the high costs of direct outlays and subsidies for growth pole ventures.

The experience of growth pole schemes in India reveals that large publicly supported industries involving major government expenditure have tended to be more successful than small and medium-sized industries (Simmons, 1979, p. 98). The failure of the latter is commonly attributed to the inadequate infrastructural support provided to them and the inadequacy of their own resources to overcome problems of isolation from supporting services, related industries, and markets.

Such considerations have led many observers in India to suggest that satellite towns should be created in the vicinity of large cities, but attempts to establish such towns near Hyderabad and elsewhere have also proved a failure. Buch observed recently that satellite towns tend to grow towards the metropolitan centre and therefore defeat the very purpose for which they are established (Times of India (New Delhi, 1 February 1979).

What is the alternative for a large country like India then? Buch suggests that the solution lies in the Punjab's experience, where flourishing villages have made possible the creation of market towns which in turn are supported by manufacturing towns like Ludhiana, Batala and Amritsar. Both market and manufacturing towns draw sustenance from a well defined hinterland. The market towns provide specialised services and commercial goods to more isolated villages, and the basic infrastructure and services necessary for small-scale industries. They act as marketing centres for the surrounding agricultural region, and as a nearby urban place to which rural residents may commute in order to find off-farm jobs. They also provide a small urban alternative for potential migrants from the surrounding area.

The development of market towns, however, requires the nurturing of the linkages both down to the rural villages and up to the bigger cities, and the commitment of considerable administrative and financial resources. It is for this reason that few countries have been able to adopt this strategy on a nation-wide basis.

Reducing the Flow of Migrants

Policies to reduce the over-all volume of migration have often included rural development programmes (including the provision or improvement of amenities in rural areas), the chief purpose of which is to retain potential migrants in the rural areas, and preferential policies for natives with a view to discouraging inter-regional migration.

(a) Rural development programmes

Rural development strategies often have the explicit goal of slowing rural-urban migration. Since rural dwellers often migrate because they lack jobs or adequate incomes, increasing the range of agricultural and non-agricultural job opportunities and raising incomes is expected to reduce migration from the rural areas.

Two types of rural development strategy have been frequently practised in the past. The first is the capital-intensive agricultural development strategy that characterised most rural development programmes in Asian countries before the mid-1970s. These programmes were aimed at increasing output through the adoption of new technology, regardless of employment or equity considerations, but they largely failed to slow the drift of population to the urban areas. One reason why the new technology has generated little employment is because it has been accompanied by excessive mechanisation on large farms. Large farms, employing wage labour and aiming at profit maximisation, are often able to increase labour productivity but they do not create as much employment or use land as intensively as small family farms (see Ishikawa, 1978).

For this reason the need for land reforms has long been felt. Some countries in Asia and other regions have already introduced land reforms with the multiple purpose of increasing production and reducing inequality on the one hand and attracting people to or retaining them in the rural areas on the other.[1] Progress in many countries, however, has often been slow. In Poland, land reforms and the associated growth of agricultural output appear to have reduced migration from rural to urban areas (see Chapter 8), but in Asia, only China, Japan, the Republic of Korea, and Sri Lanka have implemented land reform programmes that have substantially reduced inequalities and improved the farmers' incomes and security of tenure (Findley, 1977). Many of the land reform laws introduced in other Asian countries have been mainly cosmetic.

Tenancy reforms and minimum wage legislation have fared little better. Laws providing for the protection of tenants against eviction and for rent reductions have been enacted time and again in Bangladesh, India, Pakistan, Nepal, Thailand, and the Philippines, but they do not seem to have significantly improved the tenants'

---

[1] Regarding the effects of land reforms on rural out-migration in Latin America see Peek and Standing (1979).

- 20 -

position. On the contrary, in some cases tenancy reforms have actually worsened conditions, especially for small tenants, and encouraged them to migrate from the rural areas (Esman, 1978, pp. 167-168).

The second type of strategy comprises projects loosely grouped under the heading "integrated rural development"; they include land reform, provision of credit and physical infrastructure, introduction of labour-intensive agricultural technology, improvement of rural health care and housing, promotion of non-agricultural job opportunities in the rural areas, and supportive policies at the national level. A basic goal of integrated rural development programmes is the revitalisation of rural life styles by providing social and physical infrastructure in rural areas. People migrate to the towns not only for employment but also for better education, health, and housing. The improvement of living conditions that is the aim of integrated rural development should therefore have a significant effect on internal migration.

Frenkel's analysis of Polish data suggests that rural development policies in Poland during the post-war period have considerably enhanced economic opportunities in the rural areas as well as improving living conditions in the villages (see Chapter 8). As a result the shift of population from agricultural to non-agricultural activities in Poland has largely taken place without a change in place of residence. This has led to a very marked increase in the proportion of non-agricultural population in the rural areas, from 27 per cent in 1951 to 51 per cent in 1978.

In Asia, most integrated rural development projects have not been in existence long enough for the full socio-economic or migration consequences to be assessed. The major changes they aim to bring about will take years to manifest themselves. But some successes can already be reported. The slow pace of rural-urban migration in Sri Lanka, for example, is attributed to the retentive capacity of the rural sector, which is considered to have resulted from the social welfare measures introduced by successive governments since Independence, including free medical services and education, consumer subsidies, and income support for poor farmers in the form of guaranteed prices for their produce (see Chapter 4). A major scheme was also introduced in 1973 with the aim of providing better housing to the lower income groups in rural and semi-rural areas. The equitable distribution of these and other amenities reduced the disparities between rural and urban living conditions. According to an estimate made by Karunatilake (1974), average real income in the urban sector declined by 1.8 per cent a year in the period 1963-73, whereas in the rural and estate sectors taken together it rose by 2 per cent a year.[1]

In the Republic of Korea, rural development programmes have also been actively pursued, particularly
through a Korean-style community development movement
called the "Saemaul undong", which started in 1970 with
the objective of revitalising the rural areas.   After a
three-year period of experimentation the programme was
enlarged, and by 1976 it was being carried out on a
nation-wide basis.   The programme has helped to bring
about the expansion of rural roads and bridges and
improvements in housing, irrigation and organisational
infrastructure at the local level.   In fact, the movement,
along with its concurrent agricultural pricing policies, is
considered to have significantly reduced rural-urban
income inequalities.   And although the demographic
effects of the programme have not yet been fully
analysed, it has been felt that during the 10 years of its
existence the "Saemaul undong" has indirectly contributed
to keeping potential migrants in the rural sector.

Many other countries in Asia have instituted rural
development programmes so as to create a social and
physical infrastructure that will allow rural residents to
share broadly in the nation's development.   But truly
integrated rural development calls for supporting policies
aimed at the redistribution of wealth from urban to rural
areas and from rich, large-scale farmers to small farmers
and the landless.

(b) "Nativist" policies

Wherever people are free to move from place to place
in search of better opportunities for education, land and
employment, they are likely to do so.   In India, for
instance, between 1931 and 1961, the number of persons
living outside the state of their birth grew from about 8
million to some 23.7 million (Weiner, 1973, p. 191).   By
1971 the figure had increased to over 28 million.

This gives rise to problems particularly in poor
countries whose inhabitants belong to a number of distinct
linguistic, cultural and religious groups.   In Malaysia,
for example, the Malays speak of themselves as

---

1   Another factor that seems to have played an
important part in slowing down the pace of rural-urban
migration in Sri Lanka is the convenient subsidised transport network, which gives rural dwellers access to urban
employment and amenities without their having to migrate
permanently to the cities.   A recent study shows that
nearly 45 per cent of the workforce employed in Colombo
commutes to work (Dias, 1977).

"Bhumiputras", or "sons of the soil", in contrast to the ethnic Chinese, and demand special rights to employment, education, and land.   And in India opposition to migrants has developed in Bombay and Bangalore, and in the states of Assam, Andhra Pradesh, and Bihar (Weiner, 1975).

Virtually every state government in India is now committed to giving preference in employment to persons born in the state or who have resided there for a specified time, usually 10 to 15 years.   These restrictive measures, and the political agitation that followed in their wake, may have had some impact on inter-state migration, but detailed migration data are not yet available to quantify it.

Policies Influencing Urban In-migration

Until recently public policy towards migrants in the urban areas of many Asian countries was generally harsh and restrictive.   It often involved limiting access by immigrants to education and housing, demolition of shanty towns, and curtailment of services to slum and squatter communities.   By restricting access to education and housing in Manila, for example, the Government of the Philippines hoped to deter migrants, but these measures were administratively difficult to enforce and only encouraged corruption (see Ocampo, 1977).

Slowly the attitude towards migrant squatters and slum dwellers in many developing countires, particularly in Asia, is changing from a punitive to a more tolerant one (Laquian, 1979).   A number of measures have now been taken to accommodate migrants in urban areas and promote their welfare, including (a) recognition and legitimisation of the tenure of urban squatters and slum dwellers;   (b) the setting up of reception centres;   (c) improvement of slum areas;   (d) sites and services projects;   (e) provision of employment for poor migrants; and (f) minimum wage legislation.

In order to provide employment, governments have introduced urban public works programmes, promoted the expansion of the construction industry, and legislated on small-scale   enterprises.   Instead   of   discouraging hawkers, vendors and family enterprises, many countries have provided them with various types of assistance. The Malaysian Government, for example, in its efforts to encourage entrepreneurship among the Malay "sons of the soil", supports hawkers and vendors by lending them capital, training them in business methods, constructing kiosks and markets for them, and generally allowing them to sell their goods in desirable locations (ibid., p. 18). Programmes to help families build their own houses on sites provided by the government have been introduced in India, Sri Lanka, Indonesia, the Philippines, and several other Asian countries.

Although there is general agreement that something should be done to improve the plight of migrants, it is still widely feared that providing them with jobs and accommodation will encourage further migration and worsen rather than improve urban unemployment. Such fears may not, however, be justified. A priori, it is not possible to conclude unequivocally that unemployment will rise. In fact there are five major ways in which migrants may directly or indirectly raise employment levels. First, they may depress wage rates in urban areas and this may cause employment to expand. Second, the increased supply of unskilled and semi-skilled labour may stimulate more rapid industrialisation and industrial investment. Third, migrants' consumption patterns are more likely to be oriented towards "basic-needs" goods and services produced by relatively labour-intensive methods. Fourth, they may represent dynamic elements in the urban informal sector, contributing entrepreneurship, skills and small-scale working capital. And, finally, any remittances they send back to the rural areas will probably promote increased monetisation and a shift of consumption there towards industrial-urban goods; besides, when they return to their villages, they are likely to stimulate a taste for urban goods.

Ultimately, only experience can show which, if any, of these outcomes will materialise; but, since all of them are possible, it must be recognised that migration will not necessarily raise urban unemployment.

Summary and Conclusions

Planning response to the rapid urbanisation and growth of large cities in planned as well as market economies has typically involved a set of policies which include direct controls on mobility, resettlement schemes, creation of new towns, industrial and administrative decentralisation, integrated rural development programmes, and urban policies designed to encourage or discourage migrants into the urban areas.

The available evidence suggests that only a few countries, such as China and Poland, have been able to control rural-urban migration through residence permits and legal restrictions. Elsewhere attempts to do so have been largely unsuccessful because legal restrictions are difficult to enforce, licences are easily forged, monitoring entire cities is costly, and evicted persons can return.

A review of resettlement schemes shows that they have certain achievements to their credit and a very

definite potential, but to fulfil their purpose they still
have to overcome certain basic weaknesses: lack of
co-operation and co-ordination between government
departments, and inadequate provision of infrastructure,
education, housing, transport and alternative employment
opportunities in the settlement areas. In addition, such
schemes tend to be extremely expensive in relation to the
number of persons actually settled. In some cases they
also appear to have created social tensions in the areas
concerned.

The analysis of administrative decentralisation,
regional development, and industrial location programmes
suggests that they have some potential for success,
particularly if emphasis is given to the growth of rural-
based market towns. Part of the problem is that often
their redistributive aims have not been clearly stated, nor
the programmes themselves fully implemented. Moreover,
since the development of new towns, growth centres, and
industrial estates requires the commitment of substantial
administrative and financial resources, only a few
countries have been able to carry it through successfully
on a large scale.

Policies of rural development, land reform and social
welfare appear to have enhanced the retentive capacity of
the rural areas and reduced the tendency towards rural-
urban migration in East European countries such as
Poland. In Asia, most integrated rural development
programmes have been adopted only recently. Although
there is some evidence that they have considerably
reduced migration in Malaysia and Sri Lanka, the final
evaluation of their effects on migration in other countries
cannot be made for some time to come. Besides, the
land reforms necessary to support integrated rural development programmes are conspicuously absent at present in
many Asian countries.

The foregoing review of policies on urban migration
suggests that most of them have had rather limited
success, particularly in non-planned economies. There
are a number of reasons for this. First and foremost is
the general lack of high-level political commitment to a
better distribution of economic activities throughout the
country. Second, until recently urbanisation policies
have concentrated largely on the encouragement of decentralisation, overlooking the fact that other national
policies (e.g. trade, industrial, and infrastructural
policies) exert much stronger countervailing pressures,
and, third, many of the measures adopted have addressed
themselves to the symptoms and not to the causes of
resource misallocation and severe regional disparities.

In planned economies, the degree of success that has
been attained can be partly attributed to the way planning

and implementation actually take place in these countries. Public ownership of the means of production and complete command over allocation of resources facilitates greatly the manipulation of investment location decisions over national space. New growth centres are created deliberately to channel population flow towards relatively underdeveloped areas. This has to some extent reduced the rate of growth of large urban areas and given a fillip to development in hitherto undeveloped regions. But, even in centrally planned economies, the interests of socioeconomic planning and those of spatial planning do not seem to be always in harmony. In Poland, for example, the flight of youth from the farm still remains a problem and has been adversely affecting the quality and composition of the rural labour force. Despite the avowed policy of equalisation of living standards throughout the country, it has not been possible for the Polish Government to extend social services equally to all regions. Consequently, the drift of population, particularly of skilled manpower, towards the urban areas continues unabated.

The above analysis therefore suggests that the policy instruments available to governments will have little impact on internal migration until the basic factors responsible for wide rural-urban and inter-urban differentials in wages, employment opportunities, and amenities are modified. This can be achieved only if population distribution policies are an essential component of an over-all development strategy, linked and harmonised with policies on industrialisation, agriculture, and social welfare.

Chapter 3

POPULATION DISTRIBUTION AND DEVELOPMENT
STRATEGIES IN PENINSULAR MALAYSIA

By Paul Chan*

Introduction

On the basis of the 1957 and 1970 censuses of population, it is evident that internal migration in Malaysia has
become a major factor on the demographic scene. Over
the period 1950 to 1970, the number of lifetime inter-state
migrants in Peninsular Malaysia has increased by 85 per
cent. These movements are predominantly into the
states of Selengor and Pahang at the expense of Perak,
Melaka, and Kelantan. By 1970, the number of inter-
state migrants represented almost one-fifth of the total
population. In addition intra-state migration (migration
within states), both rural-to-rural and rural-to-urban has
increased significantly.

Since migration takes many forms, and has social and
economic consequences of varying importance, there is a
growing interest in Malaysia in devising programmes for
changing or controlling migratory flows. Rural-urban
migration in Malaysia inevitably calls particular attention
to the disparities between the two major segments of the
population, viz. the predominantly urban, commercially
oriented, and economically modernised Chinese, and the
heavily rural, agriculturally based Malays. This
represents a division of labour imbalance which it is the
avowed aim of the government to modify.

The government, through the New Economic Policy,
aspires to restructure society, to eradicate poverty, and
to reduce inequality among the people and regions. In
the Second Malaysia Plan (1971-75), the government thus
"...aims at accelerating the process of restructuring
society to correct economic imbalance, so as to reduce and
eventually eliminate the identifications of race with
economic function. This process involves the modernization of rural life, a rapid and balanced growth of
urban activities and the creation of a Malay commercial
and industrial community in all categories, and at all

---

* Faculty of Economics and Administration, University of Malaya, Kuala Lumpur.

levels of operation, so that the Malays and other indigenous people will become full partners in all aspects of the economic life of the nation".

Policy measures were also put forward in the Second Malaysia Plan:

"The introduction of modern industries in rural areas and the development of new growth centres in new areas and the migration of rural inhabitants to urban areas are essential to economic balance between the urban and rural areas and elimination of the identification of race with vocation as well as location. Policies will be designed to ... foster the development of modern commercial and industrial activities in rural areas generally and in selected new growth centres in present rural areas in particular. This will speed up the exposure of rural inhabitants, particularly Malays and other indigenous people, to the influences of an urban environment. Industrialization in existing areas will be further developed so that migrants, particularly Malays and other indigenous people, as well as persons living in the areas, will play an increasing role in this development both in terms of ownership and control and in terms of employment at all levels."

The Third Malaysia Plan (1976-80) emphasises in greater detail and determination what was delineated in the Second Malaysia Plan regarding the approaches and policy measures to be used: viz., regional development programmes and development schemes, relocation of industries, urban development programmes, integrated rural development projects, and so on. All these have implications for future migration trends, patterns, and directions in Peninsular Malaysia.

In attempting to reduce inequalities between ethnic groups, regions and states, the plans thus put forward a blueprint for regional development and point to the articulation of a population redistribution policy[1] which should include at least the following:

---

1   In this study the terms migration policy and population distribution policy are used interchangeably.

(a) an awareness of the dynamics of the development-population redistribution relationship, viz., "Regional mobility from depressed to more progressive areas including from rural to urban centres occurs through migration as the natural result of push and pull factors. Unchecked and unguided, this socio-economic phenomenon can enhance unemployment or poverty in the urban centres" (Third Malaysia Plan, p. 97);

(b) the formation and adoption of goals: with respect to the development of poor states the Third Malaysia Plan argues that "sizeable movements of labour from Kedah/Perlis and Kelantan are imperative if the economic position of these states is to be meaningfully improved relative to the national average" (ibid., p. 208). At the same time it also recognises that "the achievement of a balanced mobility ... is one of the biggest challenges facing Malaysia during the Third Malaysia Plan period. The government will ensure that there will be adequate urban-to-rural flow of capital and skills to provide for the employment needs of the rural population and check the rural-urban migration" (ibid., p. 97);

(c) the choice of instruments to achieve the goals: "New land development will continue to be a major means by which the government will seek to push the location of future growth in agriculture ... towards the poorer states" (ibid., p. 209); and

(d) the implementation and evaluation of monitoring of policy instruments. To illustrate, "In respect of in situ development, a concerted approach will be undertaken to integrate agency proposals for the development of the areas concerned. The focal point in this strategy will be the more effective role of the District Officer..." (ibid., p. 265).

The purpose of this study is threefold: first, to examine migration patterns in Peninsular Malaysia; second, to identify policies and programmes designed to influence migration; and third, to assess their direct and indirect effects.

For the purposes of the study, all policies and programmes are classified into two broad categories:

(a) migration-directed, and

(b) non-migration directed but with effects on migration.

Migration-directed policies include:

(a) those which are actively used to initiate the movement of people, for example, the sponsored movement of settlers into land settlement schemes; and

(b) those which are implemented to discourage or to retain potential migrants, for example, the use of incentives in integrated rural development programmes to encourage rural residents not to move out.

Non-migration directed policies which have effects on migration could be illustrated by the various remedial programmes of the government in urban centres. The upgrading of squatter areas in the capital city of Kuala Lumpur, for example, has as its main objective the improvement of the standards of living of the squatters, but it could indirectly stimulate landless urban in-migrants who would expect to be the beneficiaries of such projects.

It is obvious that the above demarcation is not always clear-cut in practice. Indeed, a mixture of the above is normally the case during the implementation of a policy and programme. However, it will help to set up the following scheme for analysis later.

Scheme of migration-related policies and programmes

Policies and programmes	Migration-directed		Non-migration directed
	Movement-oriented	Retention-oriented	
(a) Regional development policy			
(i) Land development programmes	x		
(ii) Industrial decentralisation	x	x	x
(iii) New urban growth centres	x		
(b) Integrated rural development (or in situ development) policy	x	x	x
(c) Urban restructuring policy			x
(d) Other general socio-economic development policies			x

Flows and Characteristics of Migrants

This section describes briefly the flows and characteristics of migrants in Peninsular Malaysia, and is in the nature of a background for subsequent evaluation of migration-related policies. The major sources of information are the 1947, 1957 and 1970 Population and Housing Censuses.

(a) Flows of migration

During the nineteenth century some population movements were noted. These were caused by the unsettled conditions of the time (Roff, 1967) and by seasonal agricultural demands for labour (Gosling, 1963). Such mobility, however, was cyclical and circular in nature.

The first noteworthy population redistribution was the migration which occurred during the Emergency Period. Between 1948 and 1960 the government relocated about 600,000 persons over 600 new villages (Dobby, 1952; Hamzah, 1962; Kernial, 1964). This affected about 12 per cent of the total population. The demographic profile of Peninsular Malaysia was immediately and permanently changed by this government intervention in the spatial distribution of population. Since then these new villages have had a varied experience of physical growth and socio-economic change. In 1969 the average size of the new villages was about twice that of 1959. However, only about 18 per cent experienced rapid growth (Pryor, 1979).

The period from 1947 to 1957 was quite an unsettled one, and as such population distribution and movements were somewhat distorted. It was only around the early 1960s that the mobility of people could be more meaningfully explained in terms of social and economic developments within the spatial framework. During the 1957-70 intercensal period a number of migration trends could be discerned: a significant flow of people into and out of certain states; the prevalence of short-distance migration, especially to contiguous states; and the importance of rural-to-rural migration.

Some of the major migration trends during the 1957-70 intercensal period are as follows:

1 net movement into Selangor and Pahang;

2 net movement out of Perak, Johor, Negeri Sembilan, Kelantan, Kedah, Melaka and Pinang;

3 general stability in Terengganu and Perlis;

4   net inflow to Selangor from Perak, Negeri Sembilan, Melaka and Johor;

5   net inflow to Pahang from Kelantan, Terengganu and Perak;

6   high interaction in population movement amongst the west coast states and a low one between east coast states;

7   importance of intra-state migration.

The first three characteristics of the internal migration patterns are revealed by the data in tables 1 and 2. The data on state of birth and on previous state of residence confirm the net movement of people into Pahang and Selangor, the general stability in Perlis and Terengganu, and the net out-migration from the other states. Pahang, which has vast regional land development schemes, and Selangor, the state of industrial development, had respectively gained about 66,000 and 200,000 lifetime migrants by 1970 (table 1). The data on the destination of in-migrants in table 2 show that a larger proportion of migrants to Pahang moved to the rural areas as compared with the migrants to Selangor.

The general direction of internal migration and the net inter-state migration flows are clearly depicted in map 1. It also indicates the greater movement of population among the west coast states. The matrices of interaction and inter-state migration flows are provided by the data in tables 3 and 4, from which the net inter-state migration magnitudes can be derived. The largest absolute flow was from Perak and Selangor.

The last characteristic, i.e. the importance of intra-state migration, is confirmed by the information in table 5. Selangor had the largest intra-state movement, followed by Perak and Johor. Such short distance migration is quite significant in Peninsular Malaysia. A total of 1,666,706 intra-state migrants were recorded in the 1970 census. This constituted 19 per cent of the total population.

During the period 1957-70 the population in gazetted urban areas with 10,000 and above grew at an annual compound rate of 3.2 per cent and the rural population at 2.4 per cent. The divergence in their growth rates was not substantial (Pryor, 1979). Natural increase appeared to account for 60.6 per cent of this urban growth, and migration for only 18.1 per cent. Reclassification accounted for the rest. Selangor experienced a higher rate of urban growth from in-migration than any other state, followed by Johor and Terengganu (table 6). But it was the states of Terengganu and Kelantan which

Table 1: Number of net inter-state migrants by state, 1957 and 1970

| | State of birth migrants | | State of previous residence migrants |
	1957	1970	1970
I. States with net inflows			
Pahang	17,979	65,798	48,322
Selangor	55,430	199,671	98,200
II. States with net outflows			
Johor	15,446	-4,984	-8,097
Kedah	6,052	-25,357	-21,667
Kelantan	17,109	-47,828	-32,764
Melaka	-25,209	-40,325	-11,761
Negeri Sembilan	2,887	-21,600	-12,482
Perak	-31,406	-114,312	-69,640
Pinang	-30,841	-20,087	2,738
III. States with stability			
Perlis	4,103	3,076	1,214
Terengganu	2,668	5,948	5,927

Source: Department of Statistics, Malaysia.

Table 2: Selected measures of inter-state migration by state, 1957 and 1970

| | Net migration rates | | | Destination of state of birth in-migrants (%) 1970 | | |
| | State of birth | | State of previous residence | | | |
	1957	1970	1970	Urban[1]	Rural	All
Number of migrants				363,826	589,854	953,680
I. States with net inflows						
Pahang	5.7	13.1	9.6	16.9	83.1	100.0
Selangor	5.5	12.3	6.0	55.3	44.7	100.0
II. States with net outflows						
Johor	1.7	-0.4	-0.6	43.4	56.6	100.0
Kedah	0.9	-2.7	-2.3	25.3	74.7	100.0
Kelantan	-3.4	-7.0	-4.8	37.8	62.2	100.0
Melaka	-8.7	-10.0	-2.9	26.2	73.8	100.0
Negeri Sembilan	0.8	-4.5	-2.6	23.7	76.3	100.0
Perak	-2.6	-7.3	-4.5	34.6	65.4	100.0
Pinang	-5.4	-2.6	0.4	49.7	50.3	100.0
III. States with stability						
Perlis	4.5	2.5	1.0	-	100.0	100.0
Terengganu	1.0	1.3	1.4	22.6	77.4	100.0

1 Urban areas are gazetted areas with population of 10,000+.

Source: Adapted from Pryor (1979).

Map 1: Lifetime net migration streams, Peninsular
Malaysia, 1970

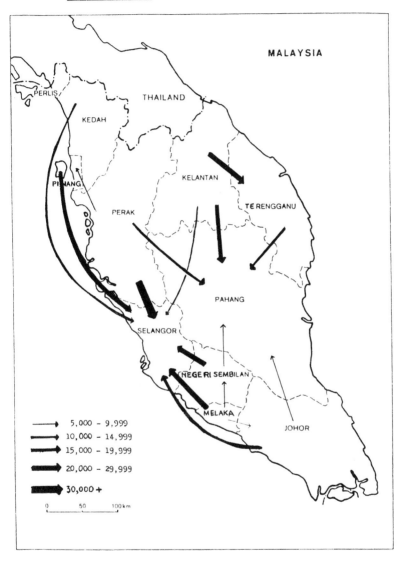

Table 3: State of birth migration matrix, 1970

State of birth (origin)	State of destination											Total
	Johor	Kedah	Kelantan	Melaka	Negeri Sembilan	Pahang	Perak	Perlis	Pinang	Selangor	Terengganu	
Johor		1,747	1,705	15,799	14,814	11,929	6,216	164	2,462	30,093	1,636	86,565
Kedah	2,983		1,741	1,396	2,221	3,914	27,162	10,613	37,718	15,317	700	103,765
Kelantan	2,912	2,735		1,159	1,877	19,876	3,495	323	1,575	9,427	24,118	67,497
Melaka	21,895	919	979		19,073	4,745	3,522	78	1,536	34,701	682	88,130
Negeri Sembilan	13,350	1,329	1,443	13,884		10,782	5,621	152	1,917	47,347	937	96,762
Pahang	5,456	877	1,676	1,322	4,064		4,430	123	1,290	17,863	4,214	41,315
Perak	12,977	24,551	3,762	4,790	8,824	19,045		2,189	35,788	106,033	2,031	219,990
Perlis	313	5,760	189	177	313	877	2,182		1,813	1,538	79	13,241
Pinang	4,368	36,302	1,981	1,726	2,738	5,135	28,413	2,218		27,464	802	111,147
Selangor	12,760	3,392	2,254	7,118	20,545	16,544	23,194	390	6,300		1,760	94,257
Terengganu	4,567	796	3,939	434	693	14,266	1,443	67	611	4,145		31,011
Total	81,581	78,408	19,669	47,905	73,162	107,113	103,678	16,317	91,060	293,928	36,959	953,680

Source: Pryor (1979).

Table 4: State of previous residence migration matrix, 1970

State of previous residence (origin)	State of destination											Total
	Johor	Kedah	Kelantan	Melaka	Negeri Sembilan	Pahang	Perak	Perlis	Pinang	Selangor	Terengganu	
Johor	–	1,424	1,533	13,501	12,011	10,013	5,673	162	2,333	21,866	1,675	70,191
Kedah	2,137	–	1,376	872	1,823	2,892	21,411	9,401	30,833	10,180	562	81,487
Kelantan	2,206	2,173	–	936	1,537	15,067	2,720	247	1,496	6,643	20,330	53,355
Melaka	14,134	573	767	–	11,536	3,256	2,175	60	968	18,827	457	52,753
Negeri Sembilan	10,457	961	1,090	11,231	–	9,938	4,463	105	1,588	30,501	677	71,011
Pahang	4,340	1,065	2,488	1,259	4,836	–	5,949	143	1,340	14,824	4,420	40,664
Perak	10,489	19,337	3,305	3,569	6,135	14,834	–	1,972	28,021	73,551	1,721	162,934
Perlis	214	5,588	177	121	248	1,016	2,346	–	1,890	1,638	79	13,317
Pinang	2,694	23,922	1,567	973	1,506	3,810	20,248	1,898	–	16,687	486	73,791
Selangor	12,209	4,093	3,505	8,193	18,295	16,721	26,993	478	7,438	–	2,164	100,089
Terengganu	3,214	684	4,783	337	602	11,439	1,316	65	622	3,572	–	26,634
Total	62,094	59,820	20,591	40,992	58,529	88,986	93,294	14,531	76,529	198,289	32,571	746,226

Source: Pryor (1979).

Table 5: Distribution of previous state of residence migrants, 1970

	Inter-state (%)	Inter-district (%)	Inter-locality (%)	Number of intra-state migrants (000s)
I. States with net inflows				
Pahang	49.9	20.8	29.3	89,474
Selangor	37.1	19.1	43.8	335,913
II. States with net outflows				
Johor	19.1	39.2	41.7	262,683
Kedah	22.0	31.9	46.1	212,296
Kelantan	14.3	48.8	36.9	123,941
Melaka	50.7	15.7	33.6	39,862
Negeri Sembilan	41.7	25.0	33.3	81,646
Perak	22.3	31.1	46.6	325,342
Pinang	49.5	23.0	33.5	99,484
III. States with stability				
Perlis	38.2	0	61.8	23,520
Terengganu	31.0	30.7	38.3	72,545
Total	30.9	27.9	41.1	1,666,706

Source: Adapted from Pryor (1979).

Table 6: Distribution and growth of urban population

	Distribution 1970 (%)	Growth 1957-70 (%)	Source of growth (%)		
			Natural increase	Migration	Reclassi-fication
States with net inflows					
Pahang	3.8	67.3	48.6	22.1	29.3
Selangor	28.9	68.6	47.7	41.0	11.3
States with net outflows					
Johor	13.3	65.6	52.2	29.6	18.2
Kedah	4.8	29.2	115.0	-15.0	-
Kelantan	4.1	109.2	31.3	6.1	62.2
Melaka	4.0	45.4	72.1	-17.5	45.4
Negeri Sembilan	4.1	61.8	52.9	21.0	26.1
Perak	17.1	41.4	79.0	12.5	8.5
Pinang	15.8	21.7	150.4	-67.8	17.4
States with stability					
Perlis	-	-	-	-	-
Terengganu	4.3	160.9	20.3	22.5	57.2
Total	100.0	40.3	60.6	18.1	21.3

Source: Adapted from Pryor (1979).

experienced the highest urban growth rate, though only about 4 per cent of their population lived in the urban areas. This was largely due to the reclassification of urban-rural areas.

The evidence suggests that in general urban growth in Peninsular Malaysia over the period 1957-70 was slow. In 1957 about 73 per cent of the population was rural. This had not changed much by 1970. This was partly due to the rural-rural bias of the migration trends, which were undoubtedly influenced by the rural development programmes.

(b) Characteristics of migrants

The usual migrant selectivity characteristics of age and sex differentials, marital status, and family size mentioned in studies of other areas could also be observed in the Malaysian situation.

Following Pryor (1979) these demographic characteristics of the migrants are summarised below:

(a) The 1970 census data for five-year migrants indicated that the majority of the migrants were between 15 and 24 years of age, with emphatic focus on the age group 20-24.

(b) The migrants were predominantly males in the age group 20-24, especially among the Malays. Generally they were long-distance migrants. The sex ratio of migrants in other ethnic groups has been stabilising towards equalisation.

(c) Available evidence suggests that the majority of migrants were single, particularly those in the age group 20-24.

(d) The migrant family size was smaller, with on average one to three children, than the non-migrant family, which had four or more children.

(e) Those with more education had a greater propensity to migrate (Narayanan, 1975).

(f) Though during the intercensal period of 1947-57 the Chinese had the highest migration rate, since 1957 the Malays were the most mobile ethnic group in the country (Caldwell, 1963; Pryor, 1975).

The evidence also shows that the Malays, especially the males, were the largest migrant group, whether it is defined by state of birth or by previous state of residence. In the light of the implementation of the New Economic Policy this trend is expected to be accentuated in the future. The significance of the ethnicity factor in the population distribution will be brought into sharper focus when the various components of the government's population policy are examined in the next section.

Development Strategies Influencing
Internal Migration

(a) Regional development policy

Regional development plans generally have one or more of the following aims: to raise real incomes; to reduce income differentials between regions; to promote the use of manpower and natural resources; to provide social and physical infrastructure; to modernise rural areas; and to create or revitalise urban centres. Various socio-economic locational incentives or disincentives, which are directed at the firm or individual (or the household unit) level in order to accomplish the above objectives, have a redistributive impact on population.

Until the Second Malaysia Plan the inchoate ideas of regional development planning were framed in terms of rural development programmes aimed at solving the problems of a dualistic economy. Since the Second Malaysia Plan, and more particularly the Third Malaysia Plan, the role of regional development planning has become better defined.

A brief review of the regional disparities in growth and development is in order here. The pattern of regional disparities is shown in table 7. Selangor and Pinang are the richest states in terms of per capita GDP. Perlis, Kedah, Terengganu and Kelantan are the poorest. The economic structures of these states also reflect imbalances in the distribution of industries and urban growth centres. Lastly, the poor states have a much higher incidence of poverty. Whereas Selangor has 29.2 per cent of its households within the poverty group Kelantan has 76.1 per cent.

It is noteworthy that there is a relationship between ethnicity and poverty distribution. The data in table 7 indicate a positive correlation between the concentration of Malay population (viz. 93.9 per cent in Terengganu, 92.8 per cent in Kelantan) and the incidence of poverty in certain states. It is this ethnicity-poverty relationship on which the New Economic Policy directs its focus, and which highlights the significant role of regional development planning.

Table 7: Peninsular Malaysia: Indicators of income, economic structures and population variables by state

Indicator	State									
	Johor	Kedah/ Perlis	Kelantan	Melaka	Negeri Sembilan	Pahang	Perak	Pinang	Selangor	Terengganu
Gross domestic product (GDP) ($ millions in constant 1970 prices)	2,587.0	1,197.6	531.3	620.0	911.7	1,239.1	2,725.0	1,817.0	6,776.4	526.9
Agriculture, forestry, livestock and fishing	903.1	581.0	206.8	143.4	337.7	458.2	658.3	168.2	544.3	223.0
Mining and quarrying	15.9	9.2	1.6	3.2	4.3	25.6	307.7	4.5	211.5	57.5
Manufacturing	594.7	147.5	41.9	91.9	166.1	213.5	506.7	480.5	1,782.8	40.4
Construction	78.3	19.1	9.5	13.3	18.0	54.1	68.5	72.2	375.0	18.0
Services	995.0	440.8	271.5	368.2	385.6	487.7	1,183.8	1,091.6	3,862.8	190.0
Per capita GDP	1,572.6	900.5	629.5	1,218.1	1,482.4	1,740.3	1,414.1	1,900.6	3,033.0	1,005.5
Population (000s)	1,645	1,330	844	509	615	712	1,927	956	2,198	526
Malays as % of 1970 population	53.4	55.7	92.8	51.8	45.4	61.2	43.1	30.7	34.6	93.9
Urban as % of 1970 population	36.0	14.0	18.0	28.0	28.0	23.0	36	56.0	51.0	29.0
% of households in poverty (1975)	45.7	64.5	76.1	44.9	44.8	43.2	48.6	43.7	29.2	68.9

Source: Mid-term Review of the Third Malaysia Plan (1979).

(i) Land development programmes

Land development and settlement constitutes one of
the most important instruments of Malaysia's regional
development programme.   There is no doubt that the
land development programmes have contributed to
reducing the potential flow of surplus rural labour to the
urban areas.   The reduction in rural-urban differentials
in income and employment opportunities, and the provision
of social and economic infrastructure in rural areas, have
discouraged potential migrants from leaving the rural
areas.   In addition, the generally labour absorptive
capacity of smallholding agricultural production, the
emotive need for ownership of land, and the availability
of land for expansion have all influenced the spatial
demographic scenario of the country.
In this respect one immediately thinks of the programme of the Federal Land Development Authority
(FELDA) as an exemplary illustration of the effects of
land development programmes on migration.   When FELDA
was established in 1956 its principal objective was to
develop land for the landless and unemployed.   By 1970
it had developed 90 schemes and resettled about 21,000
families.   By 1978 about 313,700 acres of land (1 hectare
= 2.471 acres) had been developed, involving 35,531
settler families (tables 8 and 9).   Assuming that the
average settler household size is six (five dependents and
the settler), FELDA would appear to have moved more
than 213,186 people.   This does not include the additional
marginal labour needed during the initial period of establishing the land schemes, viz. the use of migrant casual
labour in land clearing, road construction, etc.   It is
estimated that FELDA was accountable for 6 to 8 per cent
of the total migrants in Peninsular Malaysia during the
intercensal period of 1957-70 (MacAndrews, 1977).   The
figure would be higher during the 1970-75 period when 77
new land schemes were set up, and FELDA helped to
implement three massive regional integrated land development schemes in Pahang (Jengka Triangle and Pahang
Tenggara) and in Johor (Johor Tenggara).
The population redistribution impact of FELDA is not
confined to actively sponsoring potential migrants.   It
also helps to regulate and stabilise rural population movement within the rural areas.   It can be seen from table 8
that FELDA schemes are located in eight different states.
The largest (with 130,600 acres) is in Pahang, followed
by Negeri Sembilan (60,300 acres) and Johor (60,200
acres).   Except in Pahang, which depends on migrants
from other states, the settlers are predominantly from
their own states (table 9).   This could be explained by
the criteria used to choose the settlers.   Most states

Table 8: Malaysia: Land development by state, 1976-78 (acres)

State	Agency				
	State agencies	FELDA	FELCRA	RISDA	Total land developed
High income:					
Selangor	31,300	900	–	–	32,200
Middle income:					
Johor	53,200	60,200	7,700	–	121,100
Melaka	1,000	–	–	–	1,000
Negeri Sembilan	7,100	60,300	3,400	4,700	75,500
Pahang	41,000	130,600	500	26,100	198,200
Perak	9,800	23,500	5,100	9,800	48,200
Pinang	–	–	–	–	–
Sabah	46,800	–	–	–	46,800
Sarawak	15,300	–	–	–	15,300
Low income:					
Kedah/Perlis	15,500	10,400	3,600	–	29,500
Kelantan	7,500	2,800	3,000	–	13,300
Terengganu	17,700	25,000	5,400	18,300	66,400
Total Malaysia	246,200	313,700	28,700	58,900	647,500
Third Malaysia Plan targets	500,000	350,000	50,000	100,000	1,000,000
% achievement 1976-78	49.2	89.6	57.4	58.9	64.7

Source: Mid-term Review of the Third Malaysia Plan.

Table 9: Peninsular Malaysia: States with settled FELDA schemes
(number of settlers)

State of destination[1]

State of origin	Johor	%	Kedah	%	Melaka	%	Negeri Sembilan	%	Pahang	%	Perak	%	Selangor	%	Terengganu	%	Total	%
Johor	8,384	94.9	-	-	51	4.7	252	5.5	760	5.7	4	0.2	28	1.6	3	0.2	9,482	26.7
Kedah	24	0.3	1,451	95.9	7	0.6	35	0.8	1,561	11.6	85	3.5	43	2.4	2	0.1	3,208	9.0
Kelantan	15	0.2	10	0.7	-	-	31	0.7	1,552	11.6	9	0.4	3	0.2	184	10.0	1,804	5.1
Melaka	121	1.4	-	-	982	89.9	375	8.1	685	5.1	1	-	14	0.8	1	0.1	2,179	6.1
Negeri Sembilan	35	0.4	1	0.1	26	2.4	3,627	78.7	339	2.5	4	0.2	6	0.3	2	0.1	4,040	11.4
Pahang	37	0.4	-	-	4	0.4	23	0.5	4,428	33.0	3	0.1	-	-	10	0.5	4,505	12.7
Perak	64	0.7	10	0.7	8	0.7	64	1.4	1,348	10.0	2,210	90.4	301	16.8	1	0.1	4,006	11.3
Perlis	1	0.0	10	0.7	-	-	3	0.1	284	2.1	3	0.1	-	-	-	-	301	0.8
Pinang	18	0.2	23	1.5	1	0.1	16	0.3	801	6.0	92	3.8	8	0.4	-	-	959	2.7
Selangor	37	0.4	1	0.1	5	0.5	155	3.4	1,056	7.9	28	1.1	1,368	76.1	2	0.1	2,652	7.5
Terengganu	47	0.5	-	-	2	0.2	10	0.2	566	4.2	2	0.1	3	0.2	1,625	88.7	2,255	6.3
Others[2]	51	0.6	7	0.5	6	0.5	16	0.4	33	0.3	3	0.1	23	1.3	1	0.1	140	0.3
Total	8,834	100.0	1,513	100.0	1,092	100.0	4,607	100.0	13,413	100.0	2,444	100.0	1,797	100.0	1,831	100.0	35,531	100.0
%	24.9		4.3		3.1		13.0		37.7		6.9		5.0		5.1		100	

[1] Kelantan, Perlis, and Pinang are excluded since these states did not have FELDA schemes when the census was carried out in 1976.

[2] Settlers not born in Peninsular Malaysia.

Source: FELDA Settler Census 1976.

have a quota requiring a minimum of 50 per cent of the settlers to be from their own states. It is also partly due to the preference on the part of migrants for making short-distance moves.

In this way the FELDA schemes succeed in retaining migrants from rural villages within the rural areas. Rural-rural migration is therefore encouraged, and this minimises rural-urban movement. It will be noticed that, except in the case of states which have a land availability problem, most of the FELDA schemes are located in states which suffer from out-migration (table 10). This deliberate location of land development projects in such states thus provides FELDA with a stabilising role. Without doubt, the rate and volume of out-migration from these states would have accelerated had it not been for this strategic rural-rural direction carved out for the settlers by FELDA.

It was earlier mentioned that one of the characteristics of migration patterns in the country is the predominance of movements to contiguous states, which is normally a short-distance move. This pattern is encouraged and reinforced by the location of FELDA schemes. Table 9 provides evidence on this matrix of contiguous state interaction in the migration behaviour of settlers.

Table 10: Comparison of net migration with location of FELDA settlers in Peninsular Malaysia, 1957-70

State	Net inter-state migration 1957-70 (000s)	Number of FELDA settlers settled	% of FELDA settlers from same states
Johor	−5.0	+6,797	95.7
Kedah	−25.4	1,547	98.6
Kelantan	−47.8	−	−
Melaka	−40.3	874	98.3
Negeri Sembilan	−21.6	3,022	83.3
Pahang	+65.8	+9,794	32.0
Perak	−114.3	2,293	91.0
Perlis	+3.1	−	−
Pinang	−20.0	−	−
Selangor	+119.7	+1,838	87.9
Terengganu	+6.0	+1,930	90.9

Source: MacAndrews (1977), table 1.

The prominent role of Pahang as a destination area for migrants has been noted. In 1976 (see map 1 and table 9) the contiguous states of Kelantan and Perak respectively accounted for 11.6 and 10.0 per cent of the total migrant settlers to Pahang. In contrast to the other states, only 32 per cent of the settlers came from within Pahang itself. The land development schemes in Pahang therefore encourage inter-state migration.

The land development situation is shown in tables 8 and 11. Projected land development in the land-rich states of Pahang, Johor and Terengganu will sustain the existing flow and pattern of population movement. In the land-poor states of Kedah and Perlis it is inevitable that the flow of labour to the land-rich states will continue unless it is minimised by the retention of rural residents who may be attracted by the rapid development of industries and growth centres. This is, however, not likely for some time to come.

FELDA land development schemes are not only an important intervening factor in migration; they have also influenced the demographic characteristics of population distribution. In particular, FELDA's selection criteria favour the young (80 per cent are between 25 and 39 years), the married, those with an agricultural background, the landless or those owning less than 2 acres of rural land, and Malays (96 per cent). This implies, therefore, that villages in rural areas will lose this energetic and young labour. This dimension of the migration effects of land development schemes on the sending areas has yet to be studied (Chan, 1981). Further, because of the ethnicity bias, FELDA land development schemes in fact stimulate Malay mobility, and at the same time direct their movement back into the rural areas. In terms of spatial population distribution, this land development strategy creates pockets of Malay settlements and Malay movement within the rural areas. The government is not unduly concerned over this. Land development in Malaysia is essentially a political issue, and as long as the land development strategy satisfies the long-term goal of reducing Malay poverty the government will support the policy and programme.

It is quite obvious that new land development and settlement, though costly, is politically the most expedient approach to solving the rural employment and land distribution problem. Land reform and changes in the tenure system are rarely, if ever, discussed in official documents and are definitely not considered as effectual instruments for a long time to come. The sole dependence on the FELDA type model is inadequate, however. One of the weaknesses is its inability to solve the employment, income and land-ownership objectives over the life cycle

Table 11: Malaysia: Availability of suitable land for agriculture (1975) and projected land development (1970-90) (000s acres)

State	Land area	Land suitable for agriculture			Projected land development
		Alienated	Available	Total	
Johor	4,693	1,791	1,282	3,073	584.4
Kedah/Perlis	2,541	1,159	250	1,409	151.1
Kelantan	3,720	710	217	927	188.4
Melaka	418	349	22	371	22.1
Negeri Sembilan	1,642	686	338	1,024	306.5
Pahang	8,870	1,847	2,545	4,392	1,183.8
Perak	5,154	1,332	519	1,851	220.4
Pinang	253	157	3	160	5.5
Sabah	17,750	948	4,357	5,305	514.0
Sarawak	30,750	6,720	6,400	13,120	594.0
Selangor	1,980	830	149	979	88.9
Terangganu	3,146	555	866	1,421	436.9
Total	80,967	17,084	16,948	34,032	4,296.0

Source: Third Malaysia Plan.

of the settler family. The so-called second-generation problem then arises with respect to employment in the land settlement schemes.

The second-generation problem is of course not confined to the land settlement schemes. It exists also in the rural areas, which experience a disequilibrium between land availability, employment and a growing labour force. When this threshold point is reached out-migration from the villages occurs unless there are other compensating factors to retain the rural people.

This problem, which was not given much consideration during the early planning period, is now being encountered in FELDA land settlement schemes. Overlooking the socio-demographic aspects of the planning process and focusing principally on the physical aspects of land development means that the employment, income, and land-ownership issues cannot be simultaneously solved by the utilisation of only one plot of land (10 to 12 acres in FELDA schemes) over the life cycle of the family. The same plot of land is thus intended to provide a minimum income for the family, utilise the family labour, and satisfy the emotive need for land ownership. This is workable during the early life cycle of the settler, when his family size is small. When it grows, however, the triple functions of land fail. One of the rigid principles of FELDA is that the settler's land cannot be subdivided, for fragmentation creates uneconomic holdings. This means that the settler's dependents have to leave the land settlement scheme to seek employment opportunities elsewhere. A new cycle of out-migration is thus generated. Already, though still not acute, this new wave of out-migration is occurring, particularly amongst those who have received a higher level of education and who have developed some inclination for urban living (Chan, 1982a).

An estimate of the second-generation employment problem is given by MacAndrews in his study on unemployment and regional planning (MacAndrews, 1977). A total of about 126,386 dependents are expected to enter the labour force during the period 1975-90 (table 12).

It is true that part of the labour force of dependents can be absorbed into other land settlement schemes. This is not the point, however. The crux of the land planning approach is that land has a limited absorption capacity and cannot satisfy the ownership, income and employment objectives of everyone. There is always a second-generation employment problem, so there is always another wave of new migrants. Thus the land development strategy, unless accompanied by other commercial and industrial developments in the rural growth centres, only physically changes the location of the rural

Table 12:   Labour force of dependents in FELDA
            schemes, 1975-90

	1975	1980	1985	1990
Working age population	16,631	53,129	124,281	205,173
Participation rate (%)	62.6	62.7	62.1	61.6
Labour force	10,411	33,312	77,179	126,386

Notes:

(a) The working age population (beginning at 15 years
of age) is calculated on the basis of an average figure
of six children per family.

(b) Participation rate is taken from the Mid-term Review
of the Second Malaysia Plan, 1971-75, p. 66.

Source: MacAndrews (1977).

population-poverty dynamics, and postpones it in terms of
time.
      It was thought that the FELDA model of land devel-
opment would induce urbanisation, or at least semi-
urbanisation, in the rural areas.   This would have
tailored neatly with the goals of the New Economic Policy:
to urbanise and modernise the Malays.   Somehow this has
not been the case.   A physical aggregation of settlers
engaged in agricultural activities does not constitute an
urban centre.   While it is true that the Malays have
migrated away from the rural villages, they have in fact
transplanted themselves to another rural and agricultural
environment which is only physically more "modernised".
If the FELDA type of land development is to function
effectively as an urbanising agent it must offer a socio-
economic environment that is different from the kampong
one.   The social, economic and commercial structure must
be different, and it must offer opportunities for the sort
of competitive endeavours that are usually found in urban
centres in the country.   Thus, whilst physically FELDA
has influenced the demographic landscape it has not really
succeeded in establishing urban growth centres.
      Partly in response to this problem, FELDA has
initiated a larger-scale type of integrated regional development.   The prototypes of this more comprehensive

approach are the Pahang Tenggara, Johor Tenggara and Terengganu Tengah. During 1976-78 a total of 521,000 acres, involving more than 265,000 settlers, was developed by FELDA. Sixteen new towns are being built in Pahang Tenggara (DARA), five in Terengganu Tengah, and two in Johor Tenggara. The projected land development is given in table 13 and the migrant dimensions are defined in table 14.

In view of the substantial labour requirements, particularly for the state of Pahang, it is expected that a large inflow of migrants will have to be encouraged. There are difficulties in attracting labour to these frontier development areas, however, especially during the initial period of establishment when basic social and economic amenities are poor. Large incentives must be offered to potential migrants from the other land-poor states in order to channel them to these three areas. This will not be an easy task. Official reports have complained of the difficulty of obtaining rural labour for such land development. Evidence from the private sector corroborates this. From daily newspaper reports it seems that even the offer of a high wage of 500 to 1,000 ringgit per month (1 US dollar = 2.25 Malaysian ringgit) to work in oil palm plantations is not sufficient to attract the labour. Even the promise of ownership of land and a high income in the FELDA schemes cannot retain rural labour. In some states such as Johor, the labour shortage is even termed a "labour crisis". All this reflects the fact that during the last few years the urban drift has definitely begun.

The planning of comprehensive regional land development programmes could still be improved on, particularly with respect to over-all consistency and co-ordination, feasibility and realism. Objectives at the regional and national level must be consistent, and co-ordination between different regional development authorities is necessary to avoid competing claims for migrant labour. At the regional planning stage the migrant types and migrant sources need to be specified in clearer terms so that the necessary incentives and infrastructure can be devised to attract them. At the national planning level, long-term consistency in defining goals is crucial. To illustrate the lack of long-term consistency, take the policy of encouraging "sizeable movements of labour from Kedah, Perlis and Kelantan [which] are imperative if the economic position of these states is to be increasingly improved" (Mid-term Review of the Third Malaysia Plan). But the gain of migrant labour, with necessary selectivity characteristics, to the land-rich states operates to the detriment of the land-poor states in the longer run, since the former take away the better

Table 13: Peninsular Malaysia: Regional land development and number of settlers, 1978 and 1980

| | 1978 | | 1980 | |
	Land development (acres)	No. of settlers	Land development (acres)	No. of settlers
Johor Tenggara	145,800	135,900	201,000	181,900
Pahang Tenggara	247,400	89,700	415,600	145,000
Terengganu Tengah	128,400	39,400	184,000	61,200
Total	521,600	265,000	800,600	388,100

Source: Mid-term Review of the Third Malaysia Plan.

Table 14: Regional land development and migrant dimensions

Region	Target year	Welfare function	Population 1970[2] (000s)	Migrant source specified	Migration type specified
Johor Tenggara	1990	NEP[1]	135 (400-500)	Not specified; expected intra-state migrants	Urban focus; 30+ new villages, 2 new towns; mainly Malays
Pahang Tenggara	1990	NEP	56 (505)	Expected from Selangor (23%); Johor (13%); Kedah (43%); Perak (9%); Pahang (11%)	Urban focus; 16 new towns under Third Malaysia Plan; new regional centre; mainly Malays
Bukit Ridon (Pahang New Town)	1990	NEP	- (20-50)	Not specified; expected same sources as in Pahang Tenggara	Mainly Malays
Terengganu State	1990	NEP	406 (700)	Zero net migration; relies on local population	Out-migration of Malay farmers

1 The objective of the New Economic Policy: to reduce poverty and restructure society.

2 Figures in brackets indicate the projected population in 1990.

Sources: Adapted from Pryor (1979), Third Malaysia Plan, and respective project documents and consultant reports.

portion of the labour force and leave behind aged dependents (Chan, 1981).   This policy of siphoning off labour is also inconsistent with that of the in situ or integrated rural development strategy, which is aimed at retaining rural people.   This point will be elaborated later. Quite apart from the above considerations, the concept of the region as used in the regional development programme of Malaysia has yet to be meaningfully explained.   As a consequence of the federal and state division of political prerogatives over land, which is controlled by the latter, regional development has followed a course which is defined by state boundaries.   The region is often taken to be an administrative-geographic unit or a sub-areal unit.   This, to state the obvious, inevitably leads to inefficient planning and inconsistent implementation of national objectives by regional authorities.

(ii)   Industrial decentralisation

Given that the labour-absorptive capacity of the agriculture sector is limited and that there are perceived benefits (at least for the potential migrants) working and living in urban centres, it is inevitable that the rate and volume of rural-urban migration will increase in the future.   Other reasons apart, it therefore becomes vital for the government to develop a more rationalised system of industrial centres and urban growth points to absorb such migrant workers.   In Peninsular Malaysia this entails the implementation of industrial decentralisation and the development of a viable hierarchy of urban centres.

Both of these broad measures must influence the spatial demographic scenario.   However, it is difficult at this stage to assess the precise effects of regional industrial decentralisation on the rate and volume of migration. First, it is too soon to evaluate the full demographic impact of the industrial decentralisation measures; second, there are inadequate data to determine the magnitude of the impact.

Nevertheless, an attempt is made in this section to describe the industrial decentralisation approach and to relate this to the probable demographic impact, especially on the migratory movement of labour.   Though the magnitude cannot be determined the likely direction of the impact of industrialisation policy measures on population mobility are indicated, and such probable effects are evaluated.

The period 1957-70 (from Independence to the beginning of the New Economic Policy) witnessed a "laissez-faire" approach to industrialisation.   The objective was to attract foreign investment and to nurture new industries. This was to be achieved by using tax-exempting investment incentives (within the Pioneer Status framework) and by providing a "conducive" environment (tariff protection) for infant industries to mature. If the industrialisation programme was success-ful in terms of import substitution (and later export promotion), it was not directed towards restructuring the "dualistic" traits of the political economy. Some observers have even claimed that this approach to national industrialisation has in fact contributed to the widening disparities between regions and between socio-economic groups. Parallel to the existence of the export enclaves in primary products, for example, new industrial enclaves were developed in the large urban centres in the developed parts of the country. Such "natural" growth points were thus further reinforced.

Recognising that the national industrial development and structure was not consistent with the national devel-opment ideology a different emphasis was given to the industrialisation programme. To reduce regional growth differentials (and that of ethnic and socio-economic groups) a policy of industrial dispersion was adopted. Some of the major features of the industrial dispersion and decentralisation policy were the following:

(a) to disperse industries from existing growth centres, particularly in the Klang Valley industrial-commercial hub, to the rest of the country;

(b) to direct industries from the more developed to the less developed parts of states;

(c) to nurture rural industrialisation.

As shown in table 15, the developed states of Selangor, Johor and Pinang are the only ones with a production location quotient larger than 1 for manufac-turing. This means they have an above average share of the economy's location of manufacturing. In contrast, all the less developed states have a production location quotient larger than 1 for agriculture but below the national average for manufacturing.

In order to check the above trend, two policy instruments have been used: first, the giving of a more dynamic role to industrial estates, initiated in 1958, to spearhead the spread of industrialisation; second, the introduction of locational incentives aimed at creating "subsidised" concentrated areas of industrial activity.

The locational incentives refer to the set of tax exemptions which a company enjoys if it complies with the conditions of the 1973 Investment Incentives (Amendment)

Table 15: Production location quotient in Peninsular Malaysia, 1975-78[1]

States		Agriculture	Mining	Manufacturing	Construction	Services
I.	States with net inflows					
Pahang	(1975)	1.67	0.14	0.85	0.51	0.86
	(1978)	1.66	0.81	0.71	0.90	0.78
Selangor	(1975)	0.39	0.92	1.34	1.44	1.17
	(1978)	0.36	0.92	1.23	1.44	1.16
II.	States with net outflows					
Johor	(1975)	1.56	0.30	1.02	0.73	0.78
	(1978)	1.56	0.18	0.99	0.79	0.78
Kedah (includes Perlis)	(1975)	2.15	0.25	0.38	0.43	0.73
	(1978)	2.17	0.23	0.57	0.42	0.75
Kelantan	(1975)	1.64	0.08	0.35	0.97	1.04
	(1978)	1.74	0.09	0.37	0.47	1.18
Melaka	(1975)	1.11	0.08	0.61	0.74	1.21
	(1978)	1.04	0.15	0.69	0.56	0.85
Negeri Sembilan	(1975)	1.54	0.15	0.88	0.68	0.85
	(1978)	1.66	0.14	0.85	0.51	0.86
Perak	(1975)	1.08	3.64	0.73	0.66	0.88
	(1978)	1.08	3.34	0.87	0.66	0.89
Pinang	(1975)	0.47	0.07	1.29	0.98	1.24
	(1978)	0.41	0.07	1.23	1.04	1.28
III.	States with stability					
Terengganu	(1975)	1.87	0.45	0.36	1.05	0.82
	(1978)	1.89	3.21	0.36	0.89	0.72

[1] The production location quotient is estimated as follows:

$$L_{ij} = \frac{Y_{ij}}{\sum\limits_{i=1}^{n} Y_{ij}} \Bigg/ \frac{\sum\limits_{j=1}^{M} Y_{ij}}{\sum\limits_{i=1}^{n} \sum\limits_{j=1}^{m} Y_{ij}}$$

where

i = state

j = industry

Y_{ij} = industry j in state i

$\sum\limits_{i=1}^{n} Y_{ij}$ = industry j in the whole economy

$\sum\limits_{j=1}^{m} Y_{ij}$ = all industries in state i

$\sum\limits_{i=1}^{n} \sum\limits_{j=1}^{m} Y_{ij}$ = all industries in the whole economy.

The national coefficient is defined to be 1. L_{ij} greater than, equal to, or less than 1 implies over, equal and under-representation in terms of location of the industry in a given state as compared to the national coefficient of 1.

Source: Kruger (1979).

Act. What is of relevance to the present study is the definition of location incentive areas. No clear guidelines are given regarding this. However, by 1977 the following areas were designated location incentive areas:

Johor Tenggara,
Kedah (excluding Kuala Muda District),
Kelantan,
Pahang,
Perlis, and
Terengganu.

It is interesting to note that essentially these are (except Johor) the less developed states, though not necessarily all land-poor ones (for instance, Pahang). Superficially, at the general level, this appears to accord with the National Economic Policy's stated goal of upgrading the less developed states.

In reinforcing the above, the role of industrial estates within the context of the New Economic Policy has also changed substantially. Industrial estates are now explicitly incorporated into the package of rural industrialisation programmes. Their expansion in the less developed states has been quite fast, and within the more developed states there has been a deliberate diversion of industrial estates to the smaller towns and semi-urban centres.

Given the above background, we can now outline some of the probable effects of the locational incentives and the industrial estates strategy on the demographic situation, particularly labour mobility.

The relocation of firms and the establishment of industrial estates create agglomeration economies and induce the development of social infrastructure. These, in turn, act as a strong incentive for other firms. The demand for labour increases and therefore employment opportunities also increase. An excellent example of this situation is the industrial estate town of Petaling Jaya in Selangor, which grew from a few thousand inhabitants during the mid-1950s to about 900,000 residents in 1978.

The location of industrial estates in the more developed states would only tend to attract more migrant labour from the other less developed states. Most likely this will occur for the industrial-commercial complex of the Klang Valley in Selangor and Pinang, which is already receiving a major part of the migration flow in the country. Unless very strong disincentives are applied by the government it is expected that both firms and migrant labour will continue to find the political and administrative capital an exciting place to move into. This is indeed confirmed in a recent study of the impact of regional industrial incentives (Chan, 1980). The evidence suggests that industrial decentralisation has failed to shift firms and labour away from the metropolitan to smaller urban or rural centres.

On the other hand, the noticeable increase in the number of industrial estates in the designated locational incentive areas is likely to affect population mobility. In the case of the poor states of Kelantan, Perlis and Kedah, however, the objective of the Third Malaysia Plan is to move a sizeable amount of labour from these to other states. This appears to be quite inconsistent with the broad purpose of rural industrialisation using locational incentives and industrial estates. The net effect, therefore, is difficult to determine a priori.

However, the nature of the migration that will occur as a result of rural industrialisation is quite predictable. The migrant labour will be expected to conform to the general characteristics of the migrants analysed in an earlier section for the 1970 Population Census. But there are two possible qualifications: first, the migrants will have more schooling. This is largely because of the increased demand for education and the recent government policy of allowing students to stay longer in the formal school system. Second, not only males but young unmarried females will join the labour flow. In recent years female migration has become a noticeable phenomenon in Malaysia. Because of the rapid socio-economic structural changes in both the rural and the urban areas, women have become active in the labour market of the monetised sector. A study of two industrial estates in the growth centre of Pinang concludes that it was "the females who profited from the large-size, labour-intensive industries..." (von der Mehden, 1973). The implications of female migration are wider than the question of more geographical mobility. Besides the social implications, it has a chain effect on other demographic factors such as age at marriage, fertility, etc. In the sending areas the supply of labour, and farm and household activities are also affected. The increasing flow of rural migrant labour, particularly Malay female workers, has far-reaching implications which are only recently being studied (Chan, 1982b).

Another predictable demographic effect of rural industrialisation is on Malay mobility - already the highest among the three ethnic groups - which will be boosted by the employment opportunities. The volume and rate of migration and the number of Malay female migrants will increase. When this occurs it will help to realise the Malay urbanisation objective of the New Economic Policy - though by how much the final social benefits will exceed the costs is difficult to judge.

During the early period of development, industrial estates were located mainly in the largest urban centres. In 1970, for instance, all the eight industrial estates were in towns with over 50,000 residents (table 16). By 1978 the situation had changed. The industrial decentralisation policy led to the development of more industrial estates in towns with less than 15,000 residents. This is planned to increase further. While not having more industrial centres located in them would somewhat, though not totally, slow the expansion of towns with more than 50,000 residents, the new industrial estates in the small and intermediate towns would definitely encourage their growth. This would fall in line with the development of a hierarchy of small urban growth centres which would absorb the rural migrants who would otherwise move to the metropolitan centres.

It was mentioned earlier that one of the characteristics of migration in Peninsular Malaysia was the preference for short-distance moves, and the importance of moving between contiguous states. Such a pattern of mobility among migrants will be further enhanced by the location of industrial estates. In spite of the emphasis on rural industrialisation, the industrial estates are still predominantly close to major urban centres. This will undoubtedly intensify short-distance mobility, including short distance inter-urban and intra-urban mobility, circular migration, and step-wise migration. With the improvement in the network of transport, workers are now willing to commute up to 60 miles to work instead of changing residential location. This is illustrated by the effect on labour mobility of the new highway between the federal capital of Kuala Lumpur and outlying towns with industrial estates. Circular migration, which is a common phenomenon in the north-eastern agricultural states of Kedah and Perlis, will also be intensified among the network of growing small, intermediate and larger urban centres, which offer increasing employment opportunities.

One important role of industrial estates and small urban centres is that they encourage step-wise migration. In a survey of 25 small towns (Jones, 1965) with a population of 1,000-5,000, it was found that they experienced only a 17 per cent growth in population during 1957-64 because of out-migration. Such sizeable out-migration is confirmed by a more recent study (Lee, 1977) of 10 small towns which had an average of 1.53 out-migrants per household. The majority of migrants (77 per cent) moved to metropolitan centres like Kuala Lumpur, Seremban, Melaka and Klang. The role of small and intermediate towns as sources of population accretion for metropolitan centres will be further enhanced with the

Table 16: Relationship of industrial estates and urban location in Peninsular Malaysia

Regions/states	No. of industrial estates in different size class of towns											
	1970			1974			1978			Planned		
	Less than 15,000	15,000–50,000	More than 50,000	Less than 15,000	15,000–50,000	More than 50,000	Less than 15,000	15,000–50,000	More than 50,000	Less than 15,000	15,000–50,000	More than 50,000
Northern states	–	–	–	1	2	3	1	3	3	3	–	1
Kedah	–	–	–	–	2	–	–	3	–	3	–	–
Kelantan	–	–	–	–	–	2	–	–	2	–	–	–
Perlis	–	–	–	–	–	1	–	–	1	–	–	–
Terengganu	–	–	–	1	–	–	1	–	–	–	–	1
Southern states	–	–	2	2	2	5	5	2	10	2	2	1
Johor	–	–	2	–	–	3	–	–	5	–	1	1
Melaka	–	–	–	1	1	2	1	1	5	1	–	–
Pahang	–	–	–	1	1	–	4	1	–	1	1	–
Western states	–	–	6	1	6	10	1	6	15	5	6	–
Negeri Sembilan	–	–	1	–	1	1	–	1	1	2	1	–
Perak	–	–	2	1	1	2	1	1	3	–	2	–
Pinang	–	–	1	–	4	4	–	4	4	–	–	–
Selangor	–	–	2	–	–	3	–	–	7	3	3	–
Total	–	–	8	4	10	18	7	11	28	10	8	2

Source: Malaysian Industrial Development Authority.

spread of industrial estates to such places, for industrial estates will facilitate the easy movement of rural migrants to small towns. They, or the second generation, will not find it difficult to move from these intermediate points to the larger urban centres. More industrial decentralisation definitely points in the direction of more labour mobility, some circular but mostly pro-urban in direction.

(iii) New urban growth centres

As part of the industrialisation and urbanisation programme to restructure the economy, the strategy of growth centre development is now given its due attention in the Third Malaysia Plan. Quite a number of master plans have been drawn up; some are already at the implementation stage. The main thrust of the strategy is to establish growth poles which would be responsible for diffusing the spread effects to the surrounding areas. A three-tier system is envisaged with the following structure:

(a) At the top level are the major growth centres in the Klang Valley, Penang, Ipoh, and Johor Baru.

(b) At the middle level are the intermediate cities like Kuantan, Muar, Kota, and Alor Setar.

(c) At the lower level are the network of new townships in the rural areas, for example, the new towns in Pahang Tenggara.

It is thought that since the metropolitan urban centres are already well ensconced growth poles there is no need to give them top priority for development. As such, the priority development poles will be the intermediate cities like Kuantan.

Kuantan is singled out to be developed as the growth pole for the eastern part of Peninsular Malaysia. It is considered to be part of the massive Pahang Tenggara regional development programme, and will serve as the future commercial-industrial hub. At the same time, Kuantan (which is also a port) will function as the outlet for the industrial estates around the region. There will be at least 12 industrial estates under its influence. The projected population target by 1990 for Kuantan is about 250,000 (now about 47,000 for the town and 81,000 for the urban periphery), which is regarded as the threshold size. The development of Kuantan in the eastern region will affect the migration stream of the country. Migrant labour will come from the contiguous states of Terengganu, Kelantan and Johor. Competition for labour between the demands of the new growth centre and the land development schemes is to be expected. It is envisaged that the land development schemes in Pahang will as a consequence face an aggravated labour shortage. As it is, Kuantan is already attracting substantial labour from the surrounding villages, to the dismay of land development planners who cannot obtain the necessary labour. If Kuantan succeeds as a growth pole area the future migration pattern of the country will be changed quite substantially.

(b) Integrated rural development policy

Integrated rural development or in situ development, as the term is used in the Third Malaysia Plan, refers to the developing or upgrading of depressed poverty areas, for example, in the states of Kedah, Kelantan, Perlis and Terengganu. The integrated rural development programme is designed to complement the land development and industrialisation policies of the country.

Whilst differing in details, integrated rural development programmes generally have the following components:

(a)　the implementation of land and tenancy reforms;

(b)　the provision of credit and subsidies;

(c)　the promotion of labour – intensive agricultural activities;

(d)　the provision of physical infrastructure;

(e)　the establishment of marketing networks for outputs and inputs;

(f)　the introduction of rural vocational education;

(g)　the expansion of rural employment opportunities;

(h)　the establishment of rural market towns.

In situ development projects in Peninsular Malaysia have incorporated many of the elements listed above. For instance, the North Kelantan Rural Development Project (74,000 acres), the West Johor Agricultural Development Project (330,000 acres in Phase I and 600,000 acres in Phase II), and the Krian/Sungai Marrik Agricultural Project (75,500 acres) have implemented such development activities in varying degrees. The emphasis is on output and productivity as the major objectives, however. The retention of rural population is also mentioned as one of the auxiliary objectives. Though the physical aspects of rural development are given much attention, institutional reforms and agrarian changes as part of the integrated rural development strategy have never been given any emphasis. In fact, it is these changes which would ultimately lead to more equity and employment opportunities for rural residents. The increased employment opportunities would help to keep the rural population from moving to urban areas. The stress on capital-intensive methods in rural production has been found to lead to more inequalities in income and land ownership (Griffin, 1973). This, in many cases, has become a major cause of out-migration.

Most of the in situ development programmes in Malaysia are not very successful in retaining potential migrants because they are not specifically designed to cater for the differentiated needs, aspirations, and motivations of rural residents.

As a case in point this is somewhat confirmed by the findings of studies on out-migration in West Johor, which is a designated poverty region in the Third Malaysia Plan (Cheong, 1979; Chan, 1982a). In 1970 the West Johor Agricultural Development Project was implemented with a package programme including extension, credit, marketing and processing services, irrigation, and drainage infrastructure. The emphasis was thus on capital inputs and infrastructural development, with no mention of agrarian reforms. However, this massive capital injection has not completely succeeded in curbing out-migration from the region, which has about a quarter of a million people. During the 1957-70 intercensal period the population growth rate in the region was less than 2 per cent (below the national average of 2.8 per cent), mainly because of out-migration. Though the latest out-migration rate for the region as a whole is not known, a recent survey of 550 respondents recorded that 70 per cent have plans to leave the region within the next two years (Chan, 1982a). This seems to indicate that the in situ development programme has so far not satisfied the needs of those who intend to move and cannot therefore stop them from migrating out of the area.

Table 17 provides a summary of the salient characteristics of potential migrants in the West Johor region. The selective nature of the migration process, especially for those indicating a rural-urban direction, is clearly shown. These potential out-migrants come from the specific age group 15-25, and have a certain level of education. Those indicating an inclination for a rural-rural move were generally landless, with large families and a preference for rural living.

The above analysis suggests that it is necessary to establish in situ development projects with differentiated features which could satisfy the different requirements and aspirations of various subgroups. Unfortunately

Table 17: Characteristics of potential rural out-migrants[1] from West Johor region

Characteristics	Intended direction	
	Rural-urban	Rural-rural
Age	Young, 15-25 years	Older, 29+
Sex	Male	Male; probably entire family
Education	On average 7 years of schooling, i.e. secondary schooling	Religious education or only a few years of primary schooling
Family size	Not relevant; unmarried, or newly married	Large household size; about 5.5 household members
Occupation/skills	Little employment experience	Agricultural background
Urban contacts	High urban awareness	More contacts with rural places
Land ownership	Landless	Own small plots or mostly landless
Modern attitudes	Ambitious; risk-taker	Generally risk averter
Motive for migration	Self-improvement; non-agricultural activities preferred	To seek land and higher income for family

[1] Refers to those with intentions to move within two years.

Source: P. Chan: Preliminary findings of survey on out-migrants in West Johor (University of Kuala Lumpur, 1982).

rural development inputs, especially the lumpy investments, are unstructured with respect to the type of impact on different subgroups of rural residents. Rural development strategies are in the nature of "blanket" policies, and the programme implicitly assumes a uniform response among the target groups. This is the weakness of in situ development programmes as a strategy in affecting the mobility of all rural residents.

In practice, it is difficult to determine the migration impact of the in situ development policy in Malaysia. First, most in situ development programmes include projects with multiple objectives. The net effects are therefore difficult to disentangle and in most cases confounded and uncertain. Second, the time lag between the introduction of such projects and their effects in reversing migration trends may be quite substantial and could not be "captured" in "spot analysis".

However, in the light of the experiences of other countries, it seems likely that in situ development in Malaysia will not be completely effective in retaining the rural population unless it is supported by land reforms. While this may not totally stop out-migration, the higher incomes, better employment opportunities, and enhanced security due to land reform programmes should slow it down. Indeed, the experiences of Venezuela, Kenya and Sri Lanka point to this. But it must be pointed out immediately that unless there is continued improvement in in situ development the slowing down of out-migration will be confined to the first-generation beneficiaries of reform, and subsequent generations will still move out.

It must also be noted that since such in situ development does not benefit all rural people equally, and neither are its migration effects uniform, it is not an efficacious strategy for influencing population movement. Besides, in designing the strategy of in situ development the government has also overlooked the fact that its efficacy will be enfeebled by the counter-strategy of encouraging rural residents to leave the poor states (Kelantan, Perlis, Kedah). This is a contradiction in the formulation of policy and in the implementation of policy instruments. Despite the huge injections of capital expenditure the retention of rural people in the poorer regions by means of an in situ development strategy is therefore not a realistic objective in the Third Malaysia Plan. Perhaps it would be more appropriate to consider in situ development as a strategy, albeit not intended, to increase the individual potential migrant's options regarding his mobility rather than to regulate it.

(c) Urban restructuring policy

The historical development of urban centres in Peninsular Malaysia was principally influenced by European intervention, the establishment of mining towns, and other infrastructural developments associated with an immigrant population. Urban development did not evolve from an indigenous base, it was grafted on to a local Malay rural environment.

One may discern two phases in the urban development of Peninsular Malaysia. The first occurred during the Emergency Period when a policy of forced redistribution of more than half a million people into about 600 new villages was implemented. This created small urban centres mainly in the western states. In a way this was a "one-shot" affair; apart from the original investment in establishing such villages there has been no vigorous policy or significant development programme to transform such places into growth points. As a consequence, a substantial number of these villages have been stagnating. Many of them have become important sources of out-migration to the larger urban centres. These out-migrants are mainly of the second and third generations.

The second phase is associated with the policy of the government in pursuing the restructuring exercise within the framework of the New Economic Policy. This is essentially the realignment of the numerical imbalance between the Malay and non-Malay population in the urban areas. It is also the thrust of the New Economic Policy to "modernise" the Malays by urbanisation, and to commercialise them by reconstructing the functional relationship between ethnic and occupational specialisation. In attempting to accomplish the task of equalising the development situation of the Malays with that of non-Malays, the government has thus embarked on a programme of creating new urban centres in rural areas and restructuring existing major metropolitan urban centres.

Table 18 shows the urban distribution by ethnic composition since 1931. Malay urban involvement has been steadily increasing since 1931. However, it is regarded as inadequate by the government in the context of the national ethnic proportion (about 54 per cent Malays, 33 per cent Chinese, 10 per cent Indian, and 1 per cent others).

Given the fact that all the larger urban centres are predominantly non-Malay, with the Malays concentrated in the rural areas, it is to be expected that if urban growth is to depend on migration it will be mainly a question of urbanising Malay migrants.

Table 18: Urban population of Peninsular Malaysia, 1931-80

| Year | Total population | Urban population (above 10,000) | % urban population | % of urban population | |
				Malay	Non-Malay
1931	3,788,000	570,513	15.1	17.3	82.7
1947	4,908,000	929,928	18.9	19.0	81.0
1957	6,268,000	1,666,969	26.6	21.0	79.0
1970	8,819,000	2,530,433	28.7	27.6	72.4
1975	10,385,000	3,341,000	32.2	29.2	70.8
1980	11,822,000	4,148,000	35.1	32.8	67.2

Sources: Third Malaysia Plan; Mid-term Review of the Third Malaysia Plan, 1976-80; Population Census data 1970 (Malaysia, Department of Statistics).

Since 1957 the growth of urbanisation has been dependent mainly, though not entirely, on natural population increase (table 19). Up to 1970, Malays constituted 37.6 per cent of rural-urban migrants (table 20). There is little variation in the extent of Malay urban migration to urban centres of different sizes. This pattern is quite different at the regional level, however. This reflects mainly the spatial distribution of Malays in areas of rural out-migration where the towns are located.

The largest urban growth rate for Malays is in Kuala Lumpur (9 per cent). This is followed by Johor Baru (6.7 per cent). The attraction of Kuala Lumpur to potential migrants is not difficult to explain: it is not only the administrative and political centre; it is also the hub of the commercial-industrial complex in the Klang Valley which offers employment and other socio-economic opportunities to migrants.

Apart from the actual attractions themselves of metropolitan centres like Kuala Lumpur to migrants, the government has a policy of encouraging people, specifically the Malays, to move to urban centres. Several measures have been adopted to achieve this objective. Some of these measures include the following:

(a) The provision of easy and liberal credit and loans to Malays for large commercial projects and small businesses. Quasi-government departments have been established for such purposes, viz. MARA (Majlis Amanah Ra'ayat) and PERNAS (Perbadanan Nasional).

(b) The implementation of an employment quota under which employers in large, important industries and commercial houses have to employ at least 30 per cent Malays. This is to be done regardless of the ethnic population ratios in the areas, mostly metropolitan urban centres, where the business firms are located.

(c) The creation and provision of job opportunities for Malays, especially in the government departments, which are located in urban centres.

(d) The provision of low-cost loans and easy credit by the private sector, as advised by the government, to Malays to buy houses.

(e) The establishment of new housing estates where a 30 per cent ownership quota for Malays has to be enforced.

Table 19: Sources of urban growth, Peninsular Malaysia, 1957-70

Size of urban centre (urban in 1957)	Urban population		Average annual increase (%)	Source of urban growth	
	1957	1970		Migration	Natural increase
100,000+	716,952	969,026	2.4	44,044	208,030
50,000-100,000	325,412	483,884	3.1	24,069	134,403
25,000-50,000	304,822	426,614	2.6	-4,106	125,989
10,000-25,000	330,794	492,078	3.1	24,658	136,626
5,000-10,000	308,107	389,589	1.8	-45,171	126,653
Total	1,986,087	2,761,191	2.6	43,494	731,610

Source: Population Census data 1970 (Malaysia, Department of Statistics).

Table 20: Malay urban migration and growth of ethnic groups, Peninsular Malaysia, 1970

Region/city	Malay migrants (%)	Average annual growth of Chinese population (%)	Average annual growth of Malay population (%)
West [1]			
Kuala Lumpur	29.8	3.8	9.0
100,000+ (excluding Kuala Lumpur)	24.9	2.7	3.7
50,000-100,000	29.6	1.5	4.6
10,000-50,000	23.3	2.7	3.7
South-east [2]			
100,000+	47.5	3.6	6.7
50,000-100,000	37.3	1.7	3.3
North-east [3]			
100,000+	–	–	–
50,000-100,000	53.8	2.7	2.5
10,000-50,000	61.8	1.4	2.4
Peninsular Malaysia			
100,000+ (including Kuala Lumpur)	33.7	3.4	6.5
50,000-100,000	40.2	2.4	4.0
10,000-50,000	39.0	1.9	3.1
Total	37.6	2.6	4.5

[1] Selangor, Perak, Pinang, Negeri Sembilan and Melaka.

[2] Johor and Pahang.

[3] Kedah, Perlis, Kelantan, and Terengganu.

Source: Population Census data 1970 (Malaysia, Department of Statistics).

(f)   The construction of new low-cost housing projects to cater for the Malay urban migrants.

(g)   A liberal attitude towards the establishment of squatters in urban areas and the upgrading of Malay squatter settlements.

(h)   The provision of financial assistance and scholar-ships for Malay education, especially in secondary and tertiary education in the urban areas.

(i)   The establishment of a good network of communi-cation systems (roads in particular) linking the rural and urban areas and thereby facilitating mobility.

All the above in one way or another increase the urban awareness of the Malays, stimulate them to move out of rural areas and smaller towns, sponsor them explicitly or implicitly to migrate, and reinforce their desire to stay in the urban areas after their arrival.

These measures, however, do not constitute a systematic set of co-ordinated policy instruments for the explicit and expressed purpose of promoting urban in-migration. They are ad hoc and uncoordinated and, as such, rather diffused in their impact. Since no specific programmes (as in the FELDA model) are designed to establish criteria regarding, for instance, the rate and source of urban in-migration, the target group of in-migrants, and the resettlement of such urban in-migrants, the efficacy of the pro-urban migration instruments is affected. Unanticipated consequences could emerge in the future which could become socio-economic-cum-political costs to the government. The divergence between the rate of growth of employment opportunities and the rate of in-migration, for example, not only leads to unemploy-ment problems, but also has political implications in a multi-ethnic context where there is a strong drive towards wealth and employment redistribution along ethnic lines.

One significant consequence of urbanisation and the pro-urban migration policy of the government is the growth of squatting. There are no up-to-date data providing a national perspective on the squatting situation. However, there are indications of a wide-spread squatting of state land. Its main characteristics are its extensive diffusion and the heterogeneous activities of the squatters.

The squatting situation in the metropolitan area of Kuala Lumpur reflects the situation in the country as a whole. During 1968, a survey conducted by the Kuala Lumpur Commissioner estimated that 26,000 squatter families were living in about 20,000 squatter units (City Hall, 1981). In 1974, the squatter population in the Federal Territory was estimated to be one-fifth of the total population, or about 153,000. The most recent estimate disclosed that during the period 1974-78 there was a 10 per cent increase in the squatter population. In 1978, there were 243,000 squatters, representing 25 per cent of the population of the Federal Territory (ibid., 1981).

The squatters of Kuala Lumpur reflect the ethnic plurality structure of the country. In 1978, the ethnic distribution was 52 per cent Chinese, 33 per cent Malays, and about 15 per cent Indians and others. In 1968 the distribution was, respectively, 68, 21 and 11 per cent for Chinese, Malays and Indians.

The rapid growth of the Malay squatter community has been due to the effects of modernisation and the New Economic Policy. Both have greatly heightened the expectations of the Malays, and broadened the opportunities for them. Malay migration to the Klang Valley region during the last few years has been increasing rapidly.

The planning and management of a growing metropolitan urban centre like Kuala Lumpur is a new experience for the government administrators. It is not difficult to administer large overgrown villages now designated as urban areas, but to devise an appropriate mix of policies and programmes for a growing metropolitan area with a large squatter population in the context of ethnic plurality and ethnic politics is not easy.

As far as the issue of squatters and squatting is concerned the government has neither coherent national policies nor consistent programmes. The major piece of legislation is the National Land Code, established in 1965. In 1969 the essential (Clearance of Squatters) regulations were enacted. The National Land Code was further strengthened in 1974. These laws are all against squatting. Squatters, being violators of such laws, are subject to various penalities, such as demolition of their dwellings, eviction, fines, and imprisonment. The National Land Code specifies a fine of 10,000 Malaysian ringgit or one year's imprisonment for squatting. Squatting is thus a criminal act.

There are some seemingly humanitarian elements built into the various pieces of legislation, however. These are concerned with the procedures for eviction, demolition, compensation and resettlement. But with amendments to the original laws, even some of this assistance is no longer obligatory. Eviction of squatters, for instance, may now be carried out without any prior notice.

The agencies of the state involved in implementing such legislation include the following: City Hall, the Land Office, the Urban Development Authority, and the Ministry of Housing and Local Government. Each agency is supposed to have its assigned role and functions. In practice, however, there is always a conflict in executing responsibilities. Above all, the political leaders, who perceive squatters as so many units of votes, have the last word in decision-making.

The strategy of the administrators in dealing with squatters and squatting, as part of an urban development programme, is based on one of the following actions:

(a) eradication (eviction of squatters and demolition of settlements), with no other tied-in programme;

(b) eradication (eviction of squatters and demolition of settlement), with follow-up relocation and settlement of squatters;

(c) in situ rehabilitation and upgrading of squatter settlements.

Unfortunately whatever action is taken is usually partial, ad hoc, and palliative. This is because the issue of squatters and squatting is not conceptualised in its totality. Urban administrators view squatters and squatting as an isolated problem. They do not perceive them as an integral part of the process of development and structural change in the economy.

As mentioned earlier, one of the overt objectives of the New Economic Policy is to restructure the ethnic composition of urban centres. This is being achieved by accelerating urban in-migration, particularly of rural Malays. Unfortunately for the urban planners, the majority of them are landless and poor. In this context, the urban planners are confronting the tail end of structural changes in the rural-urban continuum. Given an average in-migration quantum of 1,000 persons per week into metropolitan Kuala Lumpur there is very little that the administrators and planners can do to cope with, contain or check squatter development.

Besides such contradictions in development policies, co-ordinated planning efforts are also frustrated by the federal-state government structure under which land is the prerogative of each state. This is one political right which every state is reluctant to compromise in its transactions with the federal government. Consequently, land development and planning is somewhat inward-looking in terms of political boundaries. In relation to squatting, this has created the inefficient principle that each state, including the Federal Territory, is responsible for its own strategy. In effect, however, squatters can be displaced from one state to become the problem of another. Theoretically, all squatting in the Federal Territory can be eradicated by shifting them to the boundary periphery, which is in the state of Selangor. Indeed, there is at present an alarming growth of squatter settlements perching on the border of the Federal Territory.

The strategy of squatter settlement eradication without resettlement is not an effective way of dealing with the problem. It only displaces squatters, who then become floating, migrating squatters. Re-squatting eventually occurs, though in a different location. Some reverse migration may be created; if so, the squatters become rural squatters again.

Resettlement and upgrading of select squatter areas appear to be more positive approaches. By themselves, however, being piecemeal and project-by-project in implementation, they are inadequate as the basic factors responsible for squatting are not altered. A successful programme of resettlement and upgrading also depends on the availability of urban land and adequate housing facilities.

Urban land is available, but not necessarily for alienation to squatters. The decisions regarding urban land use and ownership are essentially based on the economic returns from using such land. Urban squatting is usually considered economically wasteful since the economic returns are negligible and the opportunity cost is high. The longer the duration of the squatting the larger are the economic returns forgone.

This capitalistic attitude explains the evaluation criterion suggested for evicting squatter settlements. It has been argued that all urban land which is valued at more than 3 ringgit, probably higher now, per square foot, should not be allowed for squatting (Whering, 1976). This criterion, of course, affects the regularisation of land tenure in squatter settlements, regardless of their length of occupation. Some settlements are as old as Kuala Lumpur and are still denied legal status.

Widespread regularisation of existing squatter settlements has other implications besides the economic opportunity cost. First, it means the final granting of recognition to an act which is defined as illegal. Besides being a contradiction in itself, the longer-term significance is its attractiveness to potential squatters, for regularisation of various tenurial systems in squatter settlements must encourage more squatting in other areas. It creates the expectation that a squatter settlement would eventually be regularised and legalised. Upgrading old squatter settlements has a similar outcome: it helps to increase squatting.

The present policy of the government towards urban squatters is in the nature of various ad hoc upgrading programmes and the provision of low-cost housing. The track record of supplying low-cost housing is so far a dismal one. Between 1969 and 1974, City Hall could only resettle about 1,589 families in flats, that is, an average of 318 families per year. During 1979, the target of completing 2,938 units of low-cost housing was not realised: only 714 units were built. Between 1976 and 1979 only 4 out of the 16 housing projects had been completed. The latest target is to build 16,000 units of low-cost housing during the next two years. Considering past performances, it is doubtful whether any satisfactory rate of progress can be achieved to resettle squatters and the urban poor. Besides, even such low-cost housing is now beyond the reach of the poor. It is estimated that 80 per cent of the urban poor could not afford it (Whering, 1976).

The development of policies and programmes to help squatters and to solve the problem of urban squatting involves more than physical resettlement and legal controls. What is needed is to accept squatters as social capital, and not to view them as liabilities in the development balance sheet.

Conclusions

The Malaysian situation is characterised by two dominant population movements: rural-directed migration into Pahang state and a more urban/industrial oriented movement into Selangor. From census analysis it is clear that migrants in Malaysia are relatively young, single, and educated. Malays, particularly males, account for the largest single migrant group.

Migration policy in Malaysia is affected not so much by the expedients of population pressure on resources as by the ethnicity factor. Under the New Economic Policy, regional land development schemes in Malaysia have been largely successful not only in helping the assisted migrants themselves, but also in stabilising rural populations, particularly in areas of traditional out-migration such as Kedah and Perlis. Migrants under these schemes are highly subsidised, which makes the schemes very costly. Notwithstanding this, these programmes are politically expedient. Sole dependence on resettlement per se will not suffice, however. Greater attention needs to be paid to employment, land tenure, and income objectives. Unless these problems are tackled, second-generation problems associated with worsening labour/land ratios will reduce the retentive capacities of the resettled areas.   There is a real danger that the policy may merely succeed in redistributing poverty geographically.

Most in situ development programmes have not been successful so far in retaining potential migrants, mainly because of the absence of effective land reforms.   There is also some inconsistency between the consequences of in situ development and other migration objectives.

It is difficult at this stage to assess the precise effects of regional industrial and urban decentralisation on the rate and direction of migration.   Industrial decentralisation could be a means of increasing employment and income and the general level of economic activity in the rural areas.   But the choice of technique, whether capital-intensive or labour-intensive, and access to the new benefits, could also disrupt the rural socio-economic fabric and even aggravate existing inequalities.   The demographic effects and the effects on population mobility are not easily predictable.   Industrial relocation has been effected through the designation of location incentive areas, most of which are in the less developed states. The effect on population movement is even more difficult to predict here, particularly when contradictory policies are being followed such as the establishment of industrial estates in states designated in the Third Malaysia Plan as out-migrant areas.   However, this policy is likely to increase the mobility of Malays in general and female Malays in particular, with far-reaching social and economic implications for female migrants and the sending areas.

In general, the review of policies and programmes related to migration in this study indicates that their achievements have so far been limited.   There are several reasons for this.   First, the inter-relationships between the economic, social and spatial elements are complex and not easily anticipated in development plans. In situ development projects, for example, by raising the income of the rural poor could help to retain people or increase their capability to migrate.   Economic theory and planning are not in a position to predict in which of these directions the programme will lead.   Second, whilst the National Economic Policy has been identified, the demographic goals (except for the broad ethnic balance) have not been explicitly stated.   Third, the implementation of policies and programmes is frequently erratic. Fourth, the involvement of a large number of implementation agencies (national, regional and local) generates conflict and competition for limited resources.   Consequently the implementation of policies in parallel but separate ways often leads to cancellation of each other's efforts.   And, finally, due attention is still not given to the monitoring and review of national development plans.

This is essential if the policy impact of a programme is to be fully understood, especially if the programme is later revised.

Chapter 4

MIGRATION-RELATED POLICIES: A STUDY OF THE SRI LANKA EXPERIENCE

By A.D.V. de S. Indraratna, H.M.A. Codippily,
A.W.A.D.G. Abayasekera and A.T.P.L. Abeykoon*

The population of Sri Lanka is around 15 million with an average density of 220 per square kilometre. The population distribution is extremely uneven, however. The six wet south-western districts of Colombo, Kalutara, Galle, Matara, Kegalla and Kurunegala contain over 50 per cent of the population with only 20 per cent of the land area, while the six dry northern and eastern districts of Vavuniya, Mannar, Monaragala, Polonnaruwa, Trincomalee and Batticaloa contain less than 8 per cent of the population with 34 per cent of the land area.

The largest city of Sri Lanka, Colombo, has a population over three and a half times that of the second largest city and five times that of the third. The urban population of Sri Lanka is nearly 22 per cent of the total population, and the city of Colombo alone contains nearly one-fifth of it. While the municipality of Colombo has a population of 607,000, the smallest urban unit of Kadugannawa, an urban council, has a population of only 1,600. The density of population of Colombo is 18 times that of the whole island.

The population distribution inherited from the period of colonial rule was even more uneven. The need to relieve the population pressure in the south-west quadrant of the island, comprising eight administrative districts, had been receiving the attention of the Board of Sri Lanka Ministers since 1931. This has gathered momentum since the time of Independence in 1948, and a number of social and economic policies have been implemented which have had both direct and indirect effects on internal migration.

---

* Respectively, Department of Economics, University of Sri Lanka, Colombo; Ministry of Planning and Economic Affairs, Colombo; Ministry of Planning and Economic Affairs, Colombo; and Demographic Training and Research Unit, University of Sri Lanka, Colombo.

Migration-related policies implemented in Sri Lanka include irrigation and land development policies, land settlement schemes, dispersal of industries, development of rural infrastructure, eradication of malaria, and provision of welfare services such as free education, free health services and cheap housing. The purpose of this study is to review these policies and assess their effectiveness. The policies are examined with respect to their efficacy as instruments in achieving the desired population distribution objectives and other development goals. In doing this, an attempt is made to understand the rationale behind the policies and the process and mechanisms by which they were formulated. A few policies are selected for critical appraisal on the basis of existing evidence, supplemented by two case studies.

The period selected for this study is 1946 to 1971. This period has been selected for two reasons. First, this is a period in respect of which adequate data are available; second, it roughly corresponds to the post-Independence period during which successive Sri Lankan governments have been concerned with population distribution problems.

The study is mainly based on existing data. The available sources of data on population mobility are the censuses of population. Though questions relating to place of birth were included in all censuses in Sri Lanka, data on place of birth by place of residence were collected and published for the first time in the 1946 census of population. Subsequent censuses taken in 1953, 1963, and 1971 also collected data on these two aspects. In addition, the 1971 census had questions on duration of stay at usual residence and previous residence. This information was collected only in respect of the population within a 10 per cent sample of the census blocks. The quantitative analysis of internal migration in this study will be mainly limited to the intercensal periods 1946-53, 1953-63 and 1963-71. In addition to censuses, information relating to land settlement schemes also provides relevant migration data.

A Profile of Internal Migration in Sri Lanka

The main purpose of this section is to present a profile of internal migration in Sri Lanka, to serve as a backdrop for subsequent discussions.

(a)   Inter-district and inter-regional
      migration flows

(i)   The period 1946-53

Two important studies have been carried out on internal migration related to this period. The first was by Vamathevan in 1961 and the second by Abhayaratne and Jayawardene in 1965.

Vamathevan's study revealed that out of the 20 districts, 11 were net in-migration districts. These were Colombo, Matale, Hambantota, Mannar, Vavuniya, Batticaloa, Kurunegala, Puttalam, Chilaw, Anuradhapura and Badulla. The districts of Puttalam and Chilaw were merged after 1953, and referred to as the Puttalam district. If this classification is used for purposes of comparison with latter periods, there were 10 in-migration districts in all during the period 1946-53. The out-migration districts were Kalutara, Matara, Kandy, Nuwara Eliya, Galle, Jaffna, Trincomalee, Ratnapura and Kegalla. Table 1 shows the gross in-migration into the respective districts in absolute numbers as well as in terms of percentage of their average (mid-censal period) populations.

One of the ways in which the relative popularity of a destination for a migratory move can be measured is through an index of attraction (see Appendix I). The index of attraction computed by Abhayaratne and Jayawardene showed that the highest value was for Colombo (22.8), followed by Anuradhapura (12.6) and Kurunegala (10.4). Five districts had values less than one-tenth of that of Colombo.

One drawback of the index used by Abhayaratne and Jayawardene is that it is computed as an unweighted average of a set of percentages. This leaves room for distortions; for example, an unduly large out-migration from a densely populated district may not be adequately reflected in the index. To overcome this difficulty we have suggested an alternative index. This index directly expresses the extent to which a particular district has been able to attract in-migration from the totality of out-migrants from all the districts. Table 1 shows the index of attraction by districts for the period 1946-53. In terms of this index, the highest value was obtained for Anuradhapura (25.6) followed by Colombo (23.1) and Kurunegala (12.8).

In the absence of periodic surveys of mobility of persons or continuous population registers, the only source of information on migration available is the census of population, which gives a cross-classification of place of birth by place of residence. According to the place

Table 1: Gross in-migration and index of attraction by districts, 1946-53

Districts	Gross in-migration[1]		Index of attraction I (as defined by Abhayaratne and Jayawardene)[2]	Index of attraction H (as defined in this study)
	Number of persons	% of population		
Anuradhapura	47,887	25.97	12.6	25.6
Badulla	7,546	1.80	3.8	4.1
Batticaloa	15,474	6.53	7.0	8.5
Colombo	37,708	2.41	22.8	23.1
Galle	2,538	0.51	2.1	1.5
Hambantota	3,996	2.34	1.9	2.2
Jaffna	1,386	0.30	5.1	0.8
Kalutara	1,655	0.34	2.8	0.9
Kandy	4,132	0.53	6.7	2.8
Kegalla	1,973	0.45	2.2	1.2
Kurunegala	23,528	4.23	10.4	12.8
Mannar	705	1.87	1.5	0.4
Matale	12,869	7.21	3.5	6.9
Matara	4,217	1.10	4.4	2.4
Nuwara Eliya	7,301	2.46	2.6	4.1
Puttalam	7,293	3.54	2.4	4.0
Ratnapura	2,589	0.68	2.9	1.4
Trincomalee	780	0.98	0.3	0.4
Vavuniya	4,300	14.74	3.3	2.3

1   Vamathevan (1961).

2   Abhayaratne and Jayawardene (1965).

of birth analysis carried out by Vamathevan, migrants to the Colombo district were mainly drawn from the districts of Galle, Jaffna, Kandy and Ratnapura. However, the Anuradhapura district registered the largest in-migration; migrants were drawn mainly from the districts of Kandy, Kegalla, Colombo, and Nuwara Eliya. Among the out-migration districts, Kandy recorded the largest loss, the other major out-migration districts being Galle, Kegalla and Jaffna.

The major inter-district migratory flows during the intercensal period are illustrated in map 1.[1] This map indicates that internal migration mainly took place from neighbouring districts, except in the case of Jaffna, Galle, and Batticaloa, from where migrants had moved a long distance.

The over-all picture that emerges is of a marked migration from the wet zone to the dry zone, the only exceptions being Jaffna, an out-migration district located in the dry zone, and Colombo, an in-migration district located in the wet zone.

(ii) The period 1953-63

The patterns of migration for this period were analysed using the same methodology as for the earlier period. There were seven in-migration districts during the period, namely Colombo, Mannar, Vavuniya, Batticaloa, Trincomalee, Anuradhapura and Badulla, and 12 out-migration districts, namely Kalutara, Kandy, Nuwara Eliya, Galle, Matara, Hambantota, Jaffna, Kurunegala, Ratnapura, Kegalla, Puttalam, and Matale.

It can be observed that Matale, Hambantota, Puttalam, and Kurunegala were in-migration districts during the preceding period (1946-53) but became out-migration districts during the years 1953-63. Trincomalee was an out-migration district for the period 1946-53 but became an in-migration district during 1953-63. Table 2 indicates the respective magnitudes of gross in-migration during the period 1953-63.

The index of attraction (H_j) computed in respect of this period revealed that the highest value was for Colombo (31.0) followed by Anuradhapura (21.2) and Batticaloa (9.7). It is interesting to note that in terms of the index of attraction, the Anuradhapura-Colombo ordering obtained for the period 1946-53 was reversed during 1953-63. A marked increase in the value of the

---

[1] The Amparai, Monaragala and Polonnaruwa districts shown on this map did not in fact exist as separate districts during this period.

Map 1: Net streams of migration for the districts of Sri Lanka for the intercensal period 1946-53

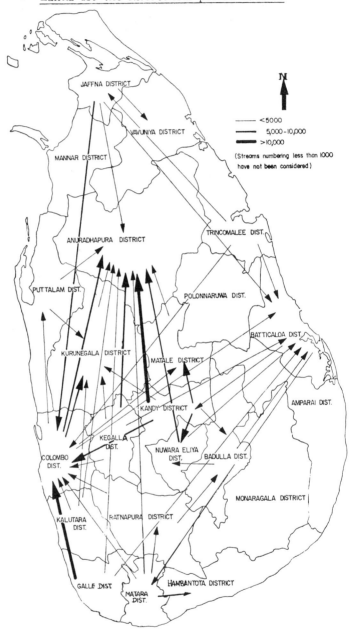

Table 2: Gross in-migration and index of attraction by districts, 1953-63

Districts	Gross in-migration[1]		Index of attraction I (as defined by Abhayaratne and Jayawardene)	Index of attraction H (as defined J in this study)
	Number of persons	% of population		
Anuradhapura	53,616	17.21	12.0	21.2
Badulla	13,151	2.35	5.9	5.2
Batticaloa	25,220	7.43	7.9	9.7
Colombo	75,271	3.84	23.3	31.0
Galle	9,644	1.65	3.1	3.9
Hambantota	6,340	2.72	1.6	2.5
Jaffna	7,068	1.28	4.9	2.7
Kalutara	1,729	0.30	3.5	0.7
Kandy	6,556	0.70	7.2	2.9
Kegalla	1,453	0.28	2.3	0.6
Kurunegala	2,782	0.38	5.5	1.2
Mannar	3,067	5.91	2.0	1.2
Matale	793	0.35	1.5	0.3
Matara	277	0.06	3.0	0.1
Nuwara Eliya	2,534	0.70	2.3	1.1
Puttalam	13,553	5.10	3.2	5.2
Ratnapura	8,800	1.82	5.1	3.6
Trincomalee	17,041	15.32	4.8	6.5
Vavuniya	11,920	22.98	5.8	4.6

1 Adapted from United Nations, Economic and Social Commission for Asia and the Pacific (1976), table 32, p. 51.

index is shown for the districts of Colombo, Trincomalee, Vavuniya, Jaffna, Puttalam, Ratnapura, and Mannar.

Map 2 shows the volume of major inter-district migratory flows for the period 1953-63. The general directions of these flows are similar to those corresponding to the period 1946-53, that is, from the wet zone districts to the dry zone districts. But, as in the previous period, Colombo and Jaffna districts had fared differently. Jaffna lost most of its out-migrants to Colombo and Vavuniya districts during the period 1953-63. Map 2 also shows an increase in the volume of migration when compared with the 1946-53 period. Another significant feature is the increase in long distance migration. In the previous period migration was predominantly over short distances.

(iii) The period 1963-71

At the time of the 1963 census there were 22 districts in all, due to the formation of three new administrative districts, the Polonnaruwa, Monaragala and Amparai districts. The Polonnaruwa district was formed out of part of the former district of Anuradhapura, while the districts of Moneragala and Amparai were respectively formed by dividing the districts of Badulla and Batticaloa. The same number of administrative districts was retained in 1971.

During this period, there were nine in-migration districts, namely, Colombo, Mannar, Vavuniya, Batticaloa, Trincomalee, Puttalam, Anuradhapura, Polonnaruwa, and Monaragala. The out-migration districts were Kalutara, Kandy, Nuwara Eliya, Galle, Matara, Hambantota, Jaffna, Matale, Amparai, Kurunegala, Badulla, Ratnapura, and Kegalla. In comparison with the previous period, there were two significant changes. First, Puttalam, which was an out-migration district during the period 1953-63, became an in-migration district during 1963-71. Second, Badulla had been an in-migration district during the previous period but became an out-migration district during 1963-71; this result is unchanged even if we take into account the in-migration to Monaragala, which formed a part of the earlier district of Badulla (see table 3).

The index of attraction H_j in table 3 clearly shows that Colombo, with an index of 37.9, continued to hold the first place followed by Anuradhapura (9.4), Batticaloa (8.0) and Kalutara (7.4). There was a marked drop in the index for Anuradhapura compared with that for the period 1953-63.

Map 2: Net streams of migration for the districts of Sri Lanka for the intercensal period 1953-63

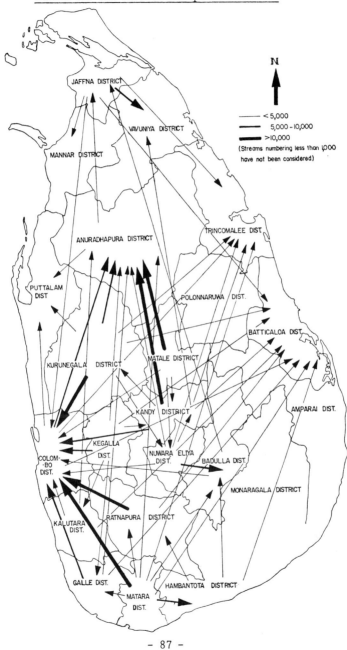

N

——— < 5,000
——— 5,000 - 10,000
━━━ > 10,000
(Streams numbering less than 1,000
have not been considered)

JAFFNA DISTRICT

VAVUNIYA DISTRICT

MANNAR DISTRICT

ANURADHAPURA DISTRICT

TRINCOMALEE DIST.

PUTTALAM DIST

POLONNARUWA DIST.

BATTICALOA DIST.

KURUNEGALA DISTRICT

MATALE DISTRICT

KANDY DISTRICT

AMPARAI DIST.

KEGALLA DIST.

COLOM-BO DIST.

NUWARA ELIYA DIST.

BADULLA DIST.

MONARAGALA DISTRICT

KALUTARA DIST.

RATNAPURA DISTRICT

GALLE DIST.

HAMBANTOTA DISTRICT

MATARA DIST.

Table 3: Gross in-migration and index of attraction by
districts, 1963-71

Districts	Gross in-migration		Index of attraction H_j (as defined in this study)
	Number of persons	% of population	
Amparai	-	-	-
Anuradhapura	22,930	4.85	9.4
Badulla	13,963	1.91	6.3
Batticaloa	18,966	4.05	8.0
Colombo	93,162	3.82	37.9
Galle	3,417	0.50	1.6
Hambantota	7,220	2.35	3.0
Jaffna	4,987	0.76	2.1
Kalutara	18,002	2.65	7.4
Kandy	1,462	0.13	0.7
Kegalla	2,353	0.38	1.0
Kurunegala	6,119	0.65	2.7
Mannar	-	-	-
Matale	9,588	3.36	4.0
Matara	3,724	0.68	1.7
Monaragala	-	-	-
Nuwara Eliya	7,831	1.85	3.4
Polonnaruwa	-	-	-
Puttalam	7,257	2.13	3.0
Ratnapura	7,059	1.17	3.0
Trincomalee	8,314	5.09	3.4
Vavuniya	12,115	14.79	4.9

Source: United Nations, Economic and Social Commission for Asia and the Pacific (1976), table 32 and Population Census, 1971.

Map 3 illustrates the main migratory flows during the period 1963-71. As before, the districts of Jaffna and Colombo fared differently from the other districts in their respective zones. Jaffna lost roughly 80 per cent of its out-migrants to Colombo, Trincomalee and Vavuniya. Kandy, which had very high out-migration, lost its migrants to Colombo, Matale, and Nuwara Eliya.

The main change that took place over the period 1946-71 was a large transfer of population from the wet zone districts to the dry zone districts, whereas no such movement was witnessed over the period 1921-46. Table 4 attempts to show the contrast in migration patterns in respect of these two periods in terms of the difference between national and district growth rates of population.

(b) Rural-urban migration

In population censuses as well as in other surveys, an area is classified as urban or rural on the basis of the types of local authority which exercise administrative powers over the area. Thus areas administered by municipal councils, urban councils, and town councils are classified as urban, whereas areas administered by village councils are classified as rural. Village councils are upgraded to the status of town councils from time to time on the basis of the type of development that takes place within their areas. The extent of development is often measured by the provision of utilities such as water supply and electricity. Considerations such as population density, housing conditions, and growth of industry and commerce are also taken into account when upgrading is done. However, these criteria have not been applied uniformly over time. This has to some extent hampered the measurement of the level of urbanisation. Table 5 shows the extent of the population classified as urban during the period 1946-71.

The data show that during the last two intercensal periods the rate of growth of the urban population has been significantly higher than in the period 1946-53. At first glance it might appear that the growth of the urban population during the latter period is due to rural-urban migration. This is not the case, however. There was in fact a significant accretion of new areas into the urban category during this period. After adjusting for changes in classification, the data indicate that the population classified as urban in 1963 had only increased from 2.016 million to 2.445 million by 1971 (see Department of Census and Statistics, 1978, table 3.6, p. 40). The implicit growth rate was therefore only 2.4 per cent, as opposed to the unadjusted rate of 4.2 per cent per annum shown in table 5. During this period the percentage of

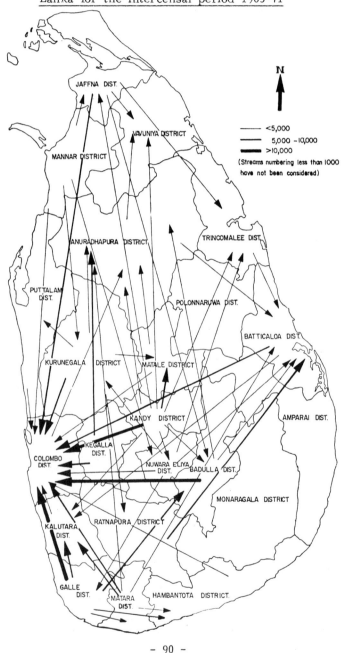

Table 4: Percentage difference between national and district annual growth rates, 1921–71

Districts	1921–46		1946–71	
	Average annual growth rate (%)	Difference between national and district annual growth rates (%)	Average annual growth rate (%)	Difference between national and district annual growth rates (%)
All Districts	1.6		2.6	
Wet zone				
Colombo	1.7	+6.2	2.6	0
Galle	1.5	-6.2	1.9	-26.9
Kalutara	1.4	-12.5	1.9	-26.9
Kandy	1.9	+18.7	2.1	-19.2
Kegalla	1.6	0	2.0	-23.1
Matara	1.6	0	2.1	-19.2
Nuwara Eliya	1.9	+18.7	2.1	-19.2
Ratnapura	2.1	+31.2	2.7	+3.8
Dry zone				
Anuradhapura	1.5	-6.2	5.7	+119.2
Badulla	1.9	+18.7	3.1	+19.2
Batticaloa	1.0	-37.5	3.9	+50.0
Hambantota	0.9	-43.7	3.3	+26.9
Jaffna	1.0	-37.5	2.0	-23.1
Kurunegala	1.3	-18.7	3.1	+19.2
Mannar	0.8	-50.0	3.7	+42.3
Matale	1.2	-25.0	2.9	+11.5
Puttalam	1.1	-31.2	3.0	+15.4
Trincomalee	3.3	+106.2	3.8	+46.2
Vavuniya	0.9	-43.7	5.8	+123.1

Source: Census reports.

Table 5: Growth of total and urban population, 1946-71

Census year	Total population (000s)	Urban population (000s)	Urban population (%)	Average annual growth rate (%)	
				Total population	Urban population
1946	6,657.3	1,023.0	15.4	–	–
1953	8,097.9	1,239.1	15.3	2.8	2.8
1963	10,582.1	2,016.3	19.1	2.7	4.9
1971	12,689.9	2,848.1	22.4	2.2	4.2

Source: Department of Census and Statistics (1978).

the population living in urban areas increased only from
19.1 per cent to 19.3 per cent. In the case of Colombo,
which is by far the most urbanised area in the country,
the population grew only at a rate of 1.2 per cent during
the period 1963-71, which is significantly below the
national average. Even if we consider Colombo and its
surrounding towns,[1] the average rate of growth was
only 2.2 per cent per annum. In the immediate suburbs
of Colombo, however, the area consisting of Kolonnawa,
Kotikawatte, Kotte, Maharagama, Dehiwala-Mount Lavinia
and Kotte-Galkissa, the population grew at a rate of 3.5
per cent per annum during the same period.

The above analysis of the patterns of internal
migration during the period 1946-71 suggests two important features. The first is the transfer of people from
the wet zone districts of the south-west to the dry zone
districts of the north and east, mainly as a result of the
opening up of new land there. Such a movement was
not witnessed during the preceding period 1921-46.
Second, there has been no marked shift of people from
the rural to the urban sector. The population classified
as urban increased by only 2.4 per cent from 2.016
million in 1963 to 2.445 million in 1971, while the total
population also increased by 2.2 per cent over the same
period.

Migration-related Policies

(a) Land settlement and development

Policies concerning land development and alienation
are considered to have had a major impact upon internal
migration patterns over the years.

(i) Land settlement schemes

With the outbreak of the First World War, the
country went through a severe period of food shortage.
This clearly indicated the need for a shift of emphasis
from plantation to food crops. This fundamental change
in land policy was brought about after the establishment
of the Donoughmore Constitution. In accordance with
the Land Commission report issued in 1929, the government assumed the sole ownership of Crown land and set

---

1   Surrounding towns include Kolonnawa UC,
Kotikawatte TC, Kotte UC, Maharagama TC, Dehiwala-
Mount Lavinia MC, Kotte-Galkissa VC, Hendala TC,
Kandana TC, Wattala-Mabole UC, Peliyagoda UC,
Battaramulla TC, and Movatuwa EC.

itself the task of developing land. With the onset of the Depression in the 1930s, there was a slump in the prices of principal export commodities. This reduced employment in the wet zone, which made development of the dry zone an absolute priority. With the introduction of state-aided settlement schemes in 1932 and the enactment of the Land Development Ordinance in 1953, the government actively pursued a policy of selecting settlers and alienating Crown land to landless people.[1]   This ordinance among other things concluded that:

(a) Crown land in a village should be reserved for village expansion and the needs of the village community;

(b) if more land was available, it was to be mapped out for alienation to middle-class Ceylonese;

(c) if still more land was available, it could be alienated to others.

With the outbreak of the Second World War, settlement was speeded up and the following inducements were given to settlers:

---

[1] In the early days of land settlements, landlessness and social need were the main criteria in selecting settlers.   Family size was also an important factor, preference being given to larger families with a view to attracting a greater population and labour force into settlement schemes in desired areas.

During the latter period of land settlements, particularly with the rising prices of agricultural commodities and the resultant profitability of agricultural work, competition for allotments in settlement schemes began to emerge.   In these circumstances, it was possible to use a number of criteria.   These include:

(a) age - with preference for the 25-39 year age group;

(b) marital status - with preference for the married;

(c) number of children - weight being given to families with three or four children;

(d) landlessness;

(e) knowledge of agriculture;

(f) qualifications in agriculture;

(g) social status and health.

1   a dwelling place for the settler and his family;

2   a subsidy for ridging or slumping his paddy allotment after the first harvest while the government continued to do the clearing;

3   a small subsistence allowance to enable him to meet initial expenses;

4   agricultural implements and buffaloes, which were made available on loan, but could become outright grants if the colonist showed he was improving his allotment;

5   arrangements for marketing his products;

6   the completion of building of houses and ridging on paddy allotments before handing over to the colonist.

The policy of land settlement and irrigation which followed had a profound impact on population redistribution. Table 6 shows a substantial increase of both irrigation schemes and the extent of irrigable land in the dry zone between 1949 and 1969. Within these 20 years, the number of irrigation schemes almost doubled while the irrigable acreage almost trebled. Two-thirds of these schemes were in the first eight dry zone districts of north and east Sri Lanka, with more than three-quarters of the irrigable acreage. The six dry-zone districts of Vavuniya, Mannar, Monaragala, Polonnaruwa, Trincomalee and Batticaloa, which contain three-quarters of the dry-zone area, had half of the schemes with nearly half the irrigable acreage.

The general policy of the government was to establish the peasant on a unit of holding consisting of a highland area as well as some irrigated land so as to enable him both to settle on the land and to derive from it an income sufficient to maintain himself and his family. Peasant families were shifted from the overcrowded wet zone to the dry zone, and in addition, of course, dry zone peasants were themselves resettled. Land area under major settlement schemes in the dry zone and the number of allottees settled in them are given in table 7. The number of allottees settled up to 1953 amounted to 3,023 on a land area of 15,192 acres. These figures had increased to 40,164 allottees and 206,268 acres by 1963 and 73,922 allottees and 332,227 acres by 1971. When these figures are compared with those for settlement schemes for the whole island it is quite evident that there was a deliberate attempt to settle as many people as possible in the sparsely populated dry zone districts.

Table 6: Major irrigation schemes in the dry zone

District	1949		1969	
	No. of schemes	Irrigable area (acres)	No. of schemes	Irrigable area (acres)
Amparai	10	32,901	9	68,651
Anuradhadura	7	15,375	18	63,195
Badulla*	12	2,396	19	11,079
Batticaloa	8	29,580	15	55,131
Hambantota	5	25,199	12	32,055
Jaffna	1	8,881	9	24,365
Kurunegala*	8	8,883	16	25,568
Mannar	2	10,102	6	26,933
Matale*	6	480	10	7,008
Monaragala	11	3,606	21	822
Polonnaruwa	2	4,203	7	52,802
Puttalam	3	2,285	7	5,968
Trincomalee	6	8,955	9	35,358
Vavuniya	15	1,414	26	18,165
All dry zone districts	96	154,260	184	427,100
Other districts	24	26,534	41	44,712
Total	120	180,794	225	471,812

* Intermediate districts (between the wet zone and the dry zone).

Source: Gunatilleke (1973), table 7.

According to the 1963 and 1971 censuses, more than 90 per cent of the total number of allottees were settled in the 13 dry zone districts (i.e. excluding Jaffna). Two other noteworthy features are discernible from the data in table 7. First, there has been an acceleration of land settlement in the dry zone since 1953, both in terms of the area and the number of allottees. Second, the area allotted per settler has decreased over the years. In the earlier schemes, each allottee was given 5 acres of irrigable land and 3 acres of highland. Allottees after 1953 were each given only 3 acres of irrigable land and 2

Table 7: Land under major settlement schemes in the dry zone

District	1953		1963		1971	
	Area (acres)	No. of allottees	Area (acres)	No. of allottees	Area (acres)	No. of allottees
Amparai	-	-	24,884	4,949	42,999	10,481
Anuradhapura	5,530	1,048	33,994	7,494	60,646	16,716
Badulla*	-	-	6,755	1,512	13,824	3,842
Batticaloa	-	-	2,751	306	15,857	3,572
Hambantota	-	-	3,366	600	5,253	1,659
Jaffna	2,186	394	17,530	3,718	31,202	6,094
Kurunegala*	1,395	310	14,403	3,168	17,073	3,962
Mannar	-	-	1,965	393	2,200	440
Matale*	-	-	4,930	1,059	16,177	4,471
Monaragala	-	-	3,872	724	4,500	881
Polonnaruwa	-	-	61,020	9,559	76,842	13,022
Puttalam	-	-	5,047	865	8,870	1,768
Trincomalee	6,081	1,271	19,668	4,489	26,460	6,165
Vavuniya	-	-	6,083	1,328	10,324	2,849
All dry zone districts	15,192	3,023	206,268	40,164	332,227	73,922
Other districts	1,589	265	21,455	5,278	6,287	1,645
Total	16,781	3,288	227,723	45,442	338,514	75,567
Area per allottee (acres)	5.10	5.01	4.48			

* Intermediate districts (between the wet zone and the dry zone).

Source: Administration reports of the Land Commissioner.

acres of highland.   At present it is fixed at 2 acres of irrigable and 1 acre of highland.   In addition to the allottees, there were the settler squatters or encroachers, who often had connections with the allottees in the settlements.   To quote the Gal Oya Board Annual Review,

"The Gal Oya Valley offers ample opportunities for agricultural and commercial encroachments. People in other parts of the country hear about employment opportunities, trade possibilities, etc., and migrate to the valley.   A realistic attitude was adopted in dealing with these encroachments.   All encroachments for commercial purposes that could be regularised were regularised by the issue of permits.   In the cases of those that could not be regularised suitable alternative sites were offered."[1]

(ii) Village expansion schemes

Unlike the large-scale land colonisation schemes in the dry zone which necessitated large inter-district movements of people, the village expansion schemes provided land to landless peasants in the same district.   Most of the land for expansion was found in the south-west wet zone and the central hill country, where landless workers were predominant.   Government land or privately owned land acquired from individuals or companies was given to landless villagers.   In some cases, the landless forced themselves into unutilised Crown land and the government later handed it over to them.   The main purposes of the village expansion schemes were:

(a)   to relieve extreme pressure on land in the developed areas of the island;

(b)   to provide employment for unemployed people in their own villages;   and

(c)   to increase the food supply.

In congested areas and in areas where people were gainfully employed, the demand was more for small blocks of land for residential purposes than for land for cultivation, and this demand was also met with suitable private land or Crown land.   Unlike under the settlement schemes, most of the land given to the peasants was

---

1   Gal Oya Board, Annual Review.

highland. A total of 303,000 acres was alienated under this scheme up to 1955 and 225,000 acres between 1955 and 1966. This type of land alienation had the effect of retaining people in their own areas. Had it not been for these schemes, a large number of landless families might have drifted from the villages either to urban areas looking for employment or to dry zone agricultural areas looking for land.

(iii) Rural development

Another important policy which appears to have slowed down rural-urban migration in Sri Lanka was concerted rural development by successive governments since Independence. Prior to Independence in 1948, the main emphasis was on the plantation sector, to the relative neglect of the peasant sector. In 1948, the Department of Rural Development was established to harness the enthusiasm and effort of the rural people themselves to better their own social and economic conditions. This was done through village organisations by bringing the village folk into closer contact and co-operation with various extension services of the government. The various organisations at the village level were village councils, rural co-operatives, rural development societies, kantha samithis (women's organ-isations), and young farmers' clubs. Minor development projects mainly in the form of provision of infrastructure services such as roads and bridges, were also undertaken through self-help schemes.

Other measures that lessened the push factor oper-ating in the rural areas were the incentives given to the rural farmers to increase their output of paddy. The guaranteed price scheme, the crop insurance scheme, the scheme of agricultural extension, and the provision of subsidised seeds and fertilisers were the most important of these incentives, in that order.

The guaranteed price scheme assured the producer of a minimum price for his product and prevented him from being exploited by the middleman or the unscrupu-lous trader. It was introduced in 1948, the year of Independence. Paddy was the first major agricultural crop to be covered by this scheme. The guaranteed price of paddy was fixed at Rs. 8 per bushel in 1948 and had been raised to Rs. 40 by 1977, in four successive steps. Several other subsidiary crops were also later brought under the scheme (Indraratna, 1966).

The crop insurance scheme was introduced in 1958-59 as a pilot project and was limited to cover approximately 28,000 acres of paddy in the four dry zone districts of Hambantota, Anuradhapura, Amparai, and Batticaloa, and the two wet zone districts of Colombo and Kegalla, for a period of four years. The scheme was extended in 1961 to provide insurance cover for subsidiary crops such as chillies, cotton, and tobacco. It was further extended to increase the paddy acreage to be covered, and by 1963-64, 16 districts had been brought under the scheme. In 1974, the crop insurance scheme was replaced by the agricultural insurance scheme as a result of the Agricultural Insurance Law of 1973. The following year, a compulsory insurance scheme exclusively for paddy cultivation in the island, and covering approximately 2.2 million acres of cultivated land over the two seasons, was started.

Government policy was also directed during this period towards creating new financial institutions to support rural agriculture. The first major step in this direction was taken in 1961 with the establishment of the People's Bank. Since its inception, the Bank has been engaged in developing and expanding credit facilities for the rural sector. In 1964, the People's Bank started its rural banking scheme to extend banking services to the villages and to provide those engaged in agriculture with credit for production and redemption of debts, as well as for housing. In 1967 the Bank launched the New Agricultural Credit Scheme whereby Central Bank finance was channelled to the rural sector.

The impact of these various measures has been a shift in terms of trade in favour of the rural sector and an increase in rural incomes. It has been estimated that during the period 1963-73, the average real income in the rural and estate sectors taken together has risen at the rate of 2 per cent per annum, in contrast to a decline of 1.8 per cent in the urban sector (Karunatilake, 1974).

(iv) Land reform

The first in the series of tenurial reforms that was effected in Sri Lanka was the Paddy Land Act of 1958. This Act ensured the tenant farmer's security of tenure. The rent was fixed as one-quarter share of the crop. The tenancy rights were made hereditary unless the owner himself wanted to cultivate the land. The Act also made provision for farmers' organisations at the village level to develop and manage the paddy sector.

The system of tenancy that prevailed before the introduction of the Paddy Land Act was not conducive to growth in productivity, as adequate incentives for cultivation were lacking and the landowners were ultimately receiving the major share of the crop. The Act not only gave the tenants security of tenure but also gave them a three-quarters share of the crop, thereby relieving them somewhat of their poverty and indebtedness.

A major step in land policy came in 1972 with the enactment of the Land Reform Law. As discussed earlier, the problem of landlessness in the high density areas had been tackled mainly by the resettlement of peasants in the dry zone. This was a slow process, however, and most of the population, especially in the south-west quadrant of the country, suffered from severe landlessness in the midst of the large estates in the plantation sector. A drastic change in agricultural land policy therefore became a matter of high priority. As a result, the Land Reform Law was enacted in August 1972. It stipulated a ceiling of 25 acres of paddy or 50 acres of other agricultural land. Any land in excess of this ceiling was vested in the Land Reform Commission, which was created to implement the law.

The total land declared to the Land Reform Commission under the new legislation was estimated to be around 1.2 million acres. Of these, 639,000 acres were under the major crops (tea, rubber, coconut, cocoa and paddy) and 204,000 areas were under forest and grass land. Paddy, which is mainly grown in smallholdings, accounted for 56,533 acres. The districts mainly affected by the law were Colombo, Kurunegala, Kandy, Ratnapura, Kegalla, Kalutara, Badulla and Matale, which were outside the dry north and east of the island.[1]

(b) Industrial development policies

In Sri Lanka, the contribution of manufacturing industry to the gross domestic product has ranged only between 12 and 14 per cent in the recent past. Nevertheless, manufacturing industry occupies a significant position in the economy because of its links with the other sectors. Its output spreads over all major sectors of the economy.

According to a survey carried out in 1975-76, almost three-quarters of the industrial establishments in operation in Sri Lanka were located in the Colombo district (Government of Sri Lanka, Ministry of Industries and Scientific Affairs, 1976). The next largest shares of industrial establishments were found to be in the districts of Kandy (4.3 per cent), Matara (4.3 per cent) and Kalutara (4.1 per cent). All these are in the wet zone, and are four of the most densely populated districts of

---

[1] Matala and Badulla are really intermediate districts between wet and dry zones.

the country.[1]

There is evidence to suggest that the spatial distribution of industry in the country has had an important bearing upon internal migration patterns, a full discussion of which will be undertaken later in this chapter. For the present, we shall examine some of the policies connected with industrial development which are considered to have had a bearing upon internal migration. The most important amongst these are:

(a) location of state industrial plants,

(b) dispersal of industries, and

(c) regional development programmes.

A few state-run factories were in operation during the pre-Independence period, as for example the plywood factory established in Gintota in 1941, the leather products factory established in Colombo in 1942, and the ceramics factory established in Negombo in 1942. In the case of the cement factory at Kankesanturai, much of the preliminary work was carried out during the pre-Independence period, but the factory was established in 1950. However, the major involvement in industry by the state began only during the post-Independence period. It was in 1953 that the government carried out a review of state-run enterprises and decided to create a corporate sector to manage them. Provision was made for the private sector to participate in these ventures. With the change of government in 1956, however, the policy of permitting joint enterprises was abandoned; from then on these ventures were to be run exclusively by the state. With this end in view, the State Industrial Corporation Act was passed in 1957, making provision for the establishment of new corporations as well as for the taking over of activities of existing state enterprises. Shortly afterwards, the government's Ten Year Plan of 1959 set out a blueprint for the expansion of existing ventures as well as for the creation of new ones. For example, the Ten Year Plan envisaged a programme of development for the cement industry on an island-wide scale with a twelvefold expansion in capacity. In fact, a tenfold expansion in capacity was achieved during the period 1963-71. Table 8 sets out the years in which respective factories and/or corporations were established.

In contrast to the private sector industries, most of which were based on the import of semi-finished goods,

_____

[1]   The spread of industry over the other districts is shown in Appendix II.

Table 8: Growth of public sector industry

Ceylon Plywoods	1941
Ceylon Leather Products	1942
Ceylon Ceramics	1942
Ceylon Cement	1950
Parantan Chemicals	1951
National Milk Board	1954
Ceylon Oils and Fats	1955
National Paper	1956
Ceylon Mineral Sands	1957
Sri Lanka Sugar	1958
National Textiles	1958
National Salt	1959
Ceylon Steel	1961
Ceylon Petroleum	1961
Ceylon Tyres	1962
Ceylon State Hardware	1963
Ceylon Fertilizer	1964
Sri Lanka State Flour Milling	1964
Ceylon Fisheries	1964
State Timber	1968
State Graphite	1971
Sri Lanka Tobacco Industries	1972
State Distilleries	1972
State Rubber Manufacturing	1972
Sri Lanka Porcelain	1975

Source: Ministry of Industries and Scientific Affairs (1976).

the public sector industries listed in table 8 were largely based on processes which converted local raw materials into finished products (e.g. cement, ceramics). In other words, they were mainly resource-based industries and as such were located close to raw material sites. In the case of the cement industry, for example, the factories were located in the Jaffna and Puttalam districts. Likewise, the mineral sands factory was located in the Vavuniya district. Thus a new set of employment centres emerged in sparsely populated regions of the country. Table 9 attempts to capture the growth of employment in these factories over the intercensal period 1963-71.

As regards the dispersal of private industry, the first explicit policy statement came in 1971 in a publication entitled Ceylon's Industrial Policy (Ministry of

Table 9: Growth of employment in state industry during the
intercensal period 1963-71

Corporation		Factory location and district	Year of estab-lishment	Employment 1963	Employment 1971
Ceylon Plywoods	(i)	Gintota, Galle D.	1941	615	980
	(ii)	Kesgama, Colombo D.	1970	–	240
Ceylon Leather	(i)	Shoe factory and tannery M'kuliya, Colombo D.	1942	363	793
	(ii)	Leather goods factory Ekala, Colombo D.	1972		
Ceylon Cement	(i)	Kankesanturai, Jaffna D.	1950	726	1102
	(ii)	Puttalam, Puttalam D.	1967	–	1044
	(iii)	Galle, Galle D.	1967	–	244
Ceylon Ceramics	(i)	Negombo, Colombo D.	1955	322	1130
	(ii)	Piliyandala, Colombo D.	1967	–	
National Paper	(i)	Valaichchenai, Batticaloa D.	1956	632	927
Ceylon Oils and Fats	(i)	Seeduwa, Colombo D.	1957	480	835
Parantan Chemicals	(i)	Parantan, Jaffna D.	1957	205	315
Ceylon Petroleum	(i)	Blending plant, Colombo D.	1960	–	115
	(ii)	Refinery, Colombo D.	1968	–	418
Ceylon Mineral Sands	(i)	Illmenita, Trincomalee D.	1961	–	494
National Textiles	(i)	Veyangoda, Colombo D.	1961	909	2376
	(ii)	Thulhiriya, Kegalla D.	1970		
	(iii)	Pugoda, Colombo D.	1973		
	(iv)	Mattegama, Kurunegala D.	1977		
Ceylon Hardware	(i)	Yakkala, Colombo D.	1966	–	870
	(ii)	Enderamulla foundry, Colombo, Colombo D.	1969	–	288
Ceylon Steel	(i)	Steel factory, Oruwela, Colombo D.	1967	–	953
Ceylon Tyres	(i)	Tyre factory. Colombo D.	1967	–	1302
State Flour Milling	(i)	Colombo, Colombo D.	1968	–	517

Source: Annual reports of Corporations.

Industries and Scientific Affairs, 1971). According to this, approval of industries in the private sector was to be restricted to four categories, one of which was small industry which was labour-intensive and located outside the Colombo region. However, there is no way of testing the impact of this policy upon internal migration since any effects it may have had would obviously belong to the period beyond the intercensal period 1963-71.

The other initiative regarding dispersal of industry came from the Regional Development Programme launched by the Ministry of Planning and Economic Affairs in 1971. The object of this programme was to shift away from modern large-scale industrial development based on imported raw materials and capital-intensive technology to a pattern of development which made minimum demands on capital, utilised local raw materials, and was based on labour-intensive techniques. This programme was also partly motivated by the desire to minimise the tendency of rural youth to migrate to urban areas (see Gunasekera and Codippily, 1971). Appendix III shows the district-wise distribution of industrial projects as at the end of June 1976. This distribution pattern shows a conscious effort to shift industries away from the densely populated districts.

(c) Social welfare policies

Education, health and housing are important components of a social welfare policy. People move from one place to another not only in search of employment but also for better education, health and housing. Policies on education, health and housing are therefore likely to have a significant influence on internal migration.

(i) Education

Prior to 1940, there were two main streams of education: education in English, which was confined to the handful of urban élite, and education in the vernacular tongues, Sinhala and Tamil, open to the vast majority of the remaining population. English education was mainly controlled by the missionaries and the "denominational system", while vernacular education was handled mainly by the state.

The Board of Ministers, at the beginning of the 1940s, felt that there should be one national system of education controlled by the state. A committee was appointed in 1940 which made two far-reaching recommendations:

(i)   that there should be free education from the kinder-
        garten up to and including university;   and

(ii)   that the denominational system of education should
        be abolished.

Several steps were taken to introduce a national
system of education in place of the existing denominational
system and to open the doors of English education to the
general population.   One of the most important steps in
this direction was the establishment of state schools called
central schools in all the important towns of Sri Lanka.
The number of such schools, which was 9 at the end of
1943, had increased to 57 at the end of 1963.   In
addition to these central schools, several senior schools
were also established.   Universal free education was
introduced in October 1945, except in denominational
schools which opted to remain outside the national system.
Prior to the establishment of these schools and the
introduction of free education, English education was
available mainly in a few large urban centres like
Colombo, Galle, Kandy, and Jaffna.   After the establishment of the central and senior schools, educational opportunities were more equalised on a geographical basis and
the incentive for people to migrate to urban centres for
the purposes of education was greatly reduced (see table
10).   The number of pupils receiving English education
had almost doubled from 93,278 in 1944 to 164,264 in 1947
(Jayasuriya, 1977).
Ten years after the introduction of the free
education system, another major change took place in the
sphere of education.   This was the adoption of Sinhala
as the official language of the country in 1956.   Sinhala
and Tamil gained added status as the media of instruction
in schools and the university, commencing in grade IX in
1956 and progressing gradually upwards to university
level in 1960.   This enabled rural children to study in
their own villages in the national languages and enter
institutions of tertiary education if they so desired,
without having to go to English medium schools elsewhere.

(ii)   Health

The major breakthrough in the field of preventive
medicine and health care in Sri Lanka was the campaign
for the eradication of malaria in 1943.   Before this
campaign gathered momentum, the crude death rate was
21.5 per 1,000 in 1945.   The island-wide spraying of
DDT and the killing of malaria larvae led to the gradual
eradication of malaria.   Mainly as a consequence of this
policy, the crude death rate started coming down

Table 10: Number of central colleges per 100,000 population, 1943-72

Districts	1943	1944	1945	1946	1947	1972
Amparai	-	-	-	-	-	-
Anuradhapura	-	-	0.72	0.71	1.35	0.54
Badulla	-	-	-	0.26	0.26	0.15
Batticaloa	1.00	0.99	0.99	0.98	0.94	0.79
Colombo	0.14	0.36	0.64	0.77	0.75	0.40
Galle	-	0.66	0.66	0.65	0.64	0.53
Hambantota	0.68	0.67	0.67	0.68	0.64	0.28
Jaffna	-	0.23	0.47	0.94	0.92	1.53
Kalutara	0.22	0.22	0.66	0.87	1.07	0.67
Kandy	-	0.28	0.42	0.84	0.82	0.41
Kegalla	-	-	0.50	0.49	0.48	0.44
Kurunegala	0.43	0.63	0.83	1.03	1.20	0.56
Mannar	-	-	-	-	-	1.24
Matale	0.66	0.65	0.64	0.64	0.62	0.30
Matara	0.29	0.58	0.57	0.85	0.83	0.50
Monaragala	-	-	-	-	-	0.57
Nuwara Eliya	-	-	0.75	1.49	0.73	0.87
Polonnaruwa	-	-	-	-	-	0.67
Puttalam	-	-	-	0.54	0.53	0.25
Ratnapura	-	0.30	0.29	0.58	0.85	0.44
Trincomalee	-	-	-	-	-	0.51
Vavuniya	-	-	-	-	-	-

Source: Census reports.

dramatically to a level as low as 12.4 per 1,000 in 1949, a fall of 42.4 per cent in a matter of four years.[1]   The policy of malaria eradication not only eliminated one of the major health hazards experienced by the country but also removed one of the major impediments to the movement of people from densely populated districts to sparsely populated regions of the country which offered greater potential for development.

[1]   Although there are sharp differences in opinion regarding the degree of impact of malaria eradication on the fall in the death rate, the consensus of opinion seems to be that it was the major factor in the fall in the death rate during this particular period.

Endemic malaria was one of the key factors in the depopulation of two-thirds of the land area of the country, and had defied all attempts to resettle in that area in the nineteenth century. During the epidemic in 1935, 5,454,781 visits for malaria treatment were made to government hospitals and dispensaries when the population of the country was around 5,608,000. The infant mortality rate, possibly the most sensitive index of adverse public health conditions, reached a peak in these epidemic years.

Malaria was prevalent in the dry zone of the country, which receives less than 50 centimetres of rainfall per year. The disease was hyper-endemic in this area. The two exceptions were the districts of Badulla and Jaffna. The wet zone in the south-west quadrant, which receives over 100 centimetres of rainfall annually, was generally free of malaria. However, it was affected by malaria epidemics during periods of drought.

Prior to 1945, anti-malaria measures were mainly confined to campaign centres established at important railway stations in urban areas. Only anti-larval measures were carried out to reduce the mosquito densities. The advent of DDT in 1945 revolutionised malaria control in Sri Lanka. By 1947 the entire area affected by malaria was sprayed with DDT. This resulted in the annihilation of the malaria mosquito and its breeding grounds. There was thus a phenomenal reduction in the morbidity rate, and in the spleen and parasite rates, in the endemic zone during the period 1947-50 (Meegama, 1969).

The population density of the non-malarious area was eight times that of the area with hyper-endemic malaria before malaria eradication in 1946, and six times after malaria was almost completely eradicated by 1963. It is evident from table 11 that the densities of population in the dry zone increased between 1946 and 1963.

As with education, the government decided to introduce a policy of free health services. As part of this policy, not only was treatment at existing hospitals and dispensaries made free but the Ministry of Health also began to establish cottage and rural hospitals in all parts of the island where hospital facilities were inadequate, thereby attempting to equalise facilities on a geographical basis. This is shown by the province-wise distribution of hospitals (cottage and rural only) from 1948 to 1963 in table 12.

The policy of equalising health facilities in the country continued unabated until the early sixties. The number of hospitals alone had increased from 2.3 per 100,000 in 1945 to 2.92 per 100,000 in 1960, an increase of more than 25 per cent in a matter of 15 years. The

Table 11: Indicators of malaria before and after its eradication

District and zones of malaria prevalence	Average spleen rates		Average parasite rates		Climatic zone*	Average crude death rate (per 1000)		Average infant mortality rate (per 1000)		Density of population (per sq. km.)	
	1938–1941	1948–1950	1938–1941	1941–1950		1936–1945	1948–1950	1936–1945	1948–1950	1946	1963
Non-endemic zones											
Colombo	2.4	0.73	0.68	0.01	I	18.1	14.3	168.6	98.3	678	1054
Galle	2.9	0.33	0.93	0.00	W	19.1	13.1	115.5	79.3	272	380
Jaffna	6.7	0.87	0.95	0.03	D	22.0	12.6	146.9	72.3	164	237
Kalutara	1.4	0.07	0.57	0.00	W	15.0	11.2	93.9	73.0	283	391
Kandy	10.2	1.00	2.40	0.11	W	18.7	13.6	156.6	94.3	301	441
Kegalla	13.6	1.53	1.67	0.10	W	15.5	10.4	114.8	74.0	242	348
Matara	16.0	1.20	4.93	0.03	W	20.3	11.3	123.7	67.0	282	413
Negombo	9.4	–	–	–	I	15.4	10.4	130.4	80.0	–	–
Nuwara Eliya	10.7	2.33	3.07	0.20	W	19.4	14.3	149.9	107.0	219	323
Non-endemic zone average	8.14	1.00	1.90	0.06		18.2	12.4	133.4	82.8	310	458
Moderate zone											
Badulla	25.1	4.93	5.50	0.53	D	22.1	14.0	136.0	92.3	44	65
Chilaw	17.3	–	4.53	–	I	17.1	9.4	128.8	62.0	206	–
Ratnapura	12.2	1.38	6.33	0.10	W	18.4	12.5	129.6	82.0	106	169
Moderate zone average	18.2	3.15	5.45	0.32		19.2	12.0	131.5	78.8	94	176

/continued....

Table 11 (continued)

District and zones of malaria prevalence	Average spleen rates		Average parasite rates		Climatic zone*	Average crude death rate (per 1000)		Average infant mortality rate (per 1000)		Density of population (per sq. km.)	
	1938–1941	1948–1950	1938–1941	1941–1950		1936–1945	1948–1950	1936–1945	1948–1950	1946	1963
Endemic zone											
Anuradhapura	67.3	9.60	9.80	0.70	D	31.9	12.8	263.8	88.7	14	37
Batticaloa	37.8	4.97	11.50	0.93	D	32.4	16.6	186.5	117.7	28	72
Hambantota	62.6	14.25	8.47	0.36	I	36.0	12.7	230.9	79.7	57	105
Kurunegala	39.6	9.13	7.37	0.93	I	25.1	11.3	190.7	79.3	101	178
Mannar	35.4	5.60	5.20	0.50	D	29.9	13.9	266.9	120.3	13	24
Matale	39.2	4.53	7.40	0.30	I	24.1	13.9	163.9	95.7	67	128
Puttalam	50.4	8.63	10.17	0.73	D	25.7	12.4	281.3	97.0	18	1007**
Trincomalee	39.5	9.57	8.60	0.53	D	29.7	11.1	188.0	110.0	28	51
Vavuniya	65.3	12.43	6.55	0.50	D	30.9	14.2	243.2	102.3	6	18
Endemic zone average	48.6	8.74	8.34	0.61		29.5	13.2	223.9	99.0	38	73

* W = wet zone; I = intermediate zone; D = dry zone.

** Also includes Chilaw district.

Sources: Reports of Registrar General on Vital Statistics; Administration reports of the Director of Medical and Sanitary Services; Census reports, and Gray (1974).

Table 12: Number of cottage and rural hospitals per 100,000 population, 1948-63

Province	1948		1950		1953		1963	
	Cottage	Rural	Cottage	Rural	Cottage	Rural	Cottage	Rural
Western	0.15	0.50	0.04	0.53	0.04	0.49	0.03	-
Central	0.41	1.67	0.39	1.56	0.36	1.46	-	-
Southern	0.19	1.98	0.18	0.18	0.17	1.94	0.13	-
Eastern	0.79	2.68	0.63	2.54	0.56	2.25	-	-
Northern	0.67	1.38	0.37	1.88	0.35	2.10	0.26	-
North-Central	0.62	3.12	-	3.13	-	2.61	-	-
North-Western	0.13	2.65	-	2.56	-	2.45	-	-
Sabaragamuwa	0.12	1.14	0.12	1.32	0.11	1.11	0.08	-
Uva	0.50	0.50	0.23	1.42	0.21	1.28	-	-
Average	0.27	1.42	0.18	1.52	0.17	1.43	0.13	1.24

Source: Administration reports of the Director of Health Services.

total number of health institutions (general, provincial, district, cottage and rural hospitals, and dispensaries) had increased from 268 in 1952 to 783 in 1961.[1]   Every district (except Kegalla with 1.7) in the country had more than two beds per 1,000 population, with an all-island average of 3.2.   The total expenditure on health had increased more than fourfold from Rs. 325 per 100,000 population in 1945 to Rs. 1,406 in 1960.   The number of patients treated at health institutions had nearly trebled from 662,433 in 1948 to 1,667,414 in 1963, as shown in table 13.   The data also show that the increase in dry zone districts where facilities were relatively poor earlier was much higher than in Colombo and other districts where facilities were relatively good.   By 1951, the crude death rate had fallen to an all-time record of 8 per 1,000.

These increased health facilities may have contributed somewhat to the slowing down of migration from the dry zone districts to the wet zone districts in the second intercensal period 1953-63.

(iii) Housing

Up to 1954, there had been no declared government policy on housing in Sri Lanka.   Housing was purely a non-government activity whereby people constructed houses both for owner occupation and as capital investment for renting.   The only assistance given by the government during this period was in the form of loans through the Loans Board.

The National Housing Act was introduced in August 1954, and the Department of National Housing was set up to increase the pace of housing construction.   This department took over the functions of the Loans Board, and for the first time the public sector became involved in the construction of houses for the middle and low-income groups.

During the decade 1955-64, in addition to loans for individual houses, loans for large-scale development of housing estates were also given.   However, most activities were concentrated in the urban sector, and that mostly in the Colombo district.   The rural sector was provided with housing through other agencies such as the Land Commissioner's Department and the Gal Oya Board, but the programme was so limited that it hardly led to any improvement in the rural housing situation.

---

[1]   Data based on administration reports of the Director of Health Services.

Table 13: In-patients in all health institutions, 1948-63

Districts	1948	1953	1955	1961	1963
Amparai	-	-	-	-	30,037
Anuradhapura	25,478	32,452	33,177	42,517	47,256
Badulla	36,186	44,422	49,852	99,657	68,154
Batticaloa	8,846	21,033	22,925	44,396	21,299
Colombo	169,955	213,677	225,637	339,937	351,122
Galle	38,635	46,682	48,755	81,507	89,525
Hambantota	19,129	19,436	24,841	42,548	35,587
Jaffna	30,821	38,452	41,821	66,265	68,777
Kalutara	31,889	47,157	51,012	101,076	101,252
Kandy	75,863	85,243	87,843	152,506	159,228
Kegalla	40,591	48,966	50,147	110,418	107,210
Kurunegala	60,124	76,246	84,530	171,543	170,841
Mannar	6,533	8,611	8,006	12,838	13,825
Matale	19,896	20,721	23,846	39,886	43,141
Matara	18,911	27,513	30,805	63,718	73,935
Monaragala	-	-	-	-	28,329
Nuwara Eliya	15,890	16,727	20,650	35,805	46,563
Polonnaruwa*	-	-	-	17,453	17,296
Puttalam	14,590	22,025	22,449	45,405	45,366
Ratnapura	39,210	53,365	57,697	110,062	115,540
Trincomalee	5,919	9,559	10,155	15,501	15,805
Vavuniya	3,977	10,242	10,808	16,180	17,324
Total	662,433	842,527	904,956	1,609,218	1,667,414

* In 1961 this district was known as Thamanakaduwa.

Source: Administration reports of the Director of Health Services.

Major changes in housing policy were introduced from 1970. First, there was an increase in public sector investment in development of housing for the low-income groups; second, an attempt was made to increase individual housing construction for owner occupation through the provision of increased loan facilities and other incentives. The relative increase in public sector investment in housing was primarily in the urban areas.

The other major component of state housing construction activity was the Aided Self-help Scheme, first introduced in 1973, and primarily aimed at providing better housing facilities to the lower-income groups in rural and semi-urban areas. Under this scheme the state meets the cost of land development, building materials, and certain services while the prospective tenants provide the labour for construction. A loan scheme for the upgrading of rural and semi-urban houses was also initiated in 1978.[1] These schemes are likely to increase the retentive capacity of the rural sector.

(iv) Transport

Another factor that may have reinforced the slow pace of rural-urban migration is the convenient and subsidised transport within the country, which facilitates mobility that does not result in permanent migration. The small size of the country and the existence of a reasonably good network of roads enables a person to come to the city and get back within a day. Around 1948 the island had about 11,000 kilometres of main roads. Today there are over 27,000 kilometres of roads throughout the country. The nationalisation of bus services in 1958 meant the improvement and expansion of services to all parts of the country. The fleet strength of the bus services increased from 3,400 in 1958 to 6,733 in 1976. Similarly the distance operated rose from 165 million kilometres to 399 million during the same period (Department of Census and Statistics, 1977, p. 333). Although bus services in the rural areas are not as frequent as in urban areas, they do provide access to urban employment and amenities, thereby reducing the need for permanent migration to the urban areas.[2]

---

[1] This is part of the programme of the National Housing Development Authority, which has as its target the construction of 100,000 houses and the upgrading of 84,000 old ones, with a capital of $200 million.

[2] The subsidy on transport has been gradually eliminated by the new government since it came into office in July 1977.

An Assessment of the Impact of Migration-related Policies

In the previous section, we identified and reviewed a number of policies which are considered to have had an impact upon internal migration in Sri Lanka. The principal aim of this section is to assess the extent to which these policies have influenced migration trends, as presented earlier. Each policy is assessed on the basis of the existing information, as well as information gathered in the two case studies. A simple regression model is also used to test how significant some of these policies have been.

(a) Land development

Land development policies stand out as significantly affecting migration trends in Sri Lanka. This is corroborated by the increase of the proportion of the population living in the dry zone from 31.3 per cent in 1946 to 37.02 per cent in 1971. The total population in the major in-migration districts of Mannar, Vavuniya, Batticaloa, Trincomalee, Anuradhapura, Polonnaruwa and Amparai (formerly part of the district of Batticaloa) increased from 9.86 per cent to 14.35 per cent of the island population. Nearly half of this increase was due to net migration.[1] Table 14 clearly shows that in the areas of major land settlement schemes, a significant percentage of the respective district population has migrated from elsewhere. In terms of number of persons, about 75,000 allottees have taken up settlement in the dry zone during the 1946-71 period. This, together with an estimate for the households of the respective allottees, accounts for the settlement of nearly 4 per cent of the island's population within a period of 25 years.

The target set out in the Ten Year Plan for 1959-68 was the settlement of 99,500 allottees. Although the actual achievement was less than targeted, a shift of 4 per cent of the population from the wet zone to the dry zone not only considerably eased the population pressure

---

1 In these districts the total population changed from 656,277 to 1,821,447, an increase of 4.49 per cent per annum. The natural growth of population was 2.47 per cent during this period, and the remaining increase was due to net migration.

Table 14: In-migrant population as a percentage of district population

District	%
Mannar	21.0
Vavuniya	35.5
Trincomalee	29.4
Anuradhapura) Polonnaruwa)	32.3
Matale	21.4

in the former, but also significantly raised employment and output.[1]

However, a number of studies on land settlement schemes in Sri Lanka argue that the economic benefits reaped have not been commensurate with the costs incurred. The study by Kunasingham (1972) which covers eight projects tends to indicate that the major settlement projects are not profitable in terms of the return on capital invested. In the case of the Nagadeepa project, on the basis of an estimated yield of 50 bushels of paddy per acre, the benefit-cost ratio is estimated to range from 0.42 to 0.82 according to discount rates used, which range from 6 to 15 per cent. This study also points out the underutilisation of resources. Similar conclusions are reported by Abhayaratne on the basis of his 1972 study. He finds that a large proportion of the allottees had not brought all members of their household to the settlement schemes because of lack of housing, inadequate transport, and lack of other facilities, resulting in a shortage of family labour. In the case of the Rajangana project, 57 per cent of the paddy allotments had been underutilised. The study by

---

[1] It is estimated that 35 per cent of Sri Lanka's paddy output is produced on major irrigation schemes which have been primarily associated with the land settlement areas. However, there is no clear estimate as to how much the settlers have contributed towards this output.

Ellman (1976) draws attention to management and organisational deficiencies, and advocates self-management by settlers as both economically and socially desirable.

Over-all, the above studies indicate deficiencies of an organisational and management character. If these deficiencies can be remedied it is clear that some of the benefit-cost ratios estimated would change favourably. In such circumstances land settlement policies would not only be effective in terms of influence on internal migration, but also cost-effective.

While schemes of land settlement increased population mobility, village expansion schemes reduced it. Since most village expansion schemes were in the wet zone, they induced a large number of people to stay in their villages instead of drifting to the cities or to the major settlement schemes. About 528,000 acres were alienated for village expansion schemes, and approximately 573,049 permits were issued to landless peasants for settlement on the land. It has been estimated that nearly half the population was affected by these village expansion schemes, about four times the number of families affected by settlement schemes. This was one of the factors which slowed down the pace of rural-urban and rural-rural migration in Sri Lanka during this period.

Case study: Mahakandarawa land
settlement scheme

For the purpose of this case study, the Mahakandarawa land settlement scheme was selected as a typical scheme. Besides being a medium-sized scheme, it is situated in the Anuradhapura district, where a large number of settlement schemes have been located.[1]

The scheme covers an area of about 7,900 acres. It was opened up in stages from 1961 to 1968 and had a total of 1,967 allotments at the time of the field survey carried out in 1977. For the purpose of the survey, a random sample of 208 allottees was selected. The main purpose of the survey was to examine the socio-economic and demographic characteristics of the settlers and to assess the extent to which such schemes were successful in retaining the migrant population in the settlement areas.

Table 15 shows the distribution of settlers by district of origin and educational attainment. The data indicate that nearly 69 per cent of settlers had come from the Anuradhapura district, while Kandy and Kegalla

---

[1] The size of settlement schemes ranges from about 700 acres to about 36,000 acres (see Ellman et al., 1976).

Table 15: Distribution of settlers by district of birth and educational attainment, 1977

District of birth	No education	Primary	Secondary	All
Anuradhapura	42	101	-	143
Badulla	-	1	-	1
Colombo	1	4	-	5
Galle	-	5	-	5
Jaffna	-	1	-	1
Kalutara	-	5	-	5
Kandy	2	17	-	19
Kegalla	-	10	-	10
Kurunegala	-	2	-	2
Matale	1	2	-	3
Matara	-	5	-	5
Nuwara Eliya	-	6	-	6
Polonnaruwa	-	1	-	1
Puttalam	-	1	-	1
Vavuniya	-	1	-	1
All	46	162	-	208

accounted for almost 14 per cent. Most of the settlers from the Anuradhapura district had come from Purana (ancient) villages in the neighbourhood. As many as 78 per cent of the settlers had only a primary education, while the rest had no education at all.

Unlike in the early stages of settlement schemes in the country, where persons from the south, south-west, and other wet zone areas had been encouraged to migrate, Mahakandarawa and some other schemes in the dry zone areas attracted settlers to a great extent from neighbouring villages and districts. It is, therefore, not surprising that nearly 69 per cent of the settlers were from Anuradhapura. Most of the settlers were paddy farmers. Only one was a non-agricultural worker. This was mainly due to the process of selection of settlers, which gave considerable priority to agricultural background. Table 16 gives the distribution of settlers with agricultural background by their age, sex, and duration of residence.

The data show that the majority of the settlers had been in the scheme for over 10 years and were within the age group 35-59. Only a very small number had been resident for a period under five years. This is due to the fact that the Mahakandarawa scheme is a relatively old scheme which was filled up rapidly during its early years, leaving little room for late entrants.

Table 17 presents the total agricultural output produced by 208 settlers during the year preceding the date of the survey. The gross output per settler works out at Rs. 5,281 per annum and the net income per agricultural worker is estimated at about Rs. 250 per month. These figures are likely to be biased downwards on account of the general reluctance on the part of the settlers to divulge their output.

Other salient features which emerged from the survey are summarised below:

(a) Most of the settlers had made the settlement area their permanent home, visiting their villages of origin only occasionally. Almost all settlers were married and had large families with an average of around five children per family.

(b) About 80 per cent had migrated with their families. The average family size had increased from 5.6 before migration to 7.3 after migration.

(c) Except in a few cases, the children had remained in the colony. Of those educated up to grade 10 or GCE ("O" level) only a few had found alternative employment.

(d) Almost all the settlers surveyed had been agricultural workers prior to joining the scheme. On average, 2.6 acres of cultivable land and 1.6 acres of highland was allotted to them.

(e) As many as 84 per cent of the settlers surveyed expressed satisfaction with the scheme as a whole. But 8 per cent expressed dissatisfaction with the irrigation facilities available, while 4.3 per cent stated that the granting of ownership to land had been delayed. The remaining 3.7 per cent were not satisfied with the income they received.

(f) About 70 per cent of the settlers surveyed said that they seek advice from the agricultural extension officers.

(g) While migration from the dry zone districts other than Anuradhapura, i.e. Puttalam, Vavuniya, Polonnaruwa, Badulla, and Jaffna, had been marginal, 50 out of the 208 settlers surveyed had migrated from the wet zone districts.

Table 16: Distribution of settlers by their age, sex
and duration of residence, 1977

Characteristics	Duration of residence			
	Less than 5 years	5-9 years	10 years and over	All
Age (years)				
15-24	2	2	4	8
25-34	12	21	18	51
35-59	6	31	112	149
All	20	54	134	208
Sex				
Male	15	47	115	177
Female	5	7	19	31
All	20	54	134	208

Table 17: Agricultural production, 1976-77

Type of crop	Quantity	Value (in rupees)
Paddy	204,533 bushels	1,019,615.00
Cowpea	4,544 kg.	20,262.75
Dried chillies	284 "	6,065.00
Sorghum	323 "	10.00
Green gram	238 "	1,430.00
Black gram	3,116 "	15,168.00
Gingelly	530 "	1,760.00
Tobacco	1,869 "	14,750.00
Kurakkan	751 "	488.00
Vegetables	883 "	22,330.00
Plantain	-	1,200.00
Coconut	900 nuts	620.00
All crops		1,103,698.00

(h) About 40 per cent of the settlers surveyed had been encroachers. Some of these encroachments had been regularised in the course of time. The percentage of encroachments in the scheme was higher than that for the district as a whole.

The above analysis suggests that Mahakandarawa is relatively stable as an agricultural settlement.

(b) Industrial employment

Although a number of industries were established during the 1950s, it was in the 1960s that a major spurt of industrial development was witnessed in the country. The steady deterioration of the terms of trade during the 1960s led to import restrictions on a wide range of commodities. This gave adequate protection and hence an opportunity for setting up local industry. As reported in a study carried out by the Marga Institute in 1976, over 1,000 new industrial units were approved during the period 1960-74, in contrast to a total of only about 500 during the period 1946-60. Since the vast majority of the industries related to assembly and packing, there was no compelling necessity to locate factories close to raw material sites. Private industrial units were heavily concentrated in the Colombo district. According to a survey carried out by the Ministry of Industries and Scientific Affairs in 1975-76, as many as 72 per cent of the approved industrial units in the private sector were located in the Colombo district, accounting for over 90 per cent of total gross output by private industry, 80 per cent of the value of plant and machinery, 82 per cent of employment and 90 per cent of the wage bill. It is therefore not surprising that Colombo registered the highest index of attraction during the intercensal period 1963-71, as well as during 1953-63, whereas it had only taken second place after Anuradhapura during the period 1946-53.

In the public sector, following the broad strategy outlined in the Ten Year Plan for 1959-68, a conscious effort was made to set up industries based on local raw materials. Factories were located close to their raw material sites. As noted earlier, the new industrial centres drew a large proportion of their labour force from elsewhere and significantly affected internal migration trends. One example which is perhaps worthy of special mention is the case of the Puttalam cement factory. This factory was set up in 1967. By the end of 1971 it had a total labour force of 1,044, the majority of whom were from the Colombo district. This probably explains why Puttalam district, which had been an out-migration district during the intercensal period 1953-63, became an in-migration district during the intercensal period 1963-71.

Case study: Puttalam cement factory

The manufacture of Portland cement commenced in Sri Lanka in 1950 with the establishment of a government cement factory in Kankesanturai, a town at the northern tip of the island. Within a short period of time certain initial technical difficulties had been overcome and production had stabilised at around 80,000 tonnes per annum. The capacity of this plant was then trebled under a major expansion programme. In addition, a new factory was established at Puttalam, situated about 130 kilometres north of Colombo, and a terminal grinding and packing plant was established in Galle, a southern town located 116 kilometres away from Colombo.

The work on the Puttalam factory started in the early 1960s. The completion of stage II in 1972 had raised the installed capacity to 440,000 tonnes per annum. At the time of the survey in 1977 the factory employed more than 1,000 persons, most of whom had come to reside in an area which had been very sparsely populated prior to the commencement of this project. Settlers in the surrounding areas are made up of factory employees, their relatives, and those engaged in trade. Factory employees fall into three categories:

(a) permanent residents of the Puttalam district, but not from the immediate vicinity of the factory (these employees commute daily to their work);

(b) residents of Puttalam town and its outskirts; and

(c) employees who have migrated into the area for employment from other parts of the island.

A 10 per cent sample of employees was selected for interview. The data presented in tables 18(a) and 18(b) show that 70 per cent of the employees had migrated from Colombo district and 10 per cent from Kurunegala district, both neighbouring districts.

The data also show that over 50 per cent of employees were in the age group 25-34 and had a secondary education. As many as 46 per cent of the employees had been resident for over 10 years.

The total capital cost of the project is estimated at Rs. 289 million, of which the foreign component is Rs. 140 million. At the time of the survey the factory was operating at over 80 per cent of the installed capacity. The value added and average wage per worker was

Table 18(a): Distribution of employees by age, education and district of origin, 1977

District of origin	Age (in years)			Education			All
	15-24	25-34	34-59	Primary	Second-ary	GCE and above	
Anuradhapura	–	–	1	–	1	–	1
Badulla	–	1	–	–	1	–	1
Colombo	8	9	7	–	24	–	24
Galle	2	3	2	1	6	–	7
Hambantota	–	–	1	–	1	–	1
Jaffna	–	–	2	–	2	–	2
Kalutara	2	2	–	–	4	–	4
Kandy	–	4	3	1	6	–	7
Kegalla	–	3	3	–	6	–	6
Kurunegala	3	5	2	1	8	1	10
Matara	1	1	–	–	2	–	2
Nuwara Eliya	–	1	1	–	2	–	2
Puttalam	4	19	7	3	27	–	30
Ratnapura	–	2	–	–	2	–	2
Trincomalee	–	–	1	–	1	–	1
All	20	50	30	6	93	1	100

Table 18(b): Distribution of employees by age and duration of residence, 1977

Duration of residence (in years)	Age (in years)			All
	15-24	25-34	35-59	
0-1	13	12	2	27
2-4	3	1	1	5
5-9	–	19	3	22
10+	4	17	25	46
All	20	49	31	100

around Rs. 3,800 and Rs. 500 respectively, per month. However, the capital cost per job created works out to about Rs. 290,000, which is high compared to that in the rest of the public sector, which ranges from Rs. 25,500 to Rs. 150,000 averaging at about Rs. 50,000 (Central Bank of Ceylon, 1975, p. 60).

The survey also revealed that the corporation provides low rent housing and credit at low interest rates to its employees. The initial settlers had faced a number of difficulties such as lack of adequate transport, water, schooling, and recreational facilities. But conscious efforts have been made over the last 10 years to ameliorate the situation and the majority of employees now appear to be satisfied with the facilities available. Over-all the findings of the case study suggest that the location of this factory in Puttalam has not only influenced migrant patterns but has also generated a level of economic activity adequate to retain the migrant population.

(c) Regression analysis

In order to assess whether land settlement and industrial location policies have influenced internal migration in Sri Lanka, we have estimated the following two equations, using district level data covering the intercensal period 1963-71.

$$H = a_0 + a_1 L + a_2 E_1 + e \qquad (1)$$

$$H = a_0 + a_1 L + a_2 E_2 + e \qquad (2)$$

where:

H = the index of attraction: gross in-migration to the district as a percentage of gross out-migration from all other districts;

L = change in the area of land under major settlement schemes;

E_1 = change in employment in state industry;

E_2 = change in total industrial employment; and

e = error term.

In equation 1, E_1 refers to the change in employment in state industry only. This is largely because it is only in the public sector that the state had direct control over the location of industries. However, import substitution policies in the 1960s also led to a rapid growth of private sector industries. An attempt is therefore made to capture the impact of industrial growth by considering total industrial employment in the public and private sectors as an alternative variable (E_2) in equation 2.

The equations were estimated by the ordinary least squares method; the data used in their estimation are given below:

District	Index of attraction H	Change in area of land under settlement (acres) L	Change in industrial employment E_1	Change in industrial employment E_2
Anuradhapura[1]	9.41	42,474	0	343
Badulla[2]	6.25	7,697	0	885
Batticaloa[3]	8.00	31,221	295	4,194
Colombo	37.93	-1,510	7,763	12,323
Galle	1.57	0	849	-264
Hambantota	2.94	1,887	0	442
Jaffna	2.13	13,672	486	-3,048
Kalutara	7.40	-4,807	0	393
Kandy	0.68	-3,617	0	4,626
Kegalla	1.02	0	0	1,655
Kurunegala	2.66	2,670	0	2,614
Mannar	0	235	0	-125
Matale	3.97	11,247	0	1,042
Matara	1.67	0	0	630
Nuwara Eliya	3.39	0	0	160
Puttalam	2.94	3,823	1,044	-22
Ratnapura	2.93	-5,234	0	84
Trincomalee	3.42	6,792	494	442
Vavuniya	4.90	4,241	0	132

[1] Includes Polonnaruwa district.

[2] Includes Monaragala district.

[3] Includes Amparai district.

Source: Data on H, L, and E_1 are as discussed in earlier sections. Data on E_2 are from census reports of 1963 and 1971.

Regression results

Equation 1 (t values are given in brackets)

$$H = 2.07398* + 0.000135*L + 0.00447**E_1$$
$$\quad\;\, (2.76) \qquad\;\, (2.50) \qquad\qquad (12.02)$$

Uncorrected R^2 = 0.901;   corrected R^2 = 0.889;

$F(2,16)$ = 72.6

No. of observations = 19;   DW statistic = 1.986

** Significant at the 1 per cent level;   * significant at the 5 per cent level.

The regression results show that the land settlement variable (L) has a positive sign and its coefficient is significant at the 5 per cent level.   The variable relating to employment in state industry (E_1) also has a significant coefficient with a positive sign.   However, the latter result should be interpreted with caution since there are only six non-zero observations in respect of E_1 with a dominant figure for Colombo.   There may thus be spurious correlation.

On excluding Colombo, the results obtained are as follows:

$$H = 2.95073** + 0.000147**L + 0.00138\ E_1$$
$$\quad\;\, (5.10) \qquad\qquad (3.97) \qquad\qquad (0.95)$$

Uncorrected R^2 = 0.501;   corrected R^2 = 0.434;

$F(2,15)$ = 7.53

DW statistic = 2.0419;   No. of observations = 18

The coefficients of L and E_1 are positive as before. However, the significance of the latter coefficient shows a marked decline;   its t value drops from 18.02 to 0.95. Also, the corrected R^2 drops to 0.434 and the F statistic to 7.53, indicating a considerably lower explanatory power when compared with the previous results.

Equation 2 (t values are given in brackets)

$$H = 1.78715 + 0.000096 \ L + 0.002210^{**} \ E_2$$
$$(1.32) \quad (1.02) \quad \quad (6.04)$$

Uncorrected $R^2 = 0.697$; corrected $R^2 = 0.659$;

$F(2,16) = 18.4$

DW statistic = 2.09; No. of observations = 19

** significant at the 1 per cent level; * significant at the 5 per cent level.

The relationship between land colonisation and index of attraction is positive, although its coefficient is statistically insignificant. The variable relating to industrial employment (E_2) has a positive sign and its coefficient is significant at the 1 per cent level.

On dropping Colombo, the following results are obtained:

$$H = 2.65740^{**} + 0.000145^{**} \ L + 0.0000857 \ E_2$$
$$(4.61) \quad \quad (3.64) \quad \quad (0.30)$$

Uncorrected $R^2 = 0.475$; corrected $R^2 = 0.405$;

$F(2,15) = 6.79$

DW statistic = 2.098; No. of observations = 18

The coefficients of L and E_2 are positive, although only the coefficient of the former is significant at the 1 per cent level. The significance of the coefficient of E_2 shows a marked decline; its t value drops from 6.05 to 0.30. Again the corrected R^2 drops to 0.405, indicating that the model could explain only about 40 per cent of the total variation. The explanatory power too, as reflected by the value of the F statistic, shows considerable decline. As in the case of equation 1 these results indicate that the values in respect of Colombo district have a dominant influence upon the results obtained.

Subject to the limitations discussed, the above results do suggest that land settlement and employment in industry have acted as pull factors and have thus affected internal migration trends in Sri Lanka during the period 1963-71. Thus it seems that land settlement and industrial location policies could be effective in drawing populations to desired destinations.

Summary and Conclusions

The analysis of internal migration during the period 1946-53 shows a marked migration from the wet zone to the dry zone, exceptions being Jaffna, an out-migration district located in the dry zone, and Colombo, an in-migration district located in the wet zone. A similar pattern was observed during the period 1953-63. But during the period 1963-71, Puttalam, an out-migration district in 1953-63, became an in-migration district, and Badulla, formerly an in-migration district, became an out-migration district. Thus the main change during 1946-71 was a large transfer of population from the wet zone districts to the dry zone districts, whereas no such movement was observed during the years 1921-46. This internal migration was mainly rural-to-rural.

While policies of land settlement encouraged mobility from the wet zone to the dry zone districts, policies of rural development, village expansion, and land reform, in addition to the social welfare policies regarding housing, health, and education, enhanced the retentive capacity of the rural sector. As a result of these policies, the proportion of rural population to the total population of Sri Lanka changed very little during the period 1946-71.

However, the beneficial effects of land settlement have not been fully realised in the past due to the under-utilisation of resources, the lack of adequate social welfare facilities in the colonised areas, and the deficiencies in the organisation and management of the schemes. These could be remedied to enhance the retentive capacity of the settlements.

The eradication of malaria in the dry zone removed one of the major impediments to the movement of people to the dry zone districts. The re-emergence of malaria must be combated to prevent people from drifting back to the wet zone.

Although the period 1963-71 had witnessed shifts in population from the wet zone to the dry zone, the Lorenz Curve relating to 1971 shows a significant movement away from the diagonal (see Appendix IV). This indicates that population distribution in 1971 had worsened in relation to those of previous census years. The explanation for this reversal lies partly in the large influx of population into the Colombo district, and to the south-west quadrant as a whole. This large-scale attraction of population back into the south-west sector is perhaps mainly attributable to the advance in industry during the 1960s. This tends to indicate that industry, by virtue of higher incomes, can generate a stronger pull factor than land settlement. The policy implication is that unless efforts are made to integrate rural industry into land settlement and development schemes the retentive capacity of such schemes will be diminished.

This result assumes special significance at a time when land settlement on an unprecedented scale is to be carried out under the accelerated Mahaweli programme. This scheme would activate internal migration on a scale hitherto unknown, for it will provide land for approximately 135,000 families. It will increase agricultural production by providing irrigation to 900,000 acres of land in the dry zone, and generate its own hydro-electric power supply. However, efforts must also be made to set up rural industries in the Mahaweli settlement areas, thus generating additional incomes to the farming communities, to enhance the retention of settlers. It is gratifying to note that several steps have already been taken in this direction. One of them is the establishment of a Ministry of Rural Industries Development so as to launch a concerted effort in the development of rural industry. Another is the appointment of a minister of non-cabinet rank in each of the administrative districts and the implementation of a system of decentralised budgeting.

Another major government project that is likely to influence internal migration is the setting up of the Greater Colombo Economic Commission (GCEC) to be in charge of an area of approximately 465 square kilometres in Katunayaka, within which there would be several investment promotion zones. It is the government's intention to attract foreign investment through a number of incentives such as tax holidays, duty-free imports of raw materials and machinery, and infrastructure facilities, thereby creating direct and indirect employment for a considerable number of people. In this industrial promotion zone at Katunayaka, in a period of one year from February 1978, 91 industries were approved, of which 15 have gone into production, creating employment for 6,150 persons. It is expected to provide job opportunities for about 150,000 when it is fully under way. The wage and other differentials between the GCEC and the rest of the economy will perhaps draw surplus manpower from the rural areas to the GCEC and the surrounding areas in search of employment. This may lead to problems of congestion. It is, therefore, important that appropriate policy measures are adopted to stimulate industry in the rural sector if a balance is to be maintained. Steps in this direction have already been taken by the tax holiday offered to small and medium-scale industries (defined as those where the capital investment is less than one million rupees), provided they are located outside municipal areas. The village reawakening programme initiated in June 1978 based on the self-help principle would also go a long way in this direction. A more detailed discussion of these recent policies is outside the scope of this study, however, and it is too early to evaluate their implications.

<u>Appendix I</u>: <u>Note on the index of attraction</u>

The index of attraction used by Abhayaratne and Jayawardene is computed as follows:

Let m_{ij} = number of out-migrants from district i to district j, and

M_i = total number of out-migrants from district i.

Thus P_{ij} = $\frac{m_{ij}}{M_i} \times 100$ gives the percentage of out-migrants from district i to district j.

The index of attraction (I_j) is therefore defined as:

$$I_j = \frac{1}{n-1} \sum_{i=1}^{n} P_{ij} \qquad\qquad i \neq j \qquad\qquad (1)$$

where n is the number of districts.

A major drawback of the above index is that all percentages are given equal weightage. This could create distortions as, for example, a particularly large out-migration from a given district may not be adequately reflected in the index. This problem can be overcome by calculating a weighted index (H_j) as follows:

$$H_j = \frac{1}{M} \sum_{i \neq j}^{n} M_{ij} \times 100$$

where $M = \sum_{i \neq j}^{n} M_i$ = total number of out-migrants from all districts other than from district j.

Thus,

$$H_j = \frac{\text{Number of in-migrants into district j}}{\text{total number of out-migrants from all districts other than from district j}} \times 100$$

- 131 -

This definition has a fairly straightforward interpretation since it indicates the extent to which a particular district has been able to attract in-migrants from the totality of out-migrants from all other districts.

Appendix II: District-wise distribution of
                industries, 1975-76

District	No. of industries	%
Amparai	12	0.50
Aruradhapura	18	0.76
Badulla	22	0.92
Batticaloa	10	0.42
Colombo	1,719	72.84
Galle	48	2.02
Hambantota	7	0.29
Jaffna	59	2.49
Kalutara	95	4.06
Kandy	103	4.39
Kegalla	32	1.35
Kurunegala	55	2.32
Mannar	3	0.12
Matale	22	0.92
Matara	101	4.31
Monaragala	7	0.29
Nuwara Eliya	6	0.25
Polonnaruwa	2	0.08
Puttalam	30	1.26
Ratnapura	8	0.33
Trincomalee	6	0.25
Vavuniya	3	0.12
Sri Lanka	2,368	100.00

Source: Ministry of Industries and Scientific
Affairs, 1976.

Appendix III: District-wise distribution of population and
DDC industrial projects, 1976

District	Population 1971	%	No. of industrial projects	%
Amparai	272,605	2.15	08	0.97
Anuradhapura	388,770	3.06	29	3.53
Badulla	615,405	4.85	29	3.53
Batticaloa	256,721	2.02	04	0.49
Colombo	2,672,265	21.26	132	16.05
Galle	735,173	5.79	64	7.79
Hambantota	340,254	2.68	12	1.46
Jaffna	701,603	5.53	90	10.95
Kalutara	729,514	5.85	55	6.69
Kandy	1,187,925	9.53	46	5.60
Kegalla	654,752	5.16	52	6.33
Kurunegala	1,025,633	8.18	90	10.95
Mannar	77,780	0.06	07	0.85
Matale	314,841	2.48	32	3.89
Matara	586,443	4.62	41	4.99
Monaragala	193,020	1.52	12	1.46
Nuwara Eliya	450,278	3.55	18	2.19
Polonnaruwa	163,653	1.29	09	1.09
Puttalam	378,430	2.98	30	3.65
Ratnapura	661,344	5.21	44	5.35
Trincomalee	188,245	1.48	11	1.34
Vavuniya	95,243	0.75	07	0.85
Total	12,680,807	100.00	822	100.00

Sources: District Development Councils (1976), and
Department of Census and Statistics (1971).

Appendix IV: Lorenz Curves

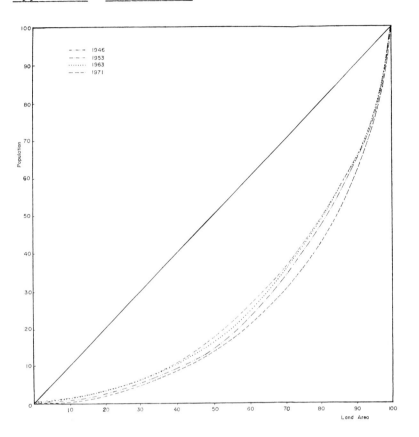

Chapter 5

MIGRATION IN INDIA: TRENDS AND POLICIES

By Ashish Bose*

Introduction

Studies on migration are very few in India because, historically speaking, migration has never been considered an important demographic issue on account of the small volume of internal migration compared to the total size of population.   The perception of internal migration has been mostly in terms of rural-to-urban migration, and especially migration to the big cities.   In other words, internal migration has been viewed almost wholly as a concomitant of urbanisation.

The last decade, however, has witnessed new patterns of internal migration in India, and the significant issue arising out of such migration is not the volume of such migration, but its political, social and economic impact, which in several cases has been profound.   The recent turmoil in Assam over the issue of "foreigners" has posed formidable problems for the government.   The violence in Tripura and other states of north-east India, arising out of the growing tension between the original tribal population, who have been vastly outnumbered by the non-tribal migrants, has highlighted the tremendous impact of migration on the life of the people.   In different regions of India, there is a growing conflict between the "sons of the soil" and the "outsiders" - migrants from other states of India (Weiner, 1978, p. 3).

The roots of the conflict between the "sons of the soil" and the "outsiders" often lie in economic factors. Religion, caste, and language become mere weapons in the struggle for survival in a situation where employment opportunities are not expanding and there is slow and even stagnating economic growth, with increasing disparities between different communities and regions.

---

*   Institute of Economic Growth, Delhi.   The author is grateful to Professor H.K. Manmohan Singh, Head of the Economics Department, Punjabi University, Patiala, for his help and co-operation, and to Miss Sakim Karim and Mrs. Manjula Bose for assisting in documentation work.

Many policies have, therefore, been introduced to achieve a more desirable and balanced spatial distribution of economic activity. These include: dispersal of industries and balanced regional development; establishment of heavy industries in new townships; land development schemes and the opening up of new agricultural areas; urban development programmes, especially those concerning slum dwellers and squatters, etc. All these have implications for migration patterns in India.

The purpose of this study is twofold: first, to examine the nature and flows of internal migration in India; and second, to assess the efficacy of some of the important migration-influencing policies.

Migration Streams

Prior to the 1951 Census of India, data on migration (based on place of birth) were available only for inter-state migration. Thanks to the extended questionnaire and the detailed tabulation of the 1961 census, it is now possible to get a detailed picture of internal migration in India.

If migrants are defined as persons born outside the state of enumeration, one comes to the conclusion that internal migration is negligible in India. But if a migrant is defined as a person born outside the place of enumeration, the figure for migration will be very large. For example, according to the 1961 census, only 3.3 per cent of the total population of India was enumerated in states outside the state of birth, while 30.7 per cent of the total population was enumerated outside the place of birth (Government of India, Census of India, 1961, pp. 16-17). In 1971, the comparable figures were 3.4 per cent and 30.4 per cent respectively (Census of India, 1971, pp. 10-11). It may be noted in this connection that the 1971 census asked a direct question on migration in respect of the place of last residence. This question was introduced to overcome the limitation of migration data based on place of birth. The 1971 census data, however, did not reveal any drastic difference between the place of birth data and the place of migration data. For example, the total number of migrants in India accounted for 30.6 per cent of the population based on the place of last residence, compared to 30.4 per cent based on the place of birth (ibid., pp. 10-11).

The fact that about one-third of India's population was enumerated outside the place of birth clearly indicates that internal migration in India is a major demographic process and needs to be studied carefully. Table 1 presents data on four lifetime migration streams:

        1   rural-to-rural;
        2   rural-to-urban;
        3   urban-to-urban; and
        4   urban-to-rural.

Migrants from abroad have been excluded since our
concern is primarily with internal migration. It must be
remembered, however, that while in the country as a
whole immigration from abroad is not important, this is
not true for individual cities where migration from
Pakistan has been quite considerable on account of the
partition of India in 1947.
        As table 1 shows, in both 1961 and 1971 the rural-
to-rural migration stream was by far the most important.
The considerable variation in the sex composition of the
different streams is shown in table 2. In contrast to the
close balance between males and females among migrants
to urban places, females constitute a significantly higher
percentage of those moving to rural places, especially
those moving from one rural place to another. Much of
this female migration is on account of marriage.

Table 1: Lifetime migration streams, 1961 and 1971 (%)

Migration streams	1961			1971		
	Total	Male	Female	Total	Male	Female
Rural-to-rural	73.7	56.7	81.3	71.3	53.5	78.8
Urban-to-rural	3.6	4.6	3.2	4.9	6.1	4.4
Rural-to-urban	14.6	25.7	9.7	15.0	26.1	10.3
Urban-to-urban	8.1	13.0	5.8	8.8	14.3	6.5
Total	100.0	100.0	100.0	100.0	100.0	100.0

Source: Bose (1980).

        Contrary to the general impression, rural-to-urban
migration is not the most important migration stream. It
is important to note, however, that in absolute terms
rural-to-urban and urban-to-urban migration accounted
for over 30 million persons in 1961, and 39 million in
1971, showing an increase of 30 per cent over the
decade.

Table 2: Lifetime migration streams by sex, 1961 and 1971
(%)

Migration streams	1961			1971		
	Male	Female	Total	Male	Female	Total
Rural-to-rural	23.7	76.3	100.0	22.4	77.6	100.0
Urban-to-rural	39.2	60.8	100.0	37.1	62.9	100.0
Rural-to-urban	54.0	46.0	100.0	52.1	47.9	100.0
Urban-to-urban	50.0	50.0	100.0	48.6	51.4	100.0

Interesting differences characterise the sex composition of the four migration streams. In both census years, females constituted a large proportion of all migrants - around 70 per cent. However, this reflected the preponderance of females in rural-to-rural migration; three out of every four rural-to-rural migrants were female in 1961 and 1971, and such migration accounted for 81.3 per cent of total female migration in India in 1961 and 78.8 per cent in 1971. For males, however, rural-to-rural migration was below 60 per cent of all migration in both decades. By contrast, the sex composition of migrants to urban places was much more balanced. But more important from the point of view of economic change is the urban-ward movement of males. In absolute numbers, the combined rural-to-urban and urban-to-urban streams involved about 10 million males in 1961 and about 21 million in 1971. They accounted for nearly 39 per cent of total male migration in 1961 and roughly 40 per cent of total male migration in 1971.

The census data also make it possible to isolate three types of migration which are roughly indicative of the distance moved, although, ideally, the geographic location of districts should also be considered:

1   short-distance migration: persons born outside the place of enumeration but living within the same district (intra-district migration);

2   medium-distance migration: persons born outside the district of residence but within the state of enumeration (inter-district or intra-state migration); and

3   long-distance migration: persons born in states of India other than the state of enumeration (inter-state migration).

An examination of table 3 clearly indicates that the predominant form of migration is short-distance. This is more common for females than males. Short-distance migration accounts for over 70 per cent of female migration, and over 50 per cent of male migration. On the other hand, nearly 20 per cent of the males were long-distance migrants compared to less than 10 per cent of the females.

Distance and rural-urban flows can be considered simultaneously. Within each category of distance, for total migrants, rural-to-rural migration predominates, although this differs in degree between males and females. Female migration in both years and for all distance categories is heavily concentrated in the rural-to-rural stream. For both sexes, but especially for males, the rural-to-rural predominance tends to decrease with distance, and for long-distance male migrants the predominance disappears. In the long-distance category, the rural-ward movement of males constitutes less than one-third of the total stream in both 1961 and 1971. The most frequent movement for males going long distances is rural to urban.

In addition to data on lifetime migration, the 1961 and 1971 censuses also collected information on duration of residence in the place of enumeration. An important limitation of these data for comparative purposes is the difference in the relative size of non-response: in 1961 only 2.8 per cent of the migrants did not report duration, while in 1971 the corresponding figure was 14.8 per cent. The broad pattern of distribution does not, however, appear to differ greatly (table 4). In 1961, more migrants reported durations of 10 years and less. The largest difference between 1961 and 1971 is in the short duration of less than one year: 9.9 per cent in 1961 and 4.4 per cent in 1971, but part of this may reflect a larger proportion of migrants not reporting duration in 1971.

It might be pointed out that the sex composition of different groups identified by duration of residence is quite similar in the two censuses. As the duration of residence in the place of enumeration increases, the proportion of males among migrants steadily declines, while the proportion of females increases. Whereas the migrants with less than one year's duration are almost equally balanced between males and females, those in the longest duration categories have only one male for every four females. This suggests that the migration of males is much less stable than that of the females, possibly reflecting that migration induced by economic factors is less stable than that induced by social factors.

Table 3: Lifetime migration streams, 1961 and 1971 (%)

Migration streams	1961			1971		
	Total	Male	Female	Total	Male	Female
Short-distance (within the district)						
Rural-to-rural	57.6	40.2	65.5	55.6	38.3	63.0
Urban-to-rural	2.0	2.3	1.8	2.5	2.9	2.4
Rural-to-urban	6.1	9.0	4.8	6.5	9.6	5.2
Urban-to-urban	2.1	3.0	1.6	1.8	2.6	1.5
Total short-distance	67.8	54.5	73.7	66.4	53.4	72.1
Medium-distance (within the state)						
Rural-to-rural	12.1	11.2	12.4	11.7	10.3	12.3
Urban-to-rural	1.1	1.5	1.0	1.6	2.0	1.4
Rural-to-urban	4.9	8.8	3.2	5.0	9.0	3.3
Urban-to-urban	3.3	5.2	2.4	3.9	6.1	2.9
Total medium-distance	21.4	26.7	19.0	22.2	27.4	19.9
Long-distance (between states)						
Rural-to-rural	4.0	5.3	3.4	3.9	4.8	3.5
Urban-to-rural	0.5	0.8	0.4	0.8	1.2	0.6
Rural-to-urban	3.6	7.8	1.8	3.6	7.6	1.8
Urban-to-urban	2.7	4.9	1.7	3.1	5.6	2.1
Total long-distance	10.8	18.8	7.3	11.4	19.2	8.0
Total	100.0	100.0	100.0	100.0	100.0	100.0

Table 4: Distribution of migrants by duration of
residence and sex, 1961 and 1971

Duration of residence	% of migrants	% of migrants		
		Male	Female	Total
1961				
Less than 1 year	9.9	48.4	51.6	100
1-5 years	22.9	40.4	59.6	100
6-10 years	16.2	30.5	69.5	100
11-15 years	12.9	27.7	72.3	100
16 years and over	35.3	20.6	79.4	100
Period not stated	2.8	35.4	64.6	100
All periods	100.0			
1971				
Less than 1 year	4.4	51.0	49.0	100
1-4 years	18.3	41.4	58.6	100
5-9 years	13.8	33.0	67.0	100
10-19 years	21.4	26.0	74.0	100
20 years and over	27.3	20.6	79.4	100
Period not stated	14.8	36.6	63.4	100
All periods	100.0			

It is notable that the volume of migration is smaller
in absolute terms according to the 1971 census compared
to the 1961 census. This may be indicative of reduced
economic mobility. In terms of general economic trends,
1961 formed part of an upward swing in economic activity
generated by the Second Five Year Plan (1956-61), while
1971 followed a period of unrest and industrial stagnation
which had made planning so uncertain that the launching
of the Fourth Plan was delayed by three years. Moreover, 1971 also followed a period of substantial progress
in agriculture. Thus it is likely that hopeful signs in
rural-based agriculture provided some compensation for
stagnation in urban-based industry. These countervailing forces seem to have exerted a restraining effect
on urban-ward migration. Another factor leading to
decreased mobility in 1971 seems to have been the impact
of information flow. In 1971 the channels of information
between rural and urban sectors were much more
advanced than in 1961. Potential migrants in rural areas

may have been discouraged from moving to urban areas by the bleak economic prospects there created by the already large reserves in the urban labour force.

Appraisal of Selected Migration-influencing Policies

(a)   Housing and human settlement policies

Housing and human settlement policies, especially the provision of mass housing for the poor, and resettlement schemes for slum-dwellers, squatters, and persons residing in unauthorised settlements (most of whom are usually migrants) are often termed accommodationist policies. Though such policies are not designed to encourage migration, they often result in doing so. We shall briefly consider the evolution of these policies in India over the last three decades, beginning with Independence in 1947.

1947-51

The partition of India in 1947 led to one of the major migratory movements in the history of the world. It witnessed the distress migration of roughly 20 million refugees between India and Pakistan. According to the 1951 Census of India, 54 per cent of the displaced persons who came from Pakistan (numbering about 10 million) settled in the urban areas of India. Considering that only 17.3 per cent of India's population was urbanised in 1951, this meant a disproportionate share of the displaced persons in urban areas. For example, 90 per cent of displaced persons who came to Uttar Pradesh were enumerated in the urban areas of that state. The quiet town of Dehra Dun in Uttar Pradesh witnessed a rate of population growth of the order of 79 per cent during 1941-51.

The major impact of refugee migration was on the big cities of India. South Dum Dum, for example, a constituent town of the Calcutta agglomeration, grew by 138 per cent during 1941-51; Greater Bombay's population increased by 76 per cent, and Delhi's by 107 per cent. No Indian city had the physical and economic infrastructure to cope with the new demands made by refugees for residential land, housing, water supply, sewerage, transport, and so on. Yet the problem had to be solved on a war footing as millions of refugees poured into the cities. New refugee colonies sprang up in almost all cities affected by partition.

The first major urban policy during the years 1947-51 was speedy rehabilitation of refugees through the creation of new refugee townships and also new refugee colonies in existing cities. There is no doubt that the government's achievement in rehabilitating refugees, especially from West Pakistan, was remarkable. It must be remembered at the same time that the refugees themselves contributed a great deal to their successful rehabilitation. In support of this thesis, we may point out that in a socio-economic survey of Greater Delhi conducted in 1955 by Rao and Desai, it was found that the average monthly income from work was Rs. 130 in the case of refugees and Rs. 117 in the case of residents excluding migrants. According to Rao, this was due to "the spirit of enterprise and hard work of the refugee population, besides of course being attributed to their higher academic qualifications and skills". Rao further observes that it is "amply borne out by the findings of this study that refugee rehabilitation in Delhi is to a considerable extent due to the efforts put in by the refugees themselves" (Rao and Desai, 1965, pp. xix-xx).

Apart from new refugee townships, two new state capitals - Bhubaneswar in Orissa and Chandigarh in the Punjab - were constructed soon after Independence; a third, Gandhinagar, in Gujarat built later.

1951-61

The 1951 census recorded the highest ever rate of growth of the urban population, namely 41.4 per cent, during the 1941-51 decade. According to our estimate, the abnormal migration of refugees contributed 6.2 per cent to this urban growth. Even so an urban growth rate of over 35 per cent due to natural increase in population and normal migration was certainly of a high order. The growth rates were the highest in cities with populations of 100,000 and over.

During the 1951-61 decade, the First and Second Five-Year Plans were implemented. A growing concern about the housing of middle- and low-income groups was reflected in these plans. It may be noted that in 1949 the Industrial Housing Scheme was formulated. This envisaged the issue of interest-free loans by the central government to the state governments or private employers, sponsored by the latter to the extent of two-thirds of the cost of housing schemes on condition that the rent charged would not exceed 12.5 per cent of the capital cost, subject to a maximum of 10 per cent of the workers' wages, the employer contributing 3 per cent of the cost of .the houses. In 1952, a new policy was announced whereby the central government was prepared to pay a subsidy of up to 20 per cent of the cost of construction, including the cost of land, provided the balance was met by the employer, who would again let out the houses to genuine workers at rates suggested under the earlier scheme. The First Plan admitted: "That these concessions have not produced the desired effect seems to indicate that the policy of paying subsidies, which has already been accepted, will have further to be liberalised as well as supplemented by loans." The plan recommended that subsidies should be paid to the state governments of up to 50 per cent of the total cost of construction of houses, including the cost of land. The plan also recognised that "for years to come the bulk of building activity will still have to be undertaken by private enterprise" (Government of India, Planning Commission, 1952, pp. 599-600). In 1954, the Low-income Group Housing Scheme was introduced. This provided for the grant of long-term house building loans at a reasonable rate of interest to persons whose income was less than Rs. 6,000 per annum.

The Second Plan (1956-61) observed that "on account of high land prices and the lack of suitably developed sites, progress in the construction of houses under the Low-income Group Housing Scheme has not been as rapid as was hoped for". The Second Plan advocated the following policy: "It would, therefore, appear desirable to provide assistance to state governments and local authorities for developing sites for sale to persons who have low incomes and wish to build houses for their own use." (Government of India, Planning Commission, 1956, p. 558).

During the Second Plan period an important development took place. The Life Insurance Corporation of India began to provide funds for house-building to middle-income groups and to state governments for undertaking rental housing for their low-paid employees.

Another significant development during the Second Plan period was the construction of steel townships in Rourkela in Orissa, Bhilai in Madhya Pradesh, and Durgapur in West Bengal, consequent upon the decision to establish three new steel plants in the public sector. The construction of the Rourkela steel plant commenced in 1955 while that of the township began in 1956. By 1961 the steel township alone had a population of about 38,000 while the over-all population, inclusive of the surrounding areas, was over 90,000. The second public sector steel plant was constructed in 1955, and the township, Bhilainagar, was built from 1956 to 1959. By 1961, Bhilainagar had a population of over 86,000. Unlike Rourkela, Bhilainagar had a small town (Durg) in close proximity.

In Durgapur, along with the steel plant, several other industries were established as a result of the decision of the West Bengal government to set up the Durgapur Industries Board. The alloy steel plant, a large plant for manufacturing coalmining machinery, and an ophthalmic glass plant were established in the public sector, and several other industries and engineering units in the private sector. By 1961, there were over 50 large, medium and small industries in the Durgapur region.

Sivaramakrishnan, in a recent study of new towns in India, points out:

> "People are usually not aware that Durgapur is more than a steel plant and its township. With an investment exceeding Rs. 6,000 million, Durgapur is the home of a dozen large and medium industries and nearly a hundred small enterprises. It is probably the largest concentration of heavy industry to be set up anew in the country. With a population of over 206,000 Durgapur is also a new town in the Class I category" (Sivaramakrishnan, 1977, p. 25).

The newest steel township is Bokaro in Bihar, where another steel plant was put up in the public sector. The Bihar government has established an industrial estate near the steel plant. According to the 1971 census, the population of Bokaro steel city was over 94,000.

Sivaramakrishnan's study brings out a very disquieting feature of these new towns:

> "Though the new towns ... have been in existence for just about 20 years, the growth of slums in and around them has been a pronounced feature ... These marginal settlements consist not only of slums and squatter settlements that have come up afresh but they also cover the villages, however small, existing in the vicinity of the new town which over a period of time have degenerated into slums. To a large extent this phenomenon has been due to ignorance of the urbanization process and defective land and development policies" (ibid., p. 75).

The figures in table 5 are relevant here.

Table 5: Marginal settlements in new steel towns (1971)

| Town | Population | | Percentage population in marginal settlements |
	Total	Marginal settlements	
Bhilai	245,124	64,685	29
Bokaro	107,159	17,565	17
Durgapur	206,638	40,004	20
Rourkela	172,502	53,363	31

Source: Sivaramakrishnan (1977), p. 74.

The failure of the public sector to build houses for persons (mostly in the services sector) who are not directly employed in public sector undertakings but who are nonetheless essential for the working of these undertakings, and the failure of the private sector to provide housing for its workers, have largely contributed to the growth of slums and marginal settlements. While the public sector in the new townships has, by and large, provided housing for its workers, this is not true of public sector undertakings in other towns and cities. The situation in selected public and private sector undertakings in one of the leading industrial cities of India – Bangalore – can be seen from table 6.

1961-75

In 1961, the Town and Country Planning Organization of the Government of India prepared a note on urban land policy, which ultimately led to the appointment of the Committee on Urban Land Policy. This committee showed a grasp of the intricate issues involved and made a series of detailed recommendations. The committee observed that "the problem of urban development is vitally connected with the problems of urban land and its values and it is impossible to conceive of improvement of cities and creation of better living conditions in urban areas without a co-ordinated, bold and realistic approach to the problem" (Government of India, Ministry of Health, 1965, p. 54).

Table 6: Housing of workers in Bangalore, 1972

Industrial concern	Total workers	No. of workers provided with housing	Percentage of workers provided with housing
Bangalore Woollen, Cotton Silk Mills	7,400	600	8.1
Bharat Electronics	10,100	1,132	11.1
Government Electric Factory	950	63	6.6
Hindustan Aeronautics	22,520	2,450	10.8
Hindustan Machine Tools and Watch Factory	7,000	2,100	30.0
Imperial Tobacco Company	2,182	196	8.9
Indian Telephone Industries	14,000	1,928	13.7
Minerva Mills	2,869	85	2.9
Motor Industries Company	5,500	–	–
Mysore Spinning and Manufacturing Company	3,027	167	5.5
New Government Electric Factory	3,000	84	2.8
Sri Krishna Spinning and Weaving Mills	1,800	263	14.6

Source: Rama Gowda (1977), p. 308.

There was, however, no evidence in the Five Year Plans of any such bold and realistic approach. The Third Plan (1961-66) devoted considerable attention to the problem of controlling urban land values. Among other things, it suggested the following measures: capital tax on transfer of freehold land, taxation of vacant plots in developed areas with power to acquire if they are not built upon within specified periods, setting a ceiling on the size of individual plots, and limiting the number of plots which a single party may be permitted to acquire.

The Fourth Plan (1969-74) observed that "the experience of public housing so far is that its unit cost is high and that with the constraint of resources it is not possible for public operations to touch even a fringe of the problem". The plan pointed out that "the private sector should standardize building components and manufacture them on a large scale" (Government of India, Planning Commission, 1969, p. 402).

The draft Fifth Five Year Plan (1974-79) spells out briefly the "strategy" of urban development, but the attitude is one of helplessness. It still harps on the old theme of formulating an urban land policy. To quote from the plan: "In view of the serious problem for urban planning and development posed by the continuous and excessive rise in urban land values in and around urban centres, the formulation of an urban land policy assumes a certain urgency". The plan then goes on to enumerate the following broad objectives in this regard:

(a) to promote optimum use of land;

(b) to make land available for purposes consistent with economic growth and social policy to different sections of the community and, in particular, to the weaker sections;

(c) to reduce and, if possible, prevent concentration of land ownership, rising land values, speculation, etc.;

(d) to allow land to be used, as a resource for financing urban development (Government of India, Planning Commission, 1973, p. 258).

Unfortunately these remained pious sentiments in the absence of any operational strategy. One significant aspect of the Draft Fifth Plan, however, was the formulation of a seven-point national programme of minimum needs. The programme included carrying out environmental improvement of slums. The Draft Fifth Plan outlay on urban development was Rs. 5,785 million, including Rs. 1,500 million for the integrated development of the Calcutta metropolitan area, and Rs. 2,500 million for extra financial assistance for metropolitan development and projects of national importance. The Fifth Plan outlays were scaled down, however, when the plan was finalised. The revised outlay on urban development was Rs. 5,055 million (Government of India, Planning Commission, 1976, p. 156).

One important development during the Fourth Plan period was the establishment of the Housing and Urban Development Corporation (HUDCO) as a government-owned company to provide financial support to state governments, housing boards, and other local authorities. HUDCO began functioning in 1970, and by the end of August 1973 it had approved schemes estimated to cost Rs. 1,100 million, with a loan commitment of Rs. 740 million. It was supposed to be an innovative institution aiming at substantially improving the housing situation by providing mass housing. But the record of HUDCO is by no means encouraging. A recent study observes:

> "HUDCO has found itself financing houses that are much too expensive for the poor man. Houses meant for the economically weaker section (EWS) whose monthly income falls short of Rs. 350 have been built at a cost of Rs. 15,000 and even more, involving a monthly repayment instalment of at least Rs. 115. Obviously such houses must eventually go to people who are not really in the EWS. HUDCO recently checked the occupancy of some of the houses it has financed; the check confirmed this suspicion" (Raj, 1978, p. 131).

The relevant data are given in table 7.

Turning to the private sector, we find that the housing provided is by and large beyond the reach of the poor. Mulkh Raj estimates that 60 per cent of private houses have three or more rooms. Hence "the poor who constitute the overwhelming majority are skipped both by the public and private sector" (ibid., p. 131). It follows from this discussion that the urban poor have no alternative but to fend for themselves and build their own "houses" wherever they can, regardless of legal formalities. This leads to the proliferation of unauthorised houses and unauthorised colonies, slums, and squatting.

Table 7:   HUDCO's housing projects

Schemes	Percentage of houses going to non-entitled families
Houses for economically weaker section (EWS)	
Baroda, Faridabad and Panipat	52.3
Madras	63.2
Madurai	44.9
Rajkot	70.0
Low-income houses	
Jaipur and Panipat	40.7
Madras	77.2

Source: Raj (1978).

1975-80:

In 1975, the Ministry of Works and Housing set up a task force to examine the planning and development of small and medium towns. The report of the task force was released in 1977. The two volumes of the report give a clear picture of the problems of small and medium towns. The task force also comments on the broad field of urban policy in India:

"While efforts are now being concentrated in tackling the problems of metropolitan and rural housing especially for the poor, there have been no policies and programmes for housing in small and medium towns and cities. The percentage of public investment in housing to total public investment had declined from 16 per cent in the First Plan to 8 per cent in the Second Plan, 7 per cent in the Third Plan, 5 per cent in the Fourth and to 3 per cent in the Fifth Plan. A large informal segment living in crowded houses without amenities is also beginning to appear in small and medium towns and cities - resulting in slums and squatter settlements" (Government of India, Ministry of Works and Housing, 1977, p. 26).

The task force came to the conclusion that "for a long-term and lasting solution of urban problems, the answer has to be found in a proper concept of urban-isation itself in the Indian context...". The task force was particularly critical of piecemeal solutions which in fact add to the urban problems. For example:

"Slum clearance as an isolated item for action and doling out of land for housing unrelated to an integrated urban policy and worse still, any urban land policy; development of industrial sites as part only of steps towards the economic rehabilitation of a group; construction of tall buildings to compete with the Qutab Minar or the beautification of a town by the installation of artificial lights in parks, in open spaces and on pavements and by painting rough-hewn ancient granite, development of places of interest for foreign tourists only with the sole objective of earning foreign exchange, without any comprehension of tending the countryside as such as a source of perennial joy to every-body" (ibid., p. 82).

(b) Urban land policy

Another important development in the field of urban planning and policy was the passing of the Urban Land Ceiling and Regulation Act of 1976. The objective of this Act was to ensure orderly urban development, check land speculation, curb luxury housing, and reduce disparities in income and wealth between different classes. For the purpose of this Act, cities were categorised as follows:

1 metropolitan cities of Delhi, Bombay, Calcutta, and Madras;

2 urban agglomerations with a population of 1 million and above including the four metropolitan cities;

3 urban agglomerations with a population between 300,000 and 1 million;

4 urban agglomerations with a population between 200,000 and 300,000.

Under the Act, the ceilings on holdings of vacant land and the plinth area of dwelling units were specified according to these four categories of cities.

This Act turned out to be a hasty piece of legislation, however, with numerous loopholes, and it posed difficult problems from the point of view of implementation. The first adverse impact of the Act was an almost complete freeze in housing activity in big cities and a rise in house rents. The Union Minister of Works and Housing hinted in 1980 that "the Urban Land Ceiling Act could be scrapped or at least drastically amended" (Indian Express, New Delhi, 26 February 1980). According to him the Act had given rise to corruption, pushed up land prices, and brought private building activity to a standstill.

(c) Dispersal of industries

In all the Five Year Plans, the need for balanced regional development, dispersal of industries, and decongestion of cities is reiterated, yet policies in this regard have, by and large, remained in the realm of wishful thinking, with very little implementation.

The most urbanised state of India, Maharashtra, has been a pioneer in the field of industrial dispersal. The Maharashtra Industrial Development Corporation (MIDC) was established in 1962 with the object of achieving more balanced industrial development. Yet, interestingly enough, Sulabha Brahme points out that of the total private fixed capital investment in factories located in the industrial area developed by the MIDC, as much as 74 per cent is concentrated in the Bombay metropolitan region. She also points out that the Bombay region received 78 per cent of the total industrial licences in Maharashtra State during 1965-69 (Brahme, 1977, p. 320). Further, the Bombay region claimed 80 per cent of new factory workers in Maharashtra State during 1956-71. The contrast between Greater Bombay and the backward Aurangabad division is briefly summarised in table 8.

Brahme's analysis leads her to conclude that "private industry and government continue to work for the growth of the Bombay metropolitan region, though the announced state policy is to discourage establishment of new industrial undertakings in overdeveloped areas of the state" (ibid., p. 320).

In June 1976, however, the government announced a comprehensive policy of industrial location in the Bombay metropolitan region. Large incentives were announced by the government to encourage industries to locate units in the developing areas of the state. These included exemptions from power cuts in developing areas, increases in power tariffs in the Bombay-Thana belt, interest subsidy schemes, promotion of resource-based industries, etc. These measures were backed by an elaborate

Table 8: Share of Greater Bombay and Aurangabad
division in Maharashtra State in 1971

Percentage of	Greater Bombay	Aurangabad division
Population	11.8	16.0
Male workers	14.8	15.9
Non-agricultural workers	34.8	8.4
Workers in manufacturing activity	50.2	2.9
Factory workers	59.4	1.5
Electricity consumption (1970)	68.9	1.3
Commercial Bank credit disbursed (1972)	85.1	0.7
Joint stock companies	87.6	0.4

Source: Brahme (1977), p. 321.

institutional set-up. Apart from the Maharashtra Industrial Development Corporation (MIDC), two of the pioneering institutions were the Maharashtra Small Scale Industries Development Corporation (MSSIDC) and the State Industrial and Investment Corporation of Maharashtra Limited (SICOM).

Godbole has evaluated the impact of industrial dispersal policies in Maharashtra and found that they had a positive impact in selected growth centres like Aurangabad, Nasik and Nagpur (Godbole, 1978). In respect of factories newly registered each year all over the state, for example, electricity consumption in the developed parts of the state declined from 70 per cent in 1969 to 64 per cent in 1974. "This is mainly due to the dual policy adopted by the government, of containing the further concentration of industries in the Bombay-Thane-Pune belt and liberal incentives, concessions and infrastructure facilities made available in the developing areas of the state" (ibid., p. 212). Godbole notes, however, that "the incentives are solely related to capital investment and have no relation to the employment potential of a unit. This has resulted in large capital intensive units getting located in the developing areas" (ibid., p. 212).

Godbole found that labour costs were a smaller percentage of total costs in the developing areas than in the developed areas. But his evaluation of industrial dispersal policies does not deal with the impact of such policies on migration. One can only surmise that to the extent that such policies succeed, the dominance of Greater Bombay will tend to decrease and a new pattern of migration to smaller places will emerge.

(d) Rural industrialisation programme

The Rural Industries Projects Programme (RIP) was launched in 1962 on a pilot basis in the 49 areas of India, comprising three to five community development blocks in each area with a population ranging between 300,000 to 500,000.

One would have expected that a programme like RIP would bring about a better diversification of the occupational structure and reduce excessive migration from villages to cities. Gupta, who has evaluated the rural industrialisation programme, has the following to say:

"It is a sad commentary on India's planning that despite several programmes of industrial development, the occupational pattern has not shown any meaningful change. Large-scale industries which were supposed to serve as centres for potential industrial development have not succeeded in fulfilling this limited objective. The employment effects of steel mills and other large industries are known to be quite disappointing. On the other hand the experiment of promoting development in the more remote and backward areas through rural industrialization has not been very encouraging" (Gupta, 1979, pp. 10-11).

Gupta and Dasgupta undertook a cost-benefit analysis of seven RIP projects and found that in terms of social cost-benefit analysis the RIP programme has been quite successful (Gupta and Dasgupta, 1979).

Gupta's study indicates that in so far as the RIP programme improves the skills of the workers, the ability of these workers to compete in the urban labour market also improves. Far from containing rural-to-urban migration, the RIP programme may in fact generate more such migration. Further, the RIP programme tends to promote substitution of labour by capital and to that extent dilutes the objective of generating employment.

(e)   The New Industrial Policy

The New Industrial Policy was formulated in December 1977. According to the then Industries Minister:

"The main thrust of the New Industrial Policy will be on effective promotion of cottage and small industries widely dispersed in rural areas and small towns ... The focal point of development ... will be taken away from the big cities and state capitals to the district headquarters. In each district there will be one agency to deal with all requirements of small and village industries. This will be called the District Industries Centre."[1]

The New Industrial Policy was expected to have a direct impact on the location of new industries as well as the dispersal of existing industries in regard to the following aspects:

1   The "tiny sector" comprising small-scale industries with investment in machinery and equipment up to one lakh (Rs. 100,000) will be encouraged only in small towns (population less than 50,000) and villages. The 1971 census figures will be applicable to these towns and villages.

2   Under the new policy, every district headquarter will have a District Industries Centre where under one single roof all the services and support required by small and village entrepreneurs will be provided.

3   No more licences will be issued to new industrial units within certain limits of large metropolitan cities having a population of more than one million.

4   No more licences will be issued to new industrial units in urban areas with a population of more than 500,000 as per the 1971 census.

5   State governments and financial institutions will deny support to new industries in these areas (those listed under (3) and (4)).

---

1   Statement on industrial policy laid before Parliament by the Minister of Industry on 23 December 1977.

The New Industrial Policy statement also asserts that "government has noted with concern that most of the industrial development that has taken place in our country since Independence has been concentrated around the metropolitan areas and large cities", leading to a rapid deterioration of living conditions, especially of the working classes, to the growth of slums, and to environmental pollution. The objectives of the new policy include acceleration of the pace of industrial growth, rapid increase in the levels of employment, productivity and income of industrial workers, and a wide dispersal of small and village industries in small towns and rural areas.

(f) Development of counter-magnets to big cities

Attempts have been made to develop ring towns as counter-magnets and divert the migration streams away from the big cities. We shall now make brief reference to the National Capital Region, the New Bombay Project and the Calcutta Metropolitan Development Authority.

The National Capital Region concept was formulated several years ago in order to develop a string of ring towns around Delhi like Faridabad, Ballabhgarh, Sonepat, Loni, Ghaziabad, etc. The revised Draft Sixth Plan (1978-83) gives an indication that this strategy did not work. For example, the plan observes: "Although a plan for preventing the growth of Delhi by the creation of a National Capital Region, involving the development of satellite towns remotely situated from the city, was approved, it has so far made negligible progress" (Government of India, Planning Commission, 1979, p. 458). One of the main hurdles was the administrative bottleneck. The National Capital Region comprised the Union Territory of Delhi and parts of western Uttar Pradesh, Haryana and Rajasthan. In spite of high level co-ordinating committees, the progress of this project was far from smooth because of the multiplicity of central and state government authorities concerned.

The New Bombay Project was taken up by the government of Maharashtra in 1970 and a draft plan was formulated in 1973 (CIDCO, 1973). Numerous studies have been conducted on various aspects of the development of the new city, but again there is very little evidence that the scheme has succeeded in making an impact on Bombay as far as migration to the city is concerned. We believe that the New Bombay Project would have succeeded if the Secretariat of the Maharashtra government had shifted to New Bombay. What is more distressing is that far from shifting the

Secretariat to the new township, recent decisions to locate the big offices of commercial establishments in the Nariman Point area, which was reclaimed from the sea for housing poor and middle-income groups, have worsened the situation in Bombay in regard to housing and transportation.

As far as Calcutta is concerned, a significant improvement was made when the Calcutta Metropolitan Development Authority (CMDA) was established in 1970. The Calcutta Metropolitan Planning Organisation (CMPO), established in 1961, had earlier formulated a Basic Development Plan for the Calcutta metropolitan region.

However, in this context, Mitra (former Secretary to the Planning Commission) observed:

> "Although the professed manifesto (of CMPO and CMDA) has been the development of the Calcutta Metropolitan Region as a whole ... yet in terms of concentration of technical appraisal, development of data, and last but not least, investment, the Calcutta Corporation area has enjoyed almost the monopoly of funds and project execution ... Calcutta's needs and political and economic weight have always loomed so much above those of the peripheral areas that funds automatically gravitated to Calcutta in spite of protests from time to time" (Mitra, 1976, pp. 13-14).

The gap between professed policies and the actual implementation of those policies is largely responsible for the worsening state of affairs in the big cities.

(g) New urbanisation policy

The "new" urbanisation policy set out in the Revised Draft Sixth Plan (1978-83) refers to a number of specific measures and also spells out the objectives and strategies of urban development.

The plan maintains that "the thrust of the urbanisation policy during the next decade must be to increase the rate of growth of the small and medium towns and to slow down and if possible, reverse the rate of growth of the metropolitan cities" (Government of India, Planning Commission, 1979, pp. 457-458). The highest priority under this policy has been given to restricting the growth of population in the larger urban conglomerations. It is hoped to achieve this by the following measures:

(i)   granting incentives to shift industries to new urban centres;

(ii)   imposing a ban on the setting up of new industries within certain limits of large cities under the New Industrial Policy statement;

(iii)   encouraging the growth of household and cottage industries under the Rural Industrialisation Programme in villages and towns with a population of less than 25,000;

(iv)   devoting special attention to the development of "tiny industries" in towns with a population of less than 50,000;

(v)   restrictions on the setting up of new offices, commercial establishments, and centres of entertainment and culture in big cities;

(vi)   similar restrictions in respect of colleges, hospitals and new telephone connections;

(vii)   efforts to move central and state government offices, banks, and other institutions to less congested areas;

(viii) fiscal measures aimed at depressing the demand on the infrastructural facilities in big cities.

Apart from these preventive measures to curb migration to big cities, positive measures are suggested to encourage the growth of small and medium towns. The Revised Draft Sixth Plan asserts that "the objectives of this policy are not merely to solve the problems of the urban environment. The small town is the hub of the rural development strategy and through it must flow all the inputs required to develop the village economy and implement the hard core of the rural conservation and environmental care programme" (ibid., p. 223).

This urbanisation policy is not really new. Almost every Five Year Plan has discussed urban development policies more or less in these terms, but over the years nothing concrete has emerged.

In this connection it is worth recalling that the Planning Commission set up a Panel of Economists in 1955 to advise on the formulation of the Second Five Year Plan. Several papers were prepared by these economists, some of which dealt with policy issues. In particular, Ganguli's paper visualised the importance of spatial aspects of planning. He proposed a policy to encourage "broad-based industrialisation ... which would involve necessary changes in the demographic structure and the economic organisation" (Ganguli, 1955, p. 521).

Ganguli wanted a nuclear township to be located in each Community Development Block. He argued that:

"These townships will become the medium through which industrial atmosphere will permeate the countryside. They will also be the channel through which energetic and enterprising workers shifting from agriculture would be initiated into the ways of modern technology without losing their moorings in the community life of the villages. It is in this way that there would be upgrading of labour and improvement in the quality of employment on a broad basis" (ibid., p. 539).

In spite of these proposals, very little was done to incorporate his ideas in the planning process. In 1962, J.P. Lewis pleaded for "town-centred" location of new economic activity, favouring towns with a population from 20,000 to 300,000. He did concede that metropolitan-centred industrialisation was natural, and "has been the pattern of other developing economies in the past; official pronouncements to the contrary, it has been the dominant pattern of Indian industrial location to date; and certainly it will be the predominant pattern for the sixties and beyond unless concerted efforts are made to check it" (Lewis, 1962, p. 174). He made a strong plea for state intervention to arrest metropolitan-dominated development.

In spite of the exhortations of Ganguli and Lewis, and the pious sentiments expressed about the need for the development of small and medium towns in successive plans, the dominance of big cities and towns increased. No evaluation of migration-influencing policies can arrive at the truth quicker than a glance at table 9 which shows the proportion of population of each size class of towns to the total urban population from 1941 to 1971. Cities with a population of over 100,000 claimed 37.9 per cent of the total urban population in 1941. This proportion had increased to 44.1 by 1951, 50.7 in 1961, and 55.8 in 1971.

In December 1979, a new centrally sponsored scheme for the integrated development of small and medium towns with a population of less than 100,000 was launched by the Ministry of Works and Housing. Under this scheme, it was proposed to select 200 towns for integrated development and give loans and assistance from the central

Table 9: Population by size class of cities and towns (in millions)
(Figures in brackets indicate percentage of total urban population)

Urban classes	1941	1951	1961	1971
Total urban population	44.15	62.44	78.94	109.11
Class I	17.73	27.56	40.02	60.91
(100,000 and above)	(37.9)	(44.1)	(50.7)	(55.8)
Class II	5.03	6.21	8.49	12.34
(50,000 to 99,999)	(11.1)	(9.9)	(10.7)	(11.3)
Class III	7.25	9.92	13.78	17.80
(20,000 to 49,999)	(16.4)	(15.9)	(17.4)	(16.3)
Class IV	7.02	8.85	10.28	12.35
(10,000 to 19,099)	(16.0)	(13.9)	(13.0)	(11.3)
Class V	6.65	8.12	5.64	5.14
(5,000 to 9,999)	(15.2)	(13.0)	(7.2)	(4.7)
Class VI	1.48	1.98	0.73	0.56
(less than 5,000)	(3.4)	(3.2)	(1.0)	(0.5)

Source: Government of India, Planning Commission (1979), p. 456.

government of the order of Rs. 4 million per town on the expectation that the states would make a contribution of a similiar amount, apart from institutional financing of such projects. Roughly, the amount to be spent per town should be of the order of Rs. 10 million.

(h) Land settlement programmes

Before Independence, the best example of migration and rural resettlement was in the canal colonies of the Punjab. This was a story of outstanding success on the part of people who took advantage of irrigation facilities and developed the entire region, bringing great prosperity both to themselves and to the state of Punjab. After Independence, there have been some cases of successful resettlement on a small scale in certain parts of India, for example in the Terai region of Uttar Pradesh, in the Rajasthan Canal Project area, etc. The most ambitious scheme of rural resettlement, however, has been in the Dandakaranya region.

The resettlement envisaged in the Dandakaranya Project was of a special type, namely the rehabilitation of displaced persons from East Pakistan who were mostly of rural origin and primarily engaged in agriculture and allied occupations. Another such example was the resettlement of displaced persons from East Pakistan in the Andaman and Nicobar Islands. But the scale of rehabilitation envisaged in the Dandakaranya Project was certainly much higher than in the Andaman and Nicobar Islands.

We shall briefly comment on the experience of the Dandakaranya Project and on the settlement schemes in the Andaman and Nicobar Islands. We shall then touch on the implications of the settlement of migrants in the Terai region of Uttar Pradesh.

(i) Dandakaranya Project

After the partition of India in 1947, one of the first major problems which the government had to tackle was the rehabilitation of displaced persons from Pakistan. The problems of displaced persons from West Pakistan and East Pakistan were qualitatively different. There was an exodus of Muslims from the rural areas of north India, so it was possible for a large number of displaced persons of rural origin from West Pakistan to settle in the rural areas of East Punjab and other states. In West Bengal, however, there was no such exodus of Muslims, and as the density of the rural population was already high the scope for resettling nearly 4 million displaced persons was extremely limited. In spite of the efforts made in Manipur, Tripura, and Assam, not more than 100,000 acres of land could be made available for the rehabilitation of refugees. The bulk of the refugee families in West Bengal thus remained in camps, awaiting dispersal to different areas. It was at this stage that the Government of India thought of the Dandakaranya Project for the resettlement of the refugees from the camps in West Bengal. The area in question was carved out from the states of Madhya Pradesh and Orissa, covering about 80,000 square kilometres and comprising the districts of Koraput and Kalahandi in Orissa and Bastar in Madhya Pradesh. A large part of this area was thickly forested.

The state governments were responsible only for the release of land. The execution of the project was entrusted to the Dandakaranya Development Authority (DDA), which was set up by the Government of India in 1958. The project was expected to "provide either rehabilitation or employment for at least 20,000 families in Dandakaranya by July 1959" (Government of India, Department of Rehabilitation, 1959, p. 34). The following norms were laid down for settling displaced persons:

Agriculturalists will be given 7 acres of partly wet and partly dry land. A house with a plot will be provided and the cost thereof will be treated as a loan repayable in ten annual instalments. The maintenance grant will be paid to each family up to a period of six months from the date the land is allotted. Loans for the purchase of implements, cattle, seeds, etc., will also be given.

Non-agriculturalists who settle in rural areas will be allotted a homestead plot for house and horticulture. Where a house or homestead plot is provided in a new village, their cost will be treated as a loan. Where no house is provided, a loan not exceeding Rs. 1,500 may be given. Small business loans ranging from Rs. 500 to Rs. 1,000 may be given.

An idea of the scale of resettlement visualised initially when the Dandakaranya Project was launched can be gained from the following observation contained in the 96th Report of the Estimates Committee of the Second Lok Sabha (April 1960):

"When the Dandakaranya Project was conceived, it seems to have been given out that it could take in two million displaced persons. It is quite likely as the campers settle down in Dandakaranya and there is greater intercourse between the Bengalis there and those in West Bengal, Assam, etc., more of the displaced persons would think of settling in Dandakaranya. It would be desirable to plan for such a contingency from now" (Government of India, Estimates Committee, 1962, pp. 34-35).

Poor performance of DDA

It is tragic to note that what was sought to be done in less than one year - that is, the rehabilitation of 20,000 families - was not accomplished in the next 20 years. According to a personal communication from the Department of Rehabilitation dated 21 November 1979, "As on 31 August 1979, 19,643 families of displaced persons from former East Pakistan settled in Dandakaranya Project were in position" (Government of India, Department of

Rehabilitation, 1979). While considering these figures, one has also to take into account the number of families which deserted the Dandakaranya area every year. The data in table 10 show that in 1972, for example, while 3,235 families were settled, 3,428 families deserted. In 1978-79, 844 families were settled while 2,504 families deserted (Estimates Committee, 1979, p. 4).

The latest report of the Estimates Committee of Parliament in April 1979 has expressed the following view on the project:

> "The Committee feel that the DDA, as it is constituted at present, has not been able to fulfil the object for which it was set up ... and there is a strong case for an independent study of the reasons responsible for its failure in the task of rehabilitation of displaced persons" (ibid., p. 84).

In the concluding chapter, the Committee sums up in statistical terms the poor performance of the DDA, and concludes: "This in brief is the painful story of the displaced persons and their rehabilitation in the Dandakaranya region" (ibid., p. 88).

The failures listed by the Committee are briefly as follows:

1 During the period 1958-59 to 1960-61, there was a shortfall of 61 per cent in achieving the land reclamation target. The shortfall has continued ever since without the DDA doing anything about it.

2 No master plan for the region has yet been prepared in spite of repeated recommendations to prepare such a plan, by successive Estimates Committees.

3 The irrigation potential of the Bhaskal Dam, completed in 1966-67, was not utilised because of deficiencies in the distribution system.

4 The completion of the Paralkote Dam has been delayed by more than two years, and the completion of the Satiguda Dam by over 15 years; the Potteru Irrigation Project is already behind schedule by three years.

5 The irrigation facilites are utterly inadequate: only 6 to 8 per cent of the cultivated land is irrigated.

Table 10: Year-wise settlement of displaced persons in Dandakaranya Project, 1960 to 1978-79

Year	No. of families settled	No. of families deserted or transferred to permanent liability homes	Net number of families settled	Cumulative total number of families settled
1960	1,265	–	1,265	1,265
1961	1,587	6	1,581	2,846
1962	2,136	13	2,123	4,969
1963	1,700	18	1,682	6,651
1964	693	11	682	7,333
1965	2,737	1,181	1,556	8,889
1966	2,360	1,859	501	9,390
1967	2,040	669	1,371	10,761
1968	1,863	10	1,853	12,614
1969	1,023	177	846	13,460
1970	1,012	486	526	13,986
1971	2,318	96	2,222	16,208
1972	3,235	3,428	-193	16,015
1973	1,443	242	1,201	17,216
1974	831	130	701	17,917
1975	961	243	718	18,635
1976	1,433	82	1,351	19,986
1977	1,526	209	1,317	21,303
1978-79	844	2,504*	-1,660	19,643

* This figure represents the net deserters after taking into account the deserters of the period 1 January 1978 to 5 July 1978 (when large scale desertions took place) who returned to their rehabilitation sites.

Source: Government of India, Department of Rehabilitation (1979).

6   As no serious attention was paid to the essential input and infrastructure for the development of small-scale industries, attempts to develop these industries have ended in failure.

7   Only 8 villages out of the 381 villages have been electrified.

8   The allotment of land per family has been reduced to 3 acres from the original 7.

9   Even though the allotment of land had been completed in many areas as far back as 1963, patta (land ownership) rights have not been conferred so far.   This has led to unrest, and was one of the major factors behind the mass exodus of displaced persons in 1978.

10 Most of the displaced persons belong to castes which are recognised as scheduled castes in West Bengal but not in Madhya Pradesh and Orissa.   This created a very unfavourable situation for the settlers in the Dandakaranya region.

11 The supply of drinking water is far from adequate.

12 As against a target of 2,641 houses to be completed in 1977-78, only 1,658 houses were constructed.

13 Out of 296 primary schools, as many as 169 are housed in temporary structures.

14 There is a shortage of medicines in the hospitals and dispensaries, and several vacancies for technical staff which have not been filled.

The Committee also observes that "it is a matter of deep regret that in spite of the fact that the Dandakaranya Development Authority has been in position for over 20 years and has spent nearly Rs. 100 crores [1,000 million] on the project, of which over Rs. 23 crores [230 million] has been spent on administration alone, the progress of the rehabilitation programme has been utterly unsatisfactory" (Estimates Committee, 1979, p. 88).
Finally, the Committee deprecates strongly "the callous neglect and unimaginative, lackadaisical and bureaucratic approach displayed by the Dandakaranya Development Authority in handling the problems of displaced persons and in executing the development projects taken up for their resettlement" (ibid., p. 88).

The exodus from Dandakaranya

The exodus of settler families from Dandakaranya has been a regular feature, culminating in the main exodus in 1978. The figure for desertions (2,504) in the last row of table 10 refers to 1978 and the first seven months of 1979, but it is worth recalling that in the first six months of 1978 alone, 10,329 families deserted the Dandakaranya area.

The Estimates Committee (1978-79) of the Sixth Lok Sabha reports a number of causes for these desertions: propaganda spread by some interested elements to the effect that there was scope for resettling displaced persons from former East Pakistan in Sunderban and other areas in West Bengal, and the intensification of such propaganda since November 1977; the misleading propaganda of Udbastu Unnayansila Samiti, which also helped raise illusory hopes of getting land in West Bengal; intimidation by local tribes at the instigation of local leaders; the apathetic attitudes of government officials; the character of the land itself, inhospitable and rocky, and incapable of producing adequate crops; delay in the implementation of two irrigation projects, Potteru and Satiguda, etc. (ibid., pp. 4-19).

According to one state government, the "main single reason for mass desertion of settlers" was the political propaganda by interested persons. But a non-official witness who gave evidence before the Estimates Committee asserted that "if economic rehabilitation was there, no amount of campaigning could have persuaded them to leave". A former chairman of the DDA said in his evidence, "The primary cause of any exodus is economic." According to him the following factors were responsible for the precarious conditions of the settlers:

1 inadequate land distribution;

2 arid, rocky and unproductive land;

3 inadequate irrigation facilities;

4 the continual failure of crops and inadequate return of agricultural produce; and

5 non-development of small-scale industries in the area.

The Estimates Committee examined all these propositions in detail and came to the following conclusions:

"Even though propaganda of an assured habitat with better living conditions in Sunderban might have been one of the major factors in inducing desertions, the Committee would like the Ministry (of Rehabilitation) not to project it as the main reason for the exodus.

The Committee agree with the view expressed by non-official experts that 'the primary cause of any exodus is economic' and that 'if economic rehabilitation was there, no amount of campaigning could have persuaded them to leave the rehabilitation sites'" (ibid., p. 15).

The Sinha Committee squarely blamed the DDA for its incompetence:

"The Committee are unhappy to note that though the move to create unrest among displaced persons had started in 1973, it remained undetected for over four years, and during this period, while the move gained momentum, the DDA did not take any effective and specific measures either to counter the move at a political level or to accelerate the pace of rehabilitation and relief to settlers suffering from drought conditions and other disabilities. In the Committee's view the steps taken by the DDA and others were belated and therefore could not have checked desertions on such a mass scale. They were in the nature of curative steps after the malady had taken a virulent form. If preventive steps had been taken well in time, mass desertions of displaced persons could have been averted.

The Committee are of the opinion that DDA as an organisation and the officers holding key positions cannot escape responsibility for their failure to detect the calculated move to create unrest among displaced persons at an early stage and to take timely measures to counter the move" (ibid., p. 14).

One of the main reasons for the instability and the periodic exoduses of the displaced persons is the denial of patta rights to settlers by the state governments. Another important reason is the failure of the DDA to develop agriculture on sound lines. The DDA suffered from an initial handicap inasmuch as the lands donated by the governments of Orissa and Madhya Pradesh were certainly not even tolerably good agricultural land for growing crops like paddy, to which the East Bengal agriculturalists were accustomed. Mostly it was forest land. The land had first to be reclaimed. This reclamation work was entrusted to a new organisation, the Rehabilitation Reclamation Organisation (RRO), directly under the Department of Rehabilitation. There is evidence to show that the RRO was not always guided by scientifically conducted surveys about the precise areas of land reclamation.

Yet another problem concerned the giving of doles. Normally, the dole was given only for six months. But as land reclamation was not carried out according to schedule, the displaced persons could not be transferred from the camp and as a result the doles had to be continued. Further, even when land was allotted to the displaced persons, it was not realised that six months is not an adequate time to make a success of agriculture, especially in areas where the land is not of good quality and irrigation facilities are poor. After six months, the amount of dole was reduced, and the displaced persons were left to the vagaries of nature. If the crops failed, there was no alternative for them except to leave the Dandakaranya area.

There is also evidence that the quantity of land allotted to the displaced persons was reduced. The evidence before the Estimates Committee shows that the allotment of agricultural land was reduced from 7 to 3 acres per family on the ground that the yield would be sufficient once irrigation was available. But no thought was given to whether the yield would be adequate before the land was irrigated.

The available evidence suggests that due to lack of employment opportunities, there is a large number of young men and women who have grown up in the Dandakaranya area and are today utterly frustrated. Some of the young men have turned to crime and there are reports of young women taking to prostitution, especially in the nearby Bhilai industrial region. The human suffering generated by the failure of the Dandakaranya Project has yet to be assessed. The DDA has also not done enough to take care of the women in the "Permanent Liability Family Camps" (PLF camps), comprising widows and unattached women with or without children and other dependents.

Whom has the DDA benefited most?

The objectives of the Dandakaranya Project were to rehabilitate the refugee families and to provide gainful employment for them. A study of the working of the DDA shows that the DDA did not give priority to displaced persons in regard to employment, even in the lower category of staff comprising clerks, peons, etc., nor is there evidence of any crash training programme to equip the displaced persons with the necessary skills.

The Estimates Committee of 1964-65 noted that only 31.6 per cent of the total staff of the DDA in the project area belonged to the category of displaced persons. The situation was worse in the case of private contractors, who were big employers of labour. To quote the report of the Estimates Committee:

> "It has come to the notice of the Committee that displaced persons and tribals are not employed in sufficient numbers by private contractors engaged by DDA in road building, irrigation works and other engineering activities in the project area. Even those that are employed are not adequately remunerated.
>
> The Committee feel that since employment in public service should make its due contribution as a means of rehabilitation of displaced persons, the DDA should have provided top priority to the displaced persons and the local tribals for employment under their own organisation" (Estimates Committee, 1965, p. 17)

The Committee also expressed the hope that the DDA "will persuade the contractors engaged by them to employ as large a number of displaced persons and tribals as possible" (ibid., p. 18).

No elaborate research is necessary to observe that the persons who benefited most from the Dandakaranya Project were the contractors and their allies.

Failure to evolve a development plan for the region

Lokanathan, the then Director-General of the National Council of Applied Economic Research, in his preface to the report on the development of Dandakaranya (mineral-based and small-scale industry), prepared by the NCAER at the request of the Dandakaranya Development Authority in 1963, says: "Dandakaranya ... was chosen by the Government of India as the most suitable area for the speedy resettlement of displaced persons from East Pakistan. In fact, no other area in India could offer the same scope for large scale reclamation and colonisation" (National Council of Applied Economic Research, 1963, p. v).

Yet the same NCAER study comes to the following conclusions:

"In this context, it will be useful to consider why the Dandakaranya region has remained underdeveloped and underpopulated. Till late the area was notorious for incidence of malaria. Since the local people were not introduced to the ideas of gainful employment, the labour in every case had to be brought from outside. In addition, the place lacks basic facilities like cheap and adequate power, water and easy means of communication. This aspect of the problem invited the special attention of the Industrial Team from the West Bengal Government that reported on the possibilities of introduction of subsidiary industries for displaced persons in Dandakaranya. The Team observed that no plan or programme could effectively function unless and until the people who would work there were having normal living conditions. It should be conceded that even rural and cottage industries would require, for their successful operation, a stable social stratum of human beings" (ibid., pp. 102-103).

While we do not deny that the Dandakaranya region had all the potential for successfully rehabilitating a large number of persons in rural areas, there is no evidence that the Planning Commission or the DDA had a concrete plan for development of the region apart from some feasibility studies, technical reports of the study team, etc. The area in question is indeed vast, greater than the total area of some Indian states. As the Estimates Committee noted, even after 19 years such a development plan for the region does not exist. To our mind, the main reason for the failure of the Dandakaranya Project was the casualness with which the project was launched by the Indian Government and the inherent limitations of the conventional governmental machinery's ability to handle the challenging problems of such a bold experiment. Because of the adverse living conditions in the region, it is understandable that the best government officers would not have been transferred there, or gone

there on their own volition.   Large funds were involved
for the purchase of machinery, building of roads, etc.
Numerous private contractors were involved.   In such a
situation, the level of corruption is likely to be high.
The organisation of the DDA itself is one of the contribu-
tory causes of the failure of the Dandakaranya Project.
The NCAER report clearly suggested in 1961 that the
DDA should operate like a corporation, importing ideas of
profit and loss into its working.   It said: "For a
concerted attack on the backwardness of the area, it
would be desirable to have a single agency, upon whom
the investors might look for help.   The two State
Governments should transfer specific sums to the
suggested   corporation   for   the   development   of
Dandakaranya" (ibid., p. 102).
     After 16 years, a similar suggestion was again made
by the Estimates Committee, in April 1979.   To quote the
report:

> "The Committee are conscious of the consti-
> tutional difficulties in converting the DDA into
> an Area Development Authority with full powers
> to take decisions in all but policy matters.
> This step would require the concurrence of the
> State Governments concerned and will also
> involve Central legislation.   They would,
> however, like the Government to examine the
> need for investing DDA with more powers,
> statutory or executive, so as to ensure that it
> is not handicapped in the task of arranging
> rehabilitation of displaced persons and develop-
> ment of the Dandakaranya region as a whole"
> (Estimates Committee, 1979, p. 84).

Integration with the tribal population

     One important factor contributing to the failure of
the Dandakaranya Project was the lack of adequate communication with the indigenous tribal population regarding
the resettlement scheme.   This led to misgivings on the
part of the tribal communities and tension between them
and the migrants.
     Mr Pannalal Dasgupta, a veteran social worker in
West Bengal, wrote a brilliant article in a Bengali journal
in February 1979 (Dasgupta, 1979, pp. 13-16) after
touring the Dandakaranya region.   We will briefly sum-
marise his arguments below.
     According to Dasgupta, the main reason for the
failure of the Dandakaranya Project is the dual control in
the   project   area: the   Dandakaranya   Development

- 173 -

Authority takes care of the refugees, and the state governments look after the tribal people. This has created enormous problems during the last 20 years, yet the dual control has carried on. Take, for example, epidemics, which break out in any area. Epidemics surely will not be selective. Both tribals and refugees will be affected. But such is the administrative procedure that the state officials will take care only of the tribal population and will not even visit the refugee settlements, while the DDA officials will take care only of the refugee settlements and will not even visit the tribal area. There is as such no communication at the administrative level; as a result, integrated development of the tribal population and the refugee population is not possible. Further, the refugee settlements are scattered over long distances, and the physical distance brings about social distance even between Bengalis. Because of the distance and loneliness no social cohesion developed; the Bengalis failed to perceive the Dandakaranya region as their new home, and the nostalgia for "Sonar Bangala" (golden Bengal) persisted.

To make matters worse, time and again there is talk of winding up the DDA, winding up the Department of Rehabilitation, etc. This compounds the sense of insecurity further.

Dasgupta refers to the unimaginative approach of the bureaucracy towards the tribal population in the Dandakaranya region. It was never explained to the tribal communities that the DDA was there to help them, to develop their area, and to promote economic growth. The distrust and suspicion on the part of the tribal people that some outsiders had come to take away their land was therefore not dispelled at the initial stage. Nor is there any evidence that joint meetings of tribal people and displaced persons were held to explain the nature of the development envisaged by the Dandakaranya Project.

(ii) Settlement in the Andaman and
      Nicobar Islands

In 1908, under British rule, a penal settlement was established in the Andaman Islands, but it was closed in 1923. In 1947, when India gained independence, the government launched a development programme. In 1956 the islands were constituted into a union territory administered by the central government. In order to develop the resources of the islands, it was necessary to encourage people to migrate there. A large number of displaced persons from East Pakistan, mostly rural people, were readily available for settlement, and the idea of colonising the island caught on. Sporadic attempts were made between 1947 and 1952 to rehabilitate East Pakistan refugees. In 1952, as part of the Five-Year Plan, the clearance of 20,000 acres of land for settling 4,000 agricultural families was undertaken, but by the end of the First Plan period (1956), only 8,100 acres of land had been cleared and 1,006 families settled. The Second Five-Year Plan (1956-61) envisaged the clearance of 11,900 acres of forest land and the settlement of 2,994 families. But by the end of the Plan, only 2,010 acres of land had been cleared and 1,506 agricultural families and 64 artisan families settled. The whole settlement programme was then reviewed, and no more families were brought into the Andaman Islands until 1964 when the Prime Minister suggested the integrated development of the islands and the rehabilitation of displaced persons from East Pakistan. Accordingly, the Department of Rehabilitation took up schemes for the resettlement of migrants, and also repatriates from Burma and Sri Lanka.

The resettlement schemes undertaken in Little Andaman were basically agriculture-oriented. According to the latest report, of the 385 families brought there, 359 were agricultural families, while 26 were engaged in small trade. In the Great Nicobar Islands, 287 ex-servicemen's families were settled in six villages. In Katchal Island, a scheme for developing a rubber plantation was started in 1968. So far 47 Sri Lankan repatriate families have been settled there (see table 11). The report of the Department of Rehabilitation concedes that "the progress of resettlement in the Andaman and Nicobar Islands has been slow mainly due to the fact that creation of necessary infrastructure in these remote islands, which is pre-requisite to any large scale resettlement programme, is a time-consuming process. Besides this, certain other important factors such as co-ordination of the reclamation programme with extraction and utilization of commercial timber and the ecological aspects of large scale deforestation programmes have to be taken into account" (Government of India, Department of Rehabilitation, 1978, p. 34).

In this connection, it may be noted that in pursuance of a ban imposed by the Prime Minister in 1974, forestry operations in the Andaman and Nicobar Islands intended to clear land for fresh settlers were halted, pending a study of the ecological aspects. An expert study team was set up by the government. After examining the recommendations of the study team, the Department of Agriculture lifted the moratorium on forest felling and released an area of 166 hectares in Little Andaman and 21 hectares in Great Nicobar in 1976.

Table 11: Settlement in the Andaman and Nicobar Islands

Name of island	Area reclaimed (acres)	No. of families settled	Remarks
Middle Andaman (Betapur)	2,050	339	Migrants from former East Pakistan
Neil	1,090	100	Migrants from former East Pakistan
Little Andaman	2,444	385	366 migrants from former East Pakistan and 19 Sri Lankan repatriates
Greater Nicobar	2,990	287	Ex-servicemen
Katchal rubber plantation	1,477	47	Sri Lanka repatriates
Rubber research-cum-development station, South Andaman	500	37	Burmese repatriates
Total	10,551	1,195	

Source: Government of India, Department of Rehabilitation (1978), p. 31.

In 1976, a Committee of Secretaries of the Government of India, headed by the Cabinet Secretary, visited the islands and recommended that another 2,000 families of ex-servicemen should be settled in Great Nicobar, ensuring at the same time that the interests of the local tribes, who were very few in number, did not suffer in any way. The Committee, however, did not favour the clearing of more land in Little Andaman, as the prospects for resettlement based on agriculture were found to be very remote there. In view of this, it was decided that no more migrants and repatriates were to be brought to Little Andaman.

On account of the similarity in geographical conditions between Bangladesh and the Andaman and Nicobar Islands, and the familiarity of the Bengali cultivators with paddy cultivation, the Andaman and Nicobar settlement project has largely succeeded.

It is unfortunate, however, that the emphasis in the resettlement scheme has been on agriculture, particularly on rice cultivation, for the islands are rich in forest resources and have about 500 types of indigenous plants, of which 300 are commercially useful. As the layer of soil is very thin in many of the islands, and much of it is below sea level, the land may not remain good for cultivation after a few harvests. In any case, it is quite likely that plantation crops may be more rewarding than rice cultivation. Some research is already under way regarding this. Similarly, the scope for expanding fisheries is enormous.

As far as the experiment of resettling ex-servicemen in the Great Nicobar group of islands is concerned, it is reported that many of the people who are settled there in response to advertisements in the newspapers were in the clerical ranks of the army and not in the fighting forces, and went there after retirement with very little energy and enterprise for settlement in such a difficult area.

On the basis of our discussions with the officials concerned, it seems that the project to develop a rubber plantation in Katchal Island referred to earlier has been halted because of objections from environmentalists. The policy of encouraging paddy cultivation as opposed to plantation crops, the possible dangers to the environment through deforestation, etc., are now being examined afresh.

On the social side, one should take note of the mounting tensions arising from the great variety of cultures and languages represented in these islands (see table 12). As against the 19,000 tribal people in Nicobar Island, the number of immigrants from the mainland is more than 120,000. Bengalis are predominant but there are also people from Kerala, Tamil Nadu, Andhra Pradesh,

Bihar, Uttar Pradesh, and other places. There is also a sizeable population of descendants of convicts who were sent to these islands during the period of British rule. It is reported that until 1960 there was some cultural fusion, and the language spoken was some kind of Hindustani, freely accepted both by the post-Independence immigrants and by the convict-settlers and their descendants. But after the taking over of a private school by the government in 1960, there has been a growing demand for the introduction of all the six major languages as media of instruction in other schools. The vigorous assertion of the linguistic identity of different groups may create conflict.

Table 12: Distribution of population by mother tongue in the Andaman and Nicobar Islands, 1971

Language	Population	%
Bengali	28,120	24.42
Hindi	18,499	16.07
Nicobarese	17,955	15.60
Tamil	14,518	12.61
Malayalam	13,953	12.12
Telegu	9,361	8.13
Urdu	2,488	2.16
Punjabi	1,023	0.89
Others	9,216	8.00

Source: Computed from Census of India, 1971, Series 23, Part II-C.

(iii) Settlement in the Terai region of Uttar Pradesh

In the context of the resettlement of population in new rural settlements, special mention must be made of the development of the Terai region in Uttar Pradesh in the foothills of the Himalayas. Nainital district offers a good example of such resettlement. After Independence, the government of Uttar Pradesh visualised the development of this malaria-infested region through the settling of different types of migrants, especially Punjabi farmers, who are known for their hard work and dynamism.

Today the entire Terai region of Nainital right up to the border of western Nepal is fully developed. In fact this region is today one of the most prosperous agricultural regions of the whole country. The mosquitoes, wild animals and bandits have disappeared and there are thousands of acres of land with excellent paddy, wheat, and sugar cane cultivation.

During our fieldwork in this region, we could identify at least 10 categories of migrants:

1 tribal settlers, mostly Tharus and Bukshas;

2 the hill people of Uttar Pradesh;

3 Punjabi refugee settlers;

4 subsequent Punjabi settlers, as a consequence of chain migration, who were not necessarily refugees;

5 Bengali refugee settlers who had come from East Pakistan after 1947;

6 Bengali refugee settlers who had come from Bangladesh after 1971;

7 repatriates from Burma;

8 ex-servicemen;

9 political sufferers and freedom fighters who were given land by the government; and

10 absentee landlords who managed to purchase land in the newly developing region and made a fortune from the land.

In spite of the diverse groups settled there, there is no doubt about the dominance of the Punjabi, especially Sikh farmers, in the Terai region. Further, the whole development of that region provided an example of capitalist farming, with the local hill people continuing to be poor and exploited. A group of intellectuals from the hill region of Uttar Pradesh summarised the situation as follows: "The almost total exclusion of the people of this area from the fruits of Terai development has meant the loss of the most important economic outlet for the common people within the region, and this has heightened the sense of helplessness. Not regional development and prosperity but depopulation, drain and exploitation - this is the grim prospect ..." (Joshi, 1980, p. 15).

In a recent seminar on the development of the backward hill areas of Uttar Pradesh held in Nainital, Joshi posed the central issues as follows:

"Are the people of the region poor and backward because they are dominated by 'outsiders' and because the region has been turned into a colony of developed parts of the country? Or, are they backward and poor because they lagged behind others in breaking away from growth-retarding values and social institutions and in undertaking much needed reforms of their social structure? Or, are they poor and backward because their natural environment required efforts and investments which were beyond their resources and abilities?" (ibid., p. 9).

Summary and Conclusions

The perception of internal migration in India has been mostly in terms of rural-to-urban migration, and the consequences of migration have been perceived more from the urban end. This analysis shows that rural-to-rural migration deserves much more attention. Further, it is not enough to be concerned with the volume and direction of migration streams. What is far more significant is to understand the political, social, and economic impact of migration. Perceived thus, the analysis of migration should transcend the conventional demographic analysis in terms of the "push and pull" factors, regarding migration as a process and not merely as a movement of people.

The recent tensions and conflicts in various parts of India arising out of migration essentially stem from the structural stagnation of the Indian economy and the inequitable distribution of the benefits of economic development between regions and between people. Language, caste, and religion are often posed as the issues behind these conflicts, but in reality these are but manifestations of the deeper malady of economic stagnation.

The "new" urbanisation policy favouring small and medium-sized towns is not really new. Almost every Five-Year Plan has discussed urban development policies more or less in these terms, but over the years nothing concrete has emerged. The persistent decline in the importance of small towns is an indication of the deterioration of economic conditions in these towns and the consequent movement of population towards the big cities in search of better economic opportunities. The preceding analysis shows that the gap between professed policies and the actual implementation of those policies is largely responsible for the worsening state of affairs in the big cities. The Urban Land and Ceiling Act (1976), for example, would be likely to affect migration to urban areas, but its effective implementation has not occurred due to a lack of political commitment and changes in government.

It is too early to judge the success or failure of the new industrial policy designed to promote small-scale and cottage industries away from the larger cities. Much will depend on the ability of the government to outwit the industrialists and entrepreneurs, who invariably take advantage of the loopholes in any such policy at the implementation level. If the policy succeeds, it will certainly reduce the distortions of urban development and the dominance of large cities.

Rural industrialisation programmes designed to increase non-agricultural activity in the rural areas have certainly helped to raise the incomes of the people in these rural areas, but there is very little evidence that the employment structure has been affected significantly. Moreover, most of these programmes, by improving the skills of the rural artisans, make them more acceptable in the urban labour market. As such the training content of the rural industrialisation programmes is likely to increase rural-to-urban migration.

The crucial factor about rural industrialisation is the location of industries. If industries are located in small villages, they will face the disadvantage of limited markets and may not survive for long. There should therefore be attempts to set up industries in small towns and rural areas with a sufficiently large population to ensure an adequate market for their products.

The analysis of the working of the Dandakaranya resettlement project, based mainly on official documents, leads to the inescapable conclusion that the project has failed to achieve the objectives for which it was set up. On the other hand, settlement schemes in the Andaman and Nicobar Islands, and in the Terai region of Uttar Pradesh, have attained some success. Nevertheless, several problems have arisen which need attention from the government. Unless the problems of integration are understood and tackled, growing tensions and conflicts between migrants and local people cannot be ruled out in the settlement areas.

The review of settlement schemes, in general, suggests that resettlement should not simply be a matter of logistics - moving people physically from one region to another - but rather should embrace more concerted and imaginative planning in the areas of destination,

emphasising the human element in the resettlement programmes. Unless this is done, there will be an
increased movement back to the areas of origin.

Over-all, the analysis in this study suggests that in
the implementation of urban policies the failures have
been far greater than the successes. In spite of the
efforts made in all the Five-Year Plans to formulate
policies and programmes to curb migration to the big
cities, there is no evidence that such migration has in
fact been contained. The role of cities with a population
of over a million continues to be increasingly dominant.
There is thus a need to consider the process of urbanisation not merely as a concomitant of industrialisation but
in the wider context of agricultural development and rural
transformation, which alone will provide an effective
deterrent to unending rural-to-urban migration and the
virtual breakdown of the urban infrastructure. There is
also a need for an imaginative and innovative approach to
the problem of unemployment in both rural and urban
areas, based on generating mobility of labour in a planned
manner so as to ensure the maximum utilisation of human
resources not in local areas alone but in the country as a
whole.

Chapter 6

TRANSMIGRATION AND ACCUMULATION IN INDONESIA

By J.P. Pérez-Sainz*

Introduction

Transmigration is a term used to denote labour migration from Java, Madura, Bali and, to a lesser extent, Lombok, to the rest of the Indonesian archipelago, the so-called Outer Islands.[1] The present study deals specifically with this migration, which has basically been and remains a government-sponsored phenomenon, made possible by state intervention in the recruitment and transfer of migrants, and in the establishment and development of settlements.[2]

Past studies of transmigration have been mainly descriptive. Although some attempts have been made to analyse the various problems affecting transmigration, the explanations given remain superficial. This is due mainly to the fact that these studies have considered transmigration as an isolated phenomenon and have not sought to relate it to the social development of Indonesia. The present study attempts to fill this gap. The analysis of transmigration in each period is preceded by a detailed examination of the historical context in which it took place.

---

* At the time this study was being prepared, the author was attached to the Institute of Social Studies, the Hague. An earlier version of this study was monitored and edited by Guy Standing. His contributions are gratefully acknowledged.

1 For the sake of simplicity we shall only refer to Java.

2 Official transmigration has induced a spontaneous migratory flow, however. The present study takes the latter into consideration in so far as it is related to and affects the former, but it does not enter into an analysis of the specific nature of voluntary migration from Java to the Outer Islands.

The Origins of Overpopulation in Java

In 1975, Indonesia as a whole had a low population density (69 inhabitants per square kilometre) but Java had one of the highest densities in the world (632). The causes for this unequal distribution of population among the islands are to be found in the uneven historical development of the Indonesian archipelago. Given the pre-capitalist nature of the relations of production which predominated throughout the territory until the end of the 19th century, the nature of the land has played an important role in differentiating regions. Thus, Geertz distinguished between "Inner Indonesia", comprising Java, except its south-western corner (i.e. south Bantam and south Priangan), Madura, southern Bali and eastern Lombok, and "Outer Indonesia", comprising the rest of the archipelago (Geertz, 1963, pp. 11 ff). The former region is basically characterised by a fertile soil which has allowed the development of an intensive form of cultivation called sawah. "Outer Indonesia", which lacks this fertile soil, has on the whole developed an extensive and shifting form of cultivation, known as ladang.[1] This distinction has constituted a material basis for the unequal growth and distribution of population in the Indonesian archipelago (ibid., pp. 36-37).

However, the equilibrium between land and other factors of production was not seriously affected until the 19th century. In the Indian Ocean area the impact of European mercantilism - aiming at the constitution of an international market as the basis of an accumulation on a world scale - was not so devastating as in other areas like Latin America, the Caribbean, or western and eastern Africa.[2] Even commercial capital from the Netherlands,

---

[1] Two other forms of cultivation of minor importance should be mentioned to give a complete picture of Indonesian agriculture. First, there is the growing of perennial tree crops in fixed gardens, though this type of cultivation did not exist separately from the ladang or sawah before 1800, after which it developed independently on specialised estates or smallholdings. Second, there is the permanent cultivation of food crops in dry fields known as tegalan. Where tegalan is combined with ladang it is difficult to distinguish one from the other (see Missen, 1972, pp. 79 ff).

[2] In this sense Wallerstein has differentiated between the "periphery" and the "external arena". The Indian Ocean area is included in the latter (Wallerstein, 1974, pp. 325 ff).

which emerged as the most important mercantilist power in the Indonesian archipelago, displacing other European competitors, remained mainly in the exchange sphere and did not affect production. It is true that the monopoly of spices, which was initially the main reason for the Dutch interest, had a direct impact on production processes in some islands, such as Halmahera, Ambon, and Banda. Nevertheless, van Leur has argued that in the 17th century most commodities from Asian trade obtained by the VOC (United East Indies Company) came from free exchange (van Leur, 1955, p. 189). The impact on production increased with the territorial expansion of the VOC, the purpose of which was the protection of its interests.[1] What concerns us here is that given the fact that previous pre-capitalist relations of production were not seriously affected, the factors checking population growth were natural disasters (epidemics, climatological disasters, etc.), internal wars among the principalities and the extra-economic coercion required by the local dominant classes or the VOC itself to carry out exploitation. The population of Java thus remained, over a long period, more or less stationary, until the 19th century (see Pelzer, 1945, p. 160).

This situation changed with the decline of Dutch commercial capital and the crisis of the VOC.[2] The

---

[1] Towards the end of the 17th century the western part of Java was occupied and a system of forced deliveries of coffee (a crop introduced by the VOC itself) was set up in the Praenger district. The eastern strip and the northern coast of Java were occupied a century later. This territorial expansion meant an increasing vassalage of the Javanese dominant classes to the VOC. Nevertheless, these territorial gains did not lead to the constitution and consolidation of a colony. As Caldwell says: "...it is really misleading to speak of Indonesia as a Dutch colony until the last quarter of the 19th century" (Caldwell, 1968, p. 41).

[2] Dietz has summarised the crisis of the VOC as follows:

"Until 1780 the VOC was a profitable enterprise, although the administration costs in Indonesia were increasing. Nevertheless the company had some chronic problems: one problem was the power of the VOC shareholders to get and use a considerable part of the profit, resulting in insufficient capital accumulation. Another problem was the lack of cash at most times,

new situation led to the first attempts to establish conditions for the appearance of capitalist relations of production, aimed at a more effective exploitation of the Indonesian archipelago, especially Java. Thus, at the beginning of the 19th century Governor Daendels, reacting to the previous overwhelming presence of the VOC, helped to introduce "private enterprise" by selling large areas of land to Europeans in western Java. The same course was taken by Governor Raffles after 1811, when the Dutch possessions were occupied by the British as an outcome of the Napoleonic Wars. The four main measures taken by him were:

1 continuation of the selling of land on an increased scale, resulting in the creation of private farms;

2 abolition of forced deliveries of crops and their substitution by a cash tax representing two-fifths of the gross output (Furnivall, 1944, p. 72);

3 opening of the internal market to British cotton goods; and

4 further weakening of the local dominant classes.[1]

The first two decades of the 19th century thus saw a twofold weakening of the pre-capitalist relations of production: at the economic level, through an increasing commercialisation, monetisation, and penetration of imports; and at the non-economic level, through an increasing loss of power by the local dominant classes.

When the Netherlands recovered its possessions, the exploitation of the Indonesian archipelago became closely

---

with the exception, of course, of the arrival of a rich cargo in the Amsterdam harbour. At the eve of the fourth Dutch war with England in 1780 the cash position was very bad. The combined loss of property in (British) India, the loss of ships and cargo and the blockade of the Dutch harbours then caused the sudden bankruptcy of the VOC. In 1798 the company was dissolved with a consolidated debt of f 120 million" (Dietz, 1979).

[1] This last measure was finally consolidated in the Regeringsreglement (government regulation) of 1818 by which the regent (top local man) became subordinated to the resident (representative of the Dutch administration).

geared to the needs of the metropolis. These needs were basically two: the creation of general conditions for expanded and accelerated capitalist production, and coverage of the budget deficit resulting from the huge debt from the Belgian War of Secession. The transfer of extracted surplus from the Dutch Indies helped to form the Batig Slot (credit balance).[1] The extraction of the surplus was based on the so-called "culture system", introduced by Governor van den Bosch in 1830,[2] which extended the system of forced deliveries of coffee, introduced years before in Praenger, to the rest of Java and to other crops. The Javanese peasantry were compelled by force either to grow commercial crops on their own lands (as was the case for sugar, indigo or tobacco, in rotation with rice) or to work part of the time on waste lands for the cultivation of state crops (coffee, tea, pepper, and, to a lesser extent, cinchona and cinnamon).[3]

No doubt the "culture system" was initially a success, as was shown by the increase in the volume and value of exports during the 1830s. But the decline of exports in the following decade indicated that this method of extracting surplus, based on pre-capitalist relations of production, could not be maintained for long. This led to the progressive disappearance of the "culture system"

---

[1] Furnival (1944, p. 134) says that "...the actual remittance averaged f 9.3 million during 1831-40, f 14.1 million during 1841-50, and reached f 15 million in 1851". As a percentage of the Dutch state income, this surplus varied from 19.3 per cent during 1840-50 to 56.8 per cent during 1860-65 (Dietz, 1977, p. 3).

[2] The main role in the extraction of surplus was played by the newly created state company, NHM (Nederlandsche Handel Maatschappij).

[3] The consequences for the peasantry are not difficult to imagine. As Dietz puts it:

"The plundering of the Javanese population was completed now: forced cultivation, forced unpaid delivery of part of the product, forced paid delivery of the other part of the production to the NHM which laid down prices, sometimes also a land tax in cash, forced labour services for the government, feudal labour services for the princes, communal labour services for the dessa, and paying usury-interest to Chinese traders" (Dietz, 1977, p. 3).

after 1870,[1] and the development of capitalist relations of production, the initial phase of which lasted until the end of the century and was known as the "liberal period".

This process of accumulation was characterised by three main features. First, there was the Agrarian Law, which established inheritable leases, lasting for a period of 75 years (under the previous legislation leases were only for 20 years and were not inheritable) and made it possible for waste land to be rented from "natives" and from the state (this land was used mainly for the production of coffee, tea and cinchona). Second, there was the Sugar Law, which allowed sugar companies to rent - but not to buy - sawah land. It thus became possible to establish capitalist relations of production in agriculture. The legislation, however, protected the desa (the local traditional community) to the extent that it made land inalienable, so that the peasant could enjoy the rent paid by the planter for the use of his land. The situation of the peasantry was nevertheless precarious because they were obliged to pay land tax. The income obtained from renting the land was not sufficient, so they were forced to work in plantations as wage labourers (Wertheim, 1956, p. 94).

Initially plantations were developed by small planters, but metropolitan capital started to accumulate in this sector, leading to a process of concentration and centralisation. This process was accelerated by the crisis of the mid-1880s (brought about by a deterioration in the terms of trade and by natural disasters), which caused the bankruptcy of many small planters and led to the consolidation of big agricultural concerns.[2]

---

1 Nevertheless, the system survived until 1920.

2 Thus the NHM (now converted into an agricultural concern) in 1915 wholly or partially owned 16 sugar factories (and effectively controlled another 22), and 14 sugar, 12 tea and 14 rubber estates. The Handel Vereeniging Amsterdam (HVA) owned 14 sugar estates and managed one tapioca plantation, one combined coffee and rubber plantation and two fibre (sisal) plantations. The Cultuur Maatschappij der Vorstendanlen controlled 20 sugar and 3 coffee factories, and 1 tobacco and one tea factory. The Deli Maatschappij, which operated mainly in tobacco, also owned rubber, oil, palm, sisal, tea and coffee plantations. All these concerns were backed by the main banks (Java Bank, Nederlands-Indische Handelsbank and others) showing a perfect fusion of productive and monetary capital (see Geertz, 1963, p. 85).

The second main feature of this accumulation process was that accumulation was also carried out in the Outer Islands. First of all, this meant that it was necessary to extend the so-called policy of "Calm and Order". This was done by gaining effective control of the Outer Islands through military expeditions to Jambi, Aceh, South-east Borneo, South Celebes, Bali, Lombok, and other areas. To facilitate accumulation in the Outer Islands contract labour (mainly landless Javanese peasants and Chinese coolies from Malaya) was used. The controlled availability of this labour required some use of extra-economic coercion to force them to work.[1] Other characteristics were the development of sectors providing raw materials (especially rubber and oil) for purposes of central accumulation, and the co-existence of petty producers with the big estates in some sectors.[2]

The last main feature of the accumulation was the attempt to broaden and consolidate the internal market as an outlet for imports, mainly from the Netherlands. This process especially favoured cotton goods from Twente (Wertheim, 1956, p. 93), which benefited from a preferential tariff policy, although it gradually decreased.[3] The increase of imports, which as we have seen had already started with Raffles, had the effect of destroying local handicrafts.

What happened to the relationship between labour and land within this process of transformation of the Indonesian social formation which led to the beginning of the accumulation process? Table 1 shows clearly an important increase in Java's population during the "culture system" period.[4] Wertheim summarises its

---

[1] The first example was the Coolie Ordinance (1880) for the east coast of Sumatra. This was followed by similar ordinances for the rest of the Outer Islands (see Furnivall, 1944, pp. 181-182).

[2] There are two reasons for this co-existence. First, the local population was already familiar with the cultivation of many of the crops. Second, international demand was large enough to allow petty producers to play a complementary role.

[3] However, the Dutch textile industry began to seek other Asian markets towards the end of the 19th century (de Jong, 1976, pp. 114 ff).

[4] The almost stagnant situation between 1845 and 1850 reflects the impact of famines as a result of the short time left for cultivation of rice and other food crops.

main causes as follows:

"The increase in population was largely the result of Western administrative measures reducing mortality, greater security, and provisions to meet the threat of famines" (Wertheim, 1956, p. 92).

Table 1: Total population of Java, 1815-1930 (in millions)

1815	4.6	1885	21.5
1845	9.5	1890	23.9
1850	9.6	1895	25.7
1855	10.9	1900	28.7
1860	12.7	1905	30.1
1865	14.2	1917	34.2
1870	16.5	1920	35.0
1875	18.3	1930	41.7
1880	19.8		

Source: Nitisastro (1970), pp. 5-6.

The claim about the improvement of health has been rejected by Nitisastro for lack of evidence (Nitisastro, 1961, pp. 40-41). Other authors tend to emphasise the other causes, especially the peace imposed by the Dutch authorities, which prevented the destruction of crops, and the improvement of the communication system, which prevented the failure of crops resulting in famines (Geertz, 1963, p. 80; Missen, 1972, p. 118). But this increase in population did not result in an increase in the area of land cultivated because cleared land would have been subject to the "culture system" (Pelzer, 1945, p. 162). The result was a dislocation of the former equilibrium between labour and land. As Geertz categorically says:

"...there is little doubt that it was during the culture system period that the saying about the Dutch growing in wealth and the Javanese in numbers first hardened into a sociological reality. By the end of it, the Javanese had, as they have today, the worst of the two possible worlds: a static economy and a burgeoning population" (Geertz, 1963, p. 70).

It can be said, therefore, that the "culture system" led to the weakening of the factors checking population growth in a pre-capitalist mode of production. In this way, one of the basic conditions for the development of capitalist relations of production was created. However, the population increase did not manifest itself as a relative surplus population because the sawah, given its characteristics, could absorb such an increase. Moreover, once the "culture system" started to decline, more land became available for cultivation.[1] This ensured that the relationship between labour and land did not deteriorate abruptly.

Colonial and Post-colonial Transmigration (1905-65)

Accumulation did not imply the immediate emergence of a relative surplus population. However, it did lead to an increasing impoverishment of the Javanese, especially of the poorest strata of the peasantry.[2] This was officially admitted in the speech from the throne in 1901, and led to the formulation of a new colonial policy, known as the "ethical policy", which aimed at the "improvement of the welfare of the native population". An improvement of the welfare of the indigenous population implied an increase in the demand for imports, which favoured Dutch metropolitan capital. Moreover, the various state interventions aiming at implementing the "ethical policy" (irrigation, education and health measures) favoured colonial capital. As Wertheim points out:

> "It can, moreover, be said that even the social services resulting from the 'ethical policy' were strongly subject to the influences of the powerful estate companies and other large-scale companies. Irrigation measures benefited the

---

[1] Although it was not possible to bring more land under cultivation in some areas, in Java as a whole land was cleared until the last years of the colonial period (see van der Leeden, 1952, pp. 91-92).

[2] This situation became evident after the crisis of 1885. The outcome of the crisis was a reduction in wages and less manpower absorption, largely due to factors such as the substitution of imported fertilisers for stable manure, the replacement of home-woven baskets by imported gunny-sacks and the introduction of light railways for carting (Furnivall, 1944, p. 214).

sugar concerns as much as the agricultural population. The health service was, in part, closely related to the need of various enterprises for physically fit labour. The fight against contagious diseases, such as plague and cholera, was a direct gain for Western business. In so far as it exceeded the elementary instruction of the 'desa' schools, education provided training for administrative personnel in the service of the government or business. The road system and the experimental stations existed chiefly for the benefit of the plantations" (Wertheim, 1956, pp. 102-103).

A couple of years earlier, in a famous article entitled "Een eereschuld" ("A debt of honour"), van Deventer had proposed, at the request of the Minister of Colonies, three possible solutions for tackling the increasing impoverishment of Java - "education, irrigation and migration". Migration existed already in the form of contract labour to the Outer Islands, as we have seen.[1]   A second type of migration, also on a labour contract basis, was represented by peasants leaving for Surinam.[2]   However, these two migratory flows were not enough to ease population pressures, so the government started to promote the transfer of Javanese peasants to settlements in the Outer Islands.   Transmigration started thus as part of the "ethical policy".

(a) Transmigration in the colonial
     period (1905-41)

In the initial phase, which lasted from 1905 to 1911, five settlements in the Lampung area of South Sumatra were created.   The first was established in Gedongtataan with 155 families from Kedol (Java).   Another settlement in Gadingredjo followed with the creation of a desa of 555 families.[3]   The first migrants received substantial

---

[1] Nitisastro (1961, p. 204) pointed out that in 1930, 84 per cent of the manpower employed in plantations on the Outer Islands was Javanese.   Of the remaining, 13 per cent was Chinese and 3 per cent local.

[2] Between 1890 and 1939, 32,886 Javanese went to Surinam: only 8,130 returned during Sukarno's period.

[3] The first action was led by the Assistant-Resident, H.G. Heyting, who was initially directed to

support from the state, consisting of a premium of 20 guilders, free transportation, and a payment of 0.4 guilders per day for a period of two years until the land was cleared and irrigation provided. The average cost per person amounted to 300 guilders until the settlement became self-sufficient (Pelzer, 1945, p. 192). This amount increased owing to deaths (caused by malaria and dysentery), desertions (to look for employment on the plantations), and rising costs associated with administration and irrigation projects.

A second phase started in 1911 and lasted until 1928.[1] In this new phase the state's support was much reduced. The premium was raised to 22.5 guilders per family and transportation was still free, but the remaining costs were financed by loans to the families amounting to a maximum of 200 guilders, with an interest of 9 per cent to be paid back in 10 years, starting from the third year of settlement. The People's Credit Bank of the Lampung district was created for this purpose. However, the limitations of the second phase soon became evident. According to Pelzer (1945, pp. 193 ff.) there were several reasons for this:

1 credits were misused by the migrants;

2 there were administrative shortcomings, especially regarding irrigation, the key element in the sawah;

3 the deficient medical facilities maintained high death rates;

4 a defective system of selection meant that desa heads saw in transmigration a means for getting rid of undesirable, sick or old people; and

5 transmigration suffered from competition with the plantations.

---

make a study of Sumatra regarding the possibilities for the settlement of Javanese peasants. His own plan was more ambitious than the one officially approved. He wanted to transfer 22,940 families over a period of 10 years (Pelzer, 1945, p. 191).

[1] In this phase the main settlement was established in Wonobobo, which together with Gedong Tataan constituted the two main Javanese colonies in the Outer Islands. Both were located in South Sumatra. Attempts to establish settlements in other islands, for instance in the Celebes (Sulawesi) and Borneo (Kalimantan), were a failure.

This last point is controversial, however. Hardjono has argued that the government was undoubtedly aware of the advantages of a large labour supply, through trans-migration, for the development of plantations in Sumatra (Hardjono, 1977, pp. 16-17). In this sense, trans-migration and contract labour migration to Sumatra should be viewed as complementary and not in competition.

Between 1928 and 1931 the migratory flow gained a new momentum due to spontaneous migration. In 1927, 914 persons migrated on their own to South Sumatra, where relatives who were already settled helped them in the initial phase. In this way, a new system based on mutual assistance among relatives developed.

The next phase of transmigration, which lasted from 1931 to 1941, was conditioned by the crisis of the 1930s, which severely affected the Dutch Indies. The value of exports declined sharply, due to a fall in the prices of primary exports. The authorities reacted by imposing restrictions on the production of the main export commodities (see Furnivall, 1944, pp. 436 ff). The crisis was also characterised by a significant increase in Japanese manufactured imports, to which the colonial authorities reacted by introducing quotas and other import restrictions. This protection created conditions for the development of an industrial base which led to a second process of accumulation, i.e. industrialisation by import substitution, and the development of an embryonic indigenous industrial bourgeoisie, especially in weaving and dyeing (with the support of the Textile Institute of Bandung) and to a lesser extent in other industries (cigarettes, matches, soap, etc.). Nevertheless, the main role in this process was played by foreign capital.

The crisis in the sugar industry affected the Javanese peasantry in two ways. First, the fall in production meant less use of the rented sawah land and therefore less rent for the landowners. Second, it reduced the need for labour and hence resulted in unem-ployment.[1] Moreover, the crisis also affected the plantations in the Outer Islands, and there was a massive return of unemployed Javanese. Only the possibility of labour absorption in the nascent industrial sector partially mitigated this situation (Wertheim, 1956, p. 113). In this catastrophic situation, migration to the Outer Islands was fostered and implemented on a large scale.

In this new phase the system of mutual aid and assistance was generalised but not on a family basis.

---

[1]   Moreover, land taxes were not scaled down until 1932-33, and even then the reduction was less than the fall in agricultural prices (Wertheim, 1956, p. 107).

Newcomers were used partially as harvest labour in the settlements. At the same time, they worked on their own plots. They were paid between one-fifth and one-quarter of what they reaped (upah bawon). In this way new migrants could survive until their own land was ready for the first harvest. The cost of settlement was reduced almost to nothing. The migrant had to pay, over two or three years, 12.5 guilders for transportation and between 10 and 12.5 guilders for household tools and utensils (Pelzer, 1945, pp. 203-204). In 1937 the government wanted to restore the family mutual assistance scheme, but this attempt was not successful because few people wanted to sponsor relatives, who constituted a greater and more permanent burden than bawoon labourers (see Hardjono, 1977, cit., p. 18).

During the 1930s the colonial authorities improved the organisation of state intervention in the transmigration process. The Central Commission for Migration and Colonisation of Natives, set up in 1937, developed activities such as comprehensive surveys, migration propaganda, and selection of migrants. The selection was based upon ten criteria known as the "Ten Commandments".

These criteria were, as Pelzer (1945, p. 210) enumerated them:

1   Select real tanis; non-farmers are a burden for a colony and endanger its success.

2   Select physically strong people: only they can stand the hardships of pioneering.

3   Select young people: by taking them one reduces future population increase in Java.

4   Select families: families are the foundation of peace and order in the colonies.

5   Don't select families with many young children: the working members of the family cannot carry that burden at the start.

6   Don't select former plantation labourers: in 90 per cent of cases they are the cause of discontent in the colonies.

7   Don't allow so-called "colonisation marriages": they are sources of unrest in the colonies.

8   Don't accept expectant mothers: the pioneer settler needs the full help of his wife during the first year.

- 195 -

9   Don't accept bachelors.

10 Allow <u>desas</u> or <u>kampongs</u> to migrate as a whole: in such cases the first nine commandments may be ignored.

The critical economic situation and the more efficient organisation made this phase of transmigration more successful than the previous one. The most successful colonial settlement (the colony of Sukadana) was established during this period, reaching a population of 90,000 persons in 1941. The number of migrants increased steadily during the second half of the 1930s, as table 2 shows. The yearly average for 1935-42 was 20,000 migrants, while for 1905-32 it was only 1,112. However, during the whole period 1904-41 the population of Java increased from 30.1 to 49.8 million, migration to the Outer Islands absorbing only 1.02 per cent of this increase. It is thus safe to conclude that transmigration failed in its official aim, that is, to reduce rural overpopulation in Java. Moreover, the nature of the transmigration policy (that is, transplanting the Javanese <u>desa</u> to the Outer Islands) gave rise to a series of problems that hindered the successful development of the settlements. The insufficient amounts of land available for the settlements meant limits to their expansion, and therefore the risk of overcrowding. For the migrant family, the small plot of land implied great difficulties in growing cash crops. As a basic characteristic of the parcellary form of production, the small plot of land was subject to fragmentation. Moreover, transactions of land took place, leading to a process of land concentration in those settlements established during colonial times. The weak economic position of the settled migrant was accentuated by his permanent indebtedness to rice-mill owners, mainly Chinese. It cannot therefore be said that transmigration meant a real improvement of the living standards of the migrants compared to their previous situation in Java (Hardjono, 1977, cit., pp. 20-21).

(b) Transmigration in Sukarno's period (1945-65)

The weakening of Dutch colonial rule with the depression of the 1930s was accelerated by the Japanese occupation (1942-45) in the Second World War, when Indonesia was harnessed to the Japanese war effort and compelled to provide crops and labour. Large numbers of labourers were shifted from Java to other parts of the Indonesian archipelago and to the Asian mainland, from

Table 2: Number of Javanese official migrants
to the Outer Islands, 1932-41

1932	7,000[a]	1937	19,369
1933	751	1938	32,259
1934	2,756	1939	45,339
1935	14,710	1940	52,885
1936	13,152	1941	60,000[a]

[a] Approximate.

Source: Pelzer, 1945, p. 211.

Burma to the Solomon Islands. Labour was also recruited from transmigration settlements (Hardjono, 1977, p. 21). This labour was devoted to military works, the workers being euphemistically called "economic soldiers" (Wertheim, 1956, pp. 263-264).

In 1950 the first post-colonial period began, lasting until 1965. In this period the crisis of primary exports continued in most sectors. Sugar production suffered from the destruction of factories by the Japanese during the Second World War. Sugar-growing fields were converted again to rice production. The drop in sugar exports, which accounted for only 3 per cent of total exports during the post-war period, was even more marked than the drop in production.[1] In the case of rubber, a distinction between big estates and petty producers ought to be made. Given the marked drop in production and exports by the former, the latter

[1] Mackie (1971, pp. 37 ff) has pointed out several causes for this fall in exports. First, there was a decrease in the number of mills as a result of the previous depression and wars. Second, the yield per hectare decreased from 160 quintals to between 100 and 130. This was due mainly to the increased proportion of cane grown independently by the peasantry, over which, moreover, the plantations had less control than before. Third, there was an increase in internal demand. Fourth, the quota given to Indonesia in the International Sugar Agreement of 1950 was only 350,000 tons. Nevertheless, this small quota was never reached.

progressively became the main rubber producers.[1] Similar trends became evident in most of the export crops.[2] However, petty producers did not represent a solid basis for carrying out accumulation, and many of these sectors faced a critical situation.

The crisis in primary exports was accentuated by the rise in internal demand fostered by the dominant classes and the higher strata of the new post-colonial bureaucracy, leading to a continuous increase in imports. The increasing flow of imports was also due to the desire to constitute an Indonesian commercial bourgeoisie which could displace the Chinese bourgeoisie. Import licences were therefore issued only to Indonesians.[3] This measure was complemented by state financial support, through the creation of the Bank Negara Indonesia. These were the two main measures of the so-called benteng programme.[4] Another attempt to strengthen Indonesian capital was made through import substitution policies. A state industrial bank was established for the purpose of promoting basic industries. The People's Bank (Bank Rakjat) was also created in order to promote small-scale industry. Nevertheless, the results were quite meagre. Few basic industries were established, and the results in small-scale industry were equally

---

[1] There were several reasons for this: a stronger labour movement demanding higher wages; insecurity of tenure; problems with staff due to the departure of Dutch personnel and the difficulties in replacing them by Indonesians; high taxation and delays in the remission of profits; the occupation of land by squatters growing rice for subsistence. These occupations also affected tobacco plantations. It has been estimated that the whole area affected by invasions of squatters amounted to 350,000 hectares, of which 115,000 were in North Sumatra (see Palte and Tempelman, 1974, p. 138).

[2] This was the case for coffee, tea, copra and tobacco (see Thomas and Panglaykim, 1966, p. 89).

[3] The Chinese bourgeoisie adapted itself to this new situation by operating through puppet Indonesian licence-holders known as "briefcase importers".

[4] This programme entered a crisis with the scandal of the issue of licences to those who gave financial support to the Nationalist Party (see Glassburner, 1962, p. 125).

disappointing.[1]   In the First Five-Year Plan (1956-60) the emphasis was put mainly on rehabilitation of existing plants, maximum utilisation of local raw materials, upgrading of labour skills, and achievement of low cost levels.   For this period there was no important increase in industrial production as a whole (see Soehoed, 1967, pp. 68-69).   In the 1960s, under the new programme known as "Guided Democracy", the emphasis was placed on industrialisation.[2]   However, the crisis in the primary export sectors and the consequent shortage of foreign exchange affected industries, whose capacity was underutilised owing to lack of imported inputs.[3]

This situation led to broad and direct state intervention through the nationalisation of Dutch-owned landed property.   Thus, 542 plantations were nationalised and put under the control of the government.   Dutch-owned manufacturing firms were also nationalised.   A second wave of nationalisations occurred in 1963, affecting mainly United Kingdom capital.   Nationalisation was completed in 1965 (Castles, 1965, pp. 21-22).

A second major issue of the "Guided Democracy" period was the attempt to carry out agrarian reform.[4] The old Agrarian Law of 1870 was replaced by a new Basic Agrarian Law in 1960.   The new legislation recognised the individual hereditary right of ownership, together with the right of adat community ownership (Pelzer, 1971, pp. 138-139).   In the same year the Emergency Law was proclaimed, determining a minimum and a maximum holding of disposable arable land.   A universal minimum of 2 hectares of arable land per peasant family was established.   The maximum depended

---

1   Only 22 of 82 programmed workshops received new machinery, only 6 were in operation (Palte and Tempelman, 1974, pp. 202-203).

2   Thirty-one per cent of the total expenditure - with the exception of 30 billion rupiahs for special projects - was allocated to the industrial sector (Paauw, 1963, p. 227).

3   One of the industrial branches which suffered most from the lack of imported inputs was textiles, wherein Indonesian interests were more rooted (Palmer and Castles, 1971, pp. 322 ff).

4   Since the 1950s the process of internal differentiation among the different strata of the Javanese peasantry had become accentuated (Wertheim, 1978, pp. 235-236).

on the population density of the area and on the kind of land (irrigated or not) (Utrecht, 1969, pp. 75-76). Within this juridical framework, the attempt to implement the agrarian reforms started in 1961. Nevertheless, the success of these reforms was limited.[1] The major problem affecting agriculture was the inadequate production of foodstuffs to guarantee a minimum level of nutrition for the population. This was only possible through a continued increase in rice and wheat flour imports.[2] In response to this situation the state launched a programme, the aim of which was to reach self-sufficiency in rice and other food substitutes (maize, cassava, etc.). Paddy centres were created with the aim of providing fertilisers, seeds, and credit to the peasants. However, the low price of rice fixed by the government discouraged peasants from repaying loans. Moreover, corruption in the paddy centres led to ijon practices which maintained the indebtedness of the peasantry.[3] The failure of this programme led to the formulation of a different strategy, as will be seen in the next section.

The instability of this first post-colonial period was reflected in the formulation of the transmigration policy in three ways. First, the purpose of transmigration became too broad and therefore too vague. Although the transfer of excess population from Java remained an objective, others were added, namely "promotion of economic development in the Outer Islands, security and national unity" (see McNicoll, 1968, p. 65). "Promotion of economic development in the Outer Islands" was directly related to the new outlook on the population

---

1 The inconsistencies in the formulation of this agrarian reform became clear during its first phase. The initial problems of land registration having been solved, there were an estimated 377,445 hectares for redistribution in Java, Madura and Bali, but in the first two islands alone there were 3 million landless families (Palte and Tempelman, 1974, pp. 210-211). For an analysis of the implementation of the land reform between 1961 and 1965, see Utrecht (1969, pp. 77 ff.

2 Pelzer (1971, pp. 140-141) points out that rice imports in 1938-40 amounted to 240,000 metric tons while in 1959 they were 603,000. In the case of wheat flour, imports for 1938-40 amounted to 94,000 metric tons and in 1955 to 132,000.

3 See Palmer (1977, p. 24). With ijon, credit was offered with the main crop as collateral.

issue. The problem was no longer population growth (Sukarno himself claimed that the country could support 250 million people) but its geographical distribution. Under this new natalist policy, transmigration as a welfare measure became even more utopian than in colonial times. "Security" was related to the need for populating disputed frontier territories, especially the frontier with Malaysia. In this sense transmigration constituted part of geo-politics, but it also acquired a new ideological function, enabling international issues to be used as a smoke-screen for internal problems, as Pluvier has suggested (Pluvier, 1965, pp. 69-70). The "Javanisation" of the Outer Islands, as a means of achieving "national unity" against separatist tendencies, was therefore an attempt to solve internal contradictions posed in geographical terms (Palte and Tempelman, 1974, p. 68). This implied the abandonment of the previous colonial policy under which settlements of migrants had been established as Javanese enclaves in the Outer Islands. In spite of criticisms of previous colonial experiments, this achieved very little because new settlements were placed in areas already opened up in the 1930s.

A second way in which the instability of the period affected the formulation of transmigration policy was the lack of serious and consistent programming. Thus, in 1952, the head of the Transmigration Service proposed to decrease Java's population from 54 million to 31 million over a period of 35 years. Somewhat more realistic were the targets formulated in the Five-Year Plan, which aimed at transferring 2 million people between 1956 and 1960, establishing 20 new settlements (19 of them in Sumatra). A new attempt followed under the Eight-Year Plan with the more modest objective of transferring 1.5 million, an average of 125,000 migrants a year (Heeren, 1967, pp. 25 ff). This figure was raised by Sukarno himself for political reasons, his declared objective being to transfer 1.5 million persons a year, the equivalent to the annual increase in the population of Java. This unrealistic figure would have meant a daily transfer of 5,000 people and the daily provision of 200 hectares of irrigated land in the Outer Islands (Palte and Tempelman, 1974, p. 71).

Finally, the instability of the period was reflected in the lack of precise and permanent institutional arrangements for the transmigration programme. From 1947 to 1965 the transmigration authority underwent eight changes (Hardjono, 1974, p. 22).

During this period the migrants were classified into four categories (Heeren, 1967, pp. 38 ff). First, there was the so-called "general transmigration" constituted by migrants who were supported by the state from their selection for the transmigration programme until the eighth month of their settlement. State aid was given in the form of a loan to be paid back in 30 years in kind, i.e. rice. This was an improvement on the last phase of migration in the colonial period. A second improvement was an increase in the size of plot from 1 to 2 hectares (Palte and Tempelman, 1974, p. 70). A second category consisted of the so-called "family transmigration", similar to that predominating in the 1930s. The only difference was that the arrival of the migrants was no longer dependent on the harvest period. Third, there was "spontaneous migration". This flow comprised people who could not wait for their turn in the transmigration programme and travelled on their own to the Outer Islands. Migrants of this kind did not receive any help from the state except some medical services for eradicating malaria (Wertheim, 1964, p. 194). Finally, there was the so-called "internal migration", which strictly speaking should not be considered as part of transmigration because it was related to labour mobility in the Outer Islands. But it was closely related to the transmigration phenomenon, being composed of members of the new generations born in the first settlements. Known as the "settlers' children", these migrants were looking for land outside their settlements.

Table 3 shows that the area of origin of migrants remained the same as in the colonial period. Central Java (including Yogyakarta) and East Java were the main areas providing migrants. Sumatra received 86 per cent of the total migratory flow, as table 4 shows, and remained the principal area of destination as in colonial times. During Sukarno's period, transmigration exceeded 50,000 a year only in 1965. For 1950-64 it totalled 343,058, which accounted for only 2.8 per cent of the increase in the population of Java in that period, which was estimated to be 12.3 million. Again transmigration was shown to be a very ineffective response to rural overpopulation in Java.

At this stage of the analysis it is possible to point out concrete problems affecting the transmigration process, most of which are not unique to Sukarno's period but are still present today. Hardjono has enumerated a number of such problems (Hardjono, 1977, p. 36). First, there was the problem of the kind of peasants who migrated, most of whom belonged to the poorest strata of the Javanese peasantry.[1] In many

---

1 In his study of three settlements in Middle Lampung, Heeren has brought out very clearly that the main motivation for migrating was the desire to possess a plot of land (Heeren, 1967, pp. 64 ff).

Table 3: Number of migrants by areas of origin, 1950-65

Year	West Java	Central Java	Yogyakarta	East Java	Bali	Local[a]	Total[b]
1950							77[c]
1951	69	1,588	390	502		402	2,951
1952	409	8,777	2,745	4,992		682	17,605
1953	3,028	12,754	4,427	14,751	1,054	3,995	40,009
1954	5,362	9,397	3,236	7,552	2,706	1,485[d]	29,738
1955	3,164	6,472	1,954	5,454	203	4,142	21,389
1956	3,236	9,700	2,724	8,116[e]		574	24,350
1957	1,935	7,653	2,094	4,739	497	6,312	23,230
1958	1,336	9,388	5,895	5,567	1,023	3,210	26,419
1959	5,991	15,311	2,654	14,514	3,948	3,678	49,096
1960	2,180	7,062	1,960	6,910[e]		3,963	22,075
1961	5,109	8,470	1,363	4,317[e]		350	19,609
1962	3,028	9,973	1,647	5,446[e]		2,035	22,129
1963	837	4,622	695	3,138	22,598	269	32,159
1964	683	7,819	4,675	59	1,986		15,222
1965	4,202	26,524	7,503	13,803	1,193		53,225

a The term "local" refers to people moving within the same province.

b This table does not include the 17,837 families resettled in southern Sumatra between 1950 and 1954 by the Bureau for National Reconstruction and the Bureau for Settlement of Ex-servicemen.

c Area of origin is not recorded.

d This figure includes 1,012 people repatriated from Surinam.

e This figure includes migrants from Bali.

Source: Hardjono, 1977, p. 24.

Table 4: Number of migrants by area of settlement
1950-65

Year	Sumatra	Kalimantan	Sulawesi	Elsewhere	Total
1950	77				77
1951	2,453		96	402	2,951
1952	16,585		338	682	17,605
1953	33,212	2,619	310	3,868	40,009
1954	26,430	1,736	1,078	494	29,738
1955	17,609	2,033	1,314	433	21,389
1956	22,135	2,119	96		24,350
1957	17,456	4,184	1,590		23,230
1958	25,700	463		256	26,419
1959	44,124	1,412	298	262	46,096
1960	19,128	2,947			22,075
1961	14,876	4,330	263	140	19,609
1962	13,966	7,543	420	200	22,129
1963	28,903	1,808	1,448		32,159
1964	11,787	2,448	987		15,222
1965	46,287	5,019	1,919		53,225

Source: Hardjono, 1977, p. 26.

cases the general prerequisites for the development of settlements were not provided at all, or provided only partially. Lack of irrigation or deficient irrigation placed important limitations on the successful development of a settlement. This was the case with the Way Seputih project in Lampung, where migrants were forced to cultivate cassava and other dry crops because the irrigation system was not ready when settlement began. Similarly, lack of communication and access to marketing centres affected many settlements in Bengkulu, given the mountainous terrain which characterises this province. Similar problems arose in the province of West Kalimantan, which had a very poor communications network.

A second set of problems affected production in the settlements. First, there was the poor quality of the soil. This was clearly a factor in the province of East Kalimantan, with the exception of the Palaran and Bukuan settlements, as well as for the provinces of South

Kalimantan and South-east Sulawesi. Second, although in the post-colonial period the size of plot per migrant family had risen from 1 to 2 hectares, this was not enough if the land was not irrigated.[1] Migrants therefore had to use the entire 2 hectares to cultivate dry crops for subsistence. Third, population growth, due to natural increase and to the inflow of independent migrants, could not be fully absorbed, given the fixed amount of land assigned to each settlement. This led to overcrowding, as at Way Seputih in Lampung. Fourth, there were problems of access to land because of disputes with the local population, arising out of a lack of clarity in the procedures by which the transmigration authorities obtained land for the establishment of settlements during Sukarno's period. Problems of this kind occurred in the Way Seputih project and in the province of Bengkulu, in the settlement provided for the victims of the Mount Agung eruption in Bali. Disputes with the local population over land claims were the major factor in forcing more than half of the 6,071 settled migrants in Bengkulu to leave.[2] Fifth, shortage of fertilisers, pesticides, seeds, and similar inputs represented another limitation on production. This was a serious problem in the province of West Kalimantan.

The most important problem affecting labour, in some cases, was the lack of appropriate skills. This was the case in the province of South-east Sulawesi, where settlements suffered from insufficient knowledge of sedentary agricultural techniques on the part of the settlers. This was because they were mainly resettled local families, who were familiar only with shifting cultivation.

Marketing problems existed only where a surplus could be produced. We have already seen the limitations imposed by the lack or inadequacy of a communications network. But even where communication facilities did not represent an obstacle, the lack of means of transport for the settled migrants implied dependence on the middle-man for selling the surplus. Normally, the product was sold at the lowest price and the migrants' income was thereby reduced.

Problems were not confined to the internal development of settlements. Relations between migrants and local population were often tense, disputes over land

---

1 Nevertheless, in the projects situated in the Hulu Mahakam area, in the province of East Kalimantan, settlers got only 1 hectare per family.

2 Such disputes were quite common in this province.

being the major issue.[1] Where attempts were made to integrate the settlers and to break the enclave policy, differences in cultivation systems and cultural differences proved to be barriers.[2] Moreover, the problem created by different cultures was accentuated by the large ethnic diversity in the Outer Islands.

These various problems were not generated by the settlers themselves. The immediate causes of most of them should be sought in the deficiencies of state intervention in the transmigration process. We have already pointed out that lack of care by the government in the selection of migrants was the main reason for the unsuitability of migrant labour. The deficiencies of state intervention were, however, apparent in two other ways. First, insufficient preparatory work was done on the selection of sites. This meant that settlements were located in areas with poor soil, or where the legal status of the land assigned to the settlement was not clear and disputes with the local population consequently arose. Often, too, settlements were located in areas far from marketing centres or with deficient communication links. Second, there was an overlapping of institutions implementing transmigration policy, in some cases leading to a lack of co-ordination. The most outstanding example in this regard was the lack of co-operation between the transmigration authorities and the Department of Public Works. Finally, problems generated by overlapping appeared in the follow-up of the transmigration projects, whose status vis-à-vis central and regional authorities was never clear. The existence of these deficiencies was the result of a lack of centralisation, a necessary condition for the success of any state

---

1 These disputes were not confined to official migrants but also occurred with spontaneous migrants (Wertheim, 1964, p. 193). Also disputes took place with demobilised soldiers in southern Sumatra (Heeren, 1977, pp. 98 ff).

2 An example of the problems created by cultural barriers is provided by Heeren. In a settlement of about 1,000 repatriated Javanese from Surinam in the northern part of the Minangkabau area of Central Sumatra, the continuous clashes between the conservative Islamic indigenous population and the "too westernised" Surinam Javanese impeded any effort at integration. The experiment finished during the attempted secession of Sumatra. The migrants had to leave the settlement, fearing a massacre due to their Javanese origin (Heeren, 1977, pp. 118 ff).

intervention. This is clearly reflected in the numerous changes in the institutional definition of the transmigration authority, as mentioned before. It can be concluded, therefore, that the immediate causes of the various impediments to transmigration lie in the deficiencies of state intervention due to a lack of centralisation.

Transmigration in the "New Order"

Sukarno's period can basically be seen as an attempt to develop a national capitalism in Indonesia. As with many other peripheral social formations, this attempt was a failure. Taylor has specified four main reasons for this (Taylor, 1974, pp. 16-17). First, the development strategy was formulated in a confused and arbitrary manner. Second, state intervention in the industrial, banking and transport sectors was not rigorously programmed. Moreover, the hypertrophy of the bureaucracy and the corruption due to the low salaries paid in the public sector led to mismanagement of the state apparatus. Third, exports and domestic production were falling and could not fill the vacuum created by the absence of foreign aid and capital. The outcome of this state of affairs was economic stagnation. Fourth, the economic crisis was accentuated by the political crisis, arising from the continuing antagonism between the Communist Party and the army. This made a very weak and unstable social base for Sukarno's regime. The equilibrium, such as it was, was upset by the manifestation of dissension within the army itself. A group of lower-ranking officers attempted a coup d'état (the Untung coup) in order to displace the dominant rightist faction of the army, which it accused of corruption (Utrecht, 1975, pp. 42-43). The failure of the attempt allowed the rightist faction to react by seizing power and smashing the Communist Party and its mass organisations. Towards the beginning of 1966 military power was consolidated, ushering in a new period in Indonesian history, labelled by the army itself the "New Order" period.

Accumulation and labour absorption

Once the political situation was consolidated, the main task of the military regime was to create conditions for giving a new impetus to the capital accumulation process. Accordingly, a stabilisation programme was formulated, following the advice of the International Monetary Fund. The government itself summarised the purpose of this programme in four main lines of action

(Arndt, 1966, p. 4):

1 It was necessary to achieve a balanced government budget.

2 A more selective and rigid credit policy should be pursued. These two kinds of intervention were aimed mainly at curbing inflation (Glassburner, 1971, p. 438).

3 A realistic exchange rate should be established in order to stimulate exports.

4 The widespread state intervention which had characterised the previous period should be reduced in order to ensure that private capital played the leading role in the accumulation process.

The stabilisation programme did not in fact create all the conditions for the recovery of economic growth, and a development programme was necessary, as we shall see later. However, three main features of the growth process are worth noting. In the first place, there has been a recovery of the existing primary export sectors - though important changes have taken place in the composition of primary exports. Tables 5 and 6 show both the recovery of the most important traditional exports and a clear movement from these traditional exports, especially rubber, towards timber and, above all, oil, which has become the main primary export since export prices soared in 1973.

As discussed in the previous section, import substitution was a major element of the growth process in Indonesia. Its recovery was delayed owing to the stabilisation policy during the first few years of the "New Order". Ineffective protection and, above all, lack of credit to finance imported inputs, kept most of the industries stagnant until the end of the 1960s (Palmer and Castle, 1978, pp. 91 ff.). Since then, the process of growth has recovered.

Table 7 shows how growth has been concentrated mainly in consumer goods industries (especially food processing, tobacco and textiles) rather than in capital goods industries.[1] This suggests a marked degree of

---

[1] Table 7 shows only the level of employment in medium-sized and large firms. According to the Indonesian definition, medium-sized firms are those which employ 10 to 99 workers without using power equipment,

Table 5: Commodity exports of Indonesia, 1965-75

Commodity	F.o.b. value (million US$)			Export composition (%)		
	1965	1970	1975	1965	1970	1975
Coffee	31.7	69.2	99.8	4.5	6.2	1.4
Copra	18.0	30.3	3.3	2.5	2.7	0.0
Palm oil	27.3	35.1	151.6	3.9	3.2	2.1
Pepper	9.0	3.2	22.8	1.3	0.3	0.3
Petroleum and petroleum products	272.0	446.3	5310.8	38.4	40.3	74.8
Rubber	222.0	253.4	358.2	31.4	22.9	5.0
Tea	16.9	18.3	51.5	2.4	1.7	0.7
Timber	2.1	104.3	500.0	0.3	9.4	7.0
Tin	39.9	53.7	103.1	5.6	4.8	1.5
Tobacco	18.7	4.2	35.2	2.6	0.4	0.5
Other products	50.1	90.1	466.2	7.1	8.1	6.6
Total	707.7	1108.1	7102.5	100.0	100.0	100.0

Source: Biro Pusat Statistik (1976).

Table 6: Volume of exports, 1965-75, indexed on base 1965

Year	Rubber	Copra	Coffee	Tobacco	Palm oil	Palm kernels	Pepper
1965	100	100	100	100	100	100	100
1966	96	96	90	97	141	96	168
1967	92	92	148	78	105	118	304
1968	108	174	79	68	121	111	200
1969	120	126	118	42	141	130	136
1970	111	149	96	81	126	129	22
1971	111	62	69	136	166	148	197
1972	111	28	89	183	184	146	201
1973	123	34	93	230	205	121	201
1974	117	–	106	189	217	74	131
1975	110	–	113	n.a.	297	55	128

Source: Palmer and Castles (1978), p. 67.

Table 7: Employment in the manufacturing industries, 1970

Industrial branch	No. of persons (000s)	Percentage of total manufacturing
Basic metals	2.6	0.3
Beverages	5.3	0.6
Clothing and footwear	9.6	1.1
Electrical machinery	2.9	0.3
Fertilisers, pesticides, petroleum products and other chemicals	32.4	3.8
Finished metal products	12.6	1.5
Food processing	285.1	33.6
Furniture	4.1	0.5
Leather and leather products	2.2	0.3
Non-electrical machinery	4.8	0.6
Non-metallic mineral products	23.2	2.7
Paper and paper products	6.8	0.8
Printed matter	14.0	1.6
Rubber	108.6	12.8
Textiles	168.6	19.9
Tobacco	134.6	15.9
Transport equipment	10.3	1.2
Wood and cork products	13.5	1.6
Miscellaneous	7.8	0.9
Total	849.0	100.0

Source: Biro Pusat Statistitik (1970).

external dependency, a suggestion which is borne out by table 8, showing the increasing proportion of raw materials and auxiliary goods, and especially capital goods, in over-all imports. The conditions of reproduction of capital thus remain external to the Indonesian social formation, and import substitution industrialisation has not been able to break this dependency.

---

or 5 to 49 workers with power equipment. When a firm employs 100 or more workers without using power equipment or 50 or more workers with power equipment, it is considered a large firm.

Table 8:   Imports by economic groups, 1966-75
           (in million US$)

Year	Consumer goods	Raw materials and auxiliary	Capital goods goods	Total
1966	224.7	180.3	121.7	526.7
1967	232.5	237.7	179.0	649.0
1968	266.5	259.7	189.6	715.8
1969	220.9	321.0	238.8	780.7
1970	251.1	376.5	373.9	1001.5
1971	210.2	428.0	464.6	1002.8
1972	251.8	597.7	712.2	1561.7
1973	648.7	973.2	1107.2	2729.1
1974	707.0	1582.3	1552.6	3841.9
1975	677.5	1961.1	2131.2	4769.8

Source: Biro Pusat Statistik (1976).

The slow recovery of import substitution considerably damaged the position of indigenous capital. During the first few years of the "New Order", local industry suffered from the competition of imports. When recovery started, local capital had to face the competition of foreign capital moving into the industrial sectors under the new law on foreign investment. The main foreign investor in industry was Japan (33.1 per cent of the total amount of foreign projects between 1967 and 1972), followed by the United States (17.9 per cent) and Hong Kong (12 per cent).

The last accumulation process in this period was a new one, namely the development of capitalist farming as a result of the Green Revolution. The development of productive forces which characterises the Green Revolution has been the outcome of the transformation of the relations of production. The replacement of the traditional hand-pounding by mechanical hulling and milling has resulted in the loss of seasonal jobs for women. As a result, the poorer strata of the peasantry have been increasingly impoverished (Mortimer, 1973, pp. 62-63). Therefore, as Hickson has observed, the Green Revolution has accelerated the development of capitalist relations of production, mainly sharecropping (Hickson, 1973, p. 330).

Table 9: Economically active population by occupation and industry, 1971

Occupation	Industry			
	Agriculture, hunting, etc.	Mining and quarrying	Manu-facturing	Electricity, gas and water
Professional, technical and related workers	10,968	4,174	9,505	1,164
Administrative and managerial workers	6,144	1,877	27,190	1,141
Clerical and related workers	56,570	16,552	65,044	13,801
Sales workers	5,500	303	16,992	585
Service workers	46,702	8,800	72,292	1,859
Farmers	25,095,174	791	13,019	133
Production and related workers transport equipment operators	70,300	53,148	2,471,763	18,487
Others	1,182,149	183	6,147	189
Total	26,473,477	85,828	2,681,952	37,359

[a] Including community services.

Source: Biro Pusat Statistik (1971).

Construc- tion	Trade, restaurants and hotels	Transport, storage and com- munication	Financing, insurance, etc.	Others[a]	Total
3,773	2,030	8,944	1,466	841,513	883,537
12,882	8,544	12,803	5,268	113,648	189,467
15,626	53,627	120,246	69,114	859,973	1,270,553
1,922	4,102,410	3,826	3,339	52,938	4,187,815
22,740	56,175	26,423	7,049	1,330,929	1,572,969
1,969	6,379	489	477	25,026	25,143,457
618,469	22,008	776,166	6,390	608,275	4,645,005
1,091	10,338	2,457	359	2,165,449	3,368,412
678,472	4,261,561	951,354	93,462	5,997,751	41,261,216

Industrialisation based on import substitution has offered limited opportunities for absorbing labour. According to table 9, manufacturing industry employed only 6.5 per cent of the total "economically active population" in 1971. It has been said that manufacturing industry was one of the sectors with the highest annual rate of growth of employment between 1961 and 1971.[1] But this increase in many cases reflects the transformation of pre-capitalist production processes into capitalist ones. But, given the more capital-intensive techniques that characterise capitalist production, not all pre-capitalist labour has been absorbed.

State programming: Repelita

We have seen how intervention at the beginning of the "New Order" period was centred on the stabilisation programme. This attempt to create conditions for fostering growth was not totally successful. The confidence of foreign investors, the key element in the growth process, was eroded. In order to restore it, a development programme (Repelita) was formulated. The first Repelita, covering the period 1969-70 to 1973-74, was aimed at a rapid increase of production in certain crucial sectors. However, the unquestioning belief that market forces would stop inflation, allocate resources optimally, and attract foreign capital together with foreign aid, made it unnecessary to specify any policy. As Rudner put it:

> "...even within this 'open' framework, the plan did not lay down policy guidelines for public finance, investment criteria, plan administration, income distribution, or social services - these having been left for later, ad hoc decision. Repelita-I involved little substantive planning; it merely set out some quinquennial sectoral priorities and related these in general terms to the constraints of economic fundamentalism on the one hand, and longer-run political goals on the other" (Rudner, 1976, p. 261).

---

[1] This rate has been estimated at 4.7 for 1961-71. According to Leiserson, four-fifths of this increase is due to labour absorption in rural small-scale industry (Leiserson, 1974, pp. 345-346). According to Sundrum, on the other hand, this absorption has taken place mainly in large and medium-sized industries which were established outside the urban territorial limits and therefore were considered as rural for statistical purposes (Sundrum, 1975, p. 60).

In this sense, state intervention played mainly a supporting role, as under the stabilisation programme and in contrast to the "étatisme" of Sukarno's period (Thomas and Panglaykim, 1969, p. 238).

The prime objective of the first Repelita was the achievement of self-sufficiency in rice by 1973 through a substantial increase in production. The early Green Revolution strategies were therefore incorporated in the Repelita scheme. Development of agriculture was not confined to rice, however. Other objectives were the diversification of cropping patterns and agricultural extension in the Outer Islands. In support of this strategy, infrastructure development was given a high priority. Repelita-I aimed mainly at the rehabilitation of existing infrastructural projects such as the irrigation and water-power projects of Jatiluhur and Asahan, but it also focused on new ones such as the dams of Cimanuk and Brantas (Palte and Tempelman, 1974, p. 215). Some selected industries, notably chemicals (provision of fertilisers, insecticides and other inputs), also played a direct or indirect supporting role vis-à-vis agriculture.

An analysis of available data indicates that timber and oil largely exceeded the estimates of Repelita-I. This was not the case for other primary exports, with the exception of palm oil. As far as industrialisation was concerned, only the textile target was achieved. Other selected industries such as cement and chemicals were not so successful. In rice production, the results seemed to be satisfactory, largely because of the Green Revolution, but this was not the case for other food crops. In sum, as Palmer says, "the realisation of the First Five-Year Plan, 1969-1974, was a mixed performance" (Palmer and Castle, 1978, p. 175).

Towards the end of Repelita-I certain problems emerged. Suhadi Mangkusuwondo points out three main ones: "unemployment", "the uneven growth of different regions", and "the question of national entrepreneurs versus foreign companies" (Mangkusuwondo, 1973, p. 32). It can be said that social policies were almost totally neglected in Repelita-I. Only education and family planning received any attention. As regards manpower absorption, it was only in 1970 that the state intervened, launching a nationwide employment programme known as the Kabupaten Programme.[1] But this programme aimed

----

[1] The central government made available an amount of 50 rupiahs per capita to 281 rural and urban autonomous areas for labour-intensive economic infrastructure works. There were other minor programmes, such as the desa programme, with subsidies of 100,000 rupiahs per village (Leiserson, 1974, p. 356).

only at the creation of complementary employment in an attempt to reduce underemployment. Even de Witt, who has been so enthusiastic about the achievements of this programme, recognised that it could offer "only a partial contribution to the solution of the employment problem" (de Witt, 1973, p. 82). Finally, the uneven geographical development was perpetuated. Primary exports continued to dominate in the Outer Islands, and the recovery of import substitution took place mainly in West Java, the less populated and less poor part of the island.

Given this situation, Repelita-II came into operation in April 1974, covering the period 1974-75 to 1978-79. Its major objectives were the following:

1 adequate supply of food and clothing of better quality and within people's purchasing power;

2 adequate household supplies and facilities;

3 better and more extensive infrastructure;

4 higher and more evenly distributed social welfare;

5 greater employment opportunities (see Grenville, 1973, p. 28).

There were three important features of Repelita-II. First it was intended to reduce the share of agriculture in the gross domestic product in favour of industry, transport, and communications. Second, contrary to Repelita-I, which was characterised by heavy financial dependence,[1] the development programme was to be financed from the oil surplus (Palte, 1976, p. 22). Third, it was designed to focus primarily on welfare issues, namely employment and income distribution (Palmer and Castle, 1978, pp. 189-190).

Transmigration since 1968

During the first few years of the "New Order" the transmigration flow was mostly minimal. The yearly average amounted to no more than 8,000 migrants. The recovery of the transmigration process started with Repelita-I. As discussed earlier, one of the main ways of developing agriculture in Repelita-I was agricultural

---

[1]   In Repelita-I, 73 per cent of the total financing came from external resources, 59 per cent from foreign aid and 14 per cent from foreign investment.

extension in the Outer Islands, where there was a shortage of manpower.[1]

Table 10 shows that during Repelita-I the same areas provided migrants as in previous periods. Sumatra remained the main island of destination for migrants, although other islands increased their share of settlers, especially Sulawesi, as table 11 shows. The persistent institutional chaos meant that a rather small number of migrants were settled up to 1972-73. Initially, state intervention in the transmigration process was focused mainly on its reorganisation. First, a Crash Programme was formulated with the aim of settling those migrants assigned to tidal projects which had not yet been prepared. The migrants were settled on dry farming areas where land was immediately available, as in Lampung, South Sumatra, Riau and South Sulawesi. Second, migrants who had been allocated to unsuitable sites were resettled. An example was the transfer of migrants from the Gunung Balak project in Central Sulawesi, placed in a reserved forest area, to the Way Abung and Panagaran projects.

During Repelita-I migrants were classified into several categories (Suratman and Guiness, 1977, pp. 85-86). General transmigrants had full support from the state. Transportation costs were covered. They received 2 hectares of land with a house and tools. Food was supplied for a period of 12 months, or 16 months in the case of tidal projects. Spontaneous migrants received land, a house, and tools, but they had to pay for transport - although in some cases it was possible to get a cash grant to cover transport costs. This kind of migration was encouraged towards the end of Repelita-I with the Banpress Programme. Special categories of migrants included those under the Crash Programme or the bedol desa programme in 1974, under which the victims of the eruption of Mount Merapi in Java were transferred. Voluntary migrants were totally self-financed. They moved to nearby areas of settlement and were not registered as in the case of spontaneous migrants. Certain criteria were applied for the selection of migrants. They were to be:

1 of Indonesian nationality;

2 not involved in the Communist movement of 30 September 1965 and not a member of any banned political or mass organisation;

---

[1] Emphasis has also been laid on rice production under the tidal projects (Suratman and Guiness, 1977, p. 85).

Table 10: Number of migrants by area of origin, 1969-74

Area of origin	1969-70	1970-71	1971-72	1972-73	1973-74	Total
West Java	2,105	3,004	2,647	7,936	8,170[a]	23,862
Central Java	4,093	5,979	4,119	15,455	27,778	57,424
Special area of Yogyakarta	5,397	2,636	2,739	5,916	6,212	22,900
East Java	4,726	3,475	4,139	16,850	24,966	54,156
Bali	1,527	4,901	5,226	5,761	4,380	21,795
Lombok					1,451	1,451
Local					108	108
Total	17,848	19,995	18,870	51,918	73,065	181,969

[a] 1,433 people from the Capital Territory of Jakarta are included.

Source: Hardjono, 1977, p. 31.

Table 11: Number of migrants by area of settlement, 1969-74

Area of settlement	1969-70	1970-71	1971-72	1972-73	1973-74	Total
Irian Jaya				485		485
Kalimantan	2,599	3,970	4,748	7,227	8,038	26,582
Maluku		233		479	1,001	1,713
Saluwesi	4,137	7,442	5,120	11,944	19,049	47,692
Sumatra	11,112	8,350	9,002	31,738	44,977	105,224
Total	17,848	19,995	18,870	51,918	73,065	181,696

Source: Hardjono, 1977, p. 32.

3   genuine farmers, or possessing other skills;

4   aged between 20 and 40;

5   with a family/legally married;

6   of sound health;

7   of some religious persuasion;

8   of good conduct;

9   with a wife not more than three months' pregnant;

10 with members of their family: aged 6 months to 60
    years.

Transmigrants who had been members of the armed forces
were given concessions in the case of age (20-54 years)
and also marital status (already or not yet married)
(Soebiantoro, 1974, p. 37).
        The main projects during Repelita-I were spread
over all provinces (Hardjono, 1977, pp. 46 ff.).   In
Lampung the majority of the 52,377 migrants were settled
in the Way Abung and Panagaran projects.   Way Abung,
which was one of the selected projects in the Crash
Programme, faced several problems.   The soil started to
deterioraite in the oldest settlements as a result of the
continuous cultivation of cassava.   Attempts to overcome
this drawback by the introduction of Bimas were not very
successful because of the late supply of inputs such as
fertilisers as well as persistent drought and lack of
appropriate skills.   Disputes with local people and
private agricultural companies were another factor hinder-
ing the development of this project.   Since the area was
overcrowded as early as 1974, overpopulation presented
an additional problem.   Moreover, there were marketing
difficulties, as was also the case in Panagaran.   In both
projects village unit co-operatives were created as a
possible solution to marketing difficulties, but the lack of
managerial skills and capital made it impossible to break
the domination of the middlemen.   In the province of
South Sumatra one of the most successful projects was
developed in the Belitang area, which received 14,787
migrants, 49.3 per cent of the total number of migrants
established in the province.   Less successful was the Air
Beliti project under the Crash Programme, which was
bedevilled by land disputes with the local population.   In
the same province, two big tidal projects were established
in the Upang Delta and Cintamanis.   The first received

- 219 -

5,378 migrants, who settled satisfactorily. Nevertheless,
lack of skills and poor health conditions (a cholera out-
break in 1972 and persistent malaria) presented problems.
Furthermore, the acidity of the soil increased owing to
sedimentation and drainage difficulties, particularly in
Cintamanis. Only 6,135 migrants were settled in the
province of Bengkulu. In the remaining provinces of
Sumatra a total of 16,723 migrants were settled during
Repelita-I. The largest number (11,379) were sent to
Jambi. In this province the tidal projects in Riau
suffered from hasty preparation under the Crash
Programme, and in the tidal project of Teluk Kiambang
there were land disputes with local people and difficult
access to markets. In general, projects in West Sumatra
suffered from the selection of inappropriate sites, while in
Aceh the historical hostility towards migrants was the
main factor obstructing transmigration.

In Kalimantan, the province of East Kalimantan
received the largest number of migrants (9,340).
Although settlements were not very successful, the timber
boom offered work opportunities for transmigrants. The
province of South Kalimantan received 7,012 migrants, of
which 4,271 were placed in the tidal project of Barambai.
This project suffered from increasing acidity of the soil
due to bad drainage, and from persistent health problems.
The second main project was Tambarang, the development
of which was hindered by lack of access to markets and
difficulties in the supply of fertilisers and other inputs.
A total of 5,809 migrants went to the province of Central
Kalimantan, 83.3 per cent of them to the Permatang Tujuh
tidal project. This was more successful than Barambai,
but faced marketing problems due to the long distances
involved. West Kalimantan received only 4,421 migrants.
The most important project was the tidal project of Sei
Rusau, which absorbed most of the migrants. Like
Permatang Tujuh, it has been doing well, although access
to markets has been one of its major problems.

Of the 47,692 migrants transferred to the island of
Sulawesi, 20,102 went to the Luwu district in the
province of South Sulawesi. Although, in general, the
settlements made progress, difficulties persisted. The
most recent settlements suffered from inadequate
irrigation and a lack of fertilisers, but the worst problem
was the lack of access to markets, due to a deficient
transport and communications network in the province.
The creation of co-operatives as a means of ending the
control of middlemen proved ineffective. Two main
projects were established in the province of Central
Sulawesi for settling 15,074 migrants. One of them,
Lembontanara Tableland, was established in a very
isolated area. In all, 9,011 migrants went to the

province of South-east Sulawesi. In general, this province suffers from a lack of fertile soil, long dry seasons, and a bad communications infrastructure. Only 3,505 migrants settled in the province of North Sulawesi.

The number of transmigrants moving to other areas was very small during Repelita-I, i.e. 1,713 to Maluku and 485 to Irian Jaya.

At the end of Repelita-I 61 projects, including 103 village units, were under official guidance. But the results, as in previous periods, were disappointing. Only in the last two years was the target for transmigration reached. Settlements continued to suffer from the old problems. Accordingly, in 1972 a Basic Transmigration Act was elaborated, which attempted to define the modalities of state intervention in a clearer way in order to achieve greater efficiency through the centralisation and co-ordination of activities in the Ministry of Manpower, Transmigration and Co-operatives.

Transmigration received a new lease of life with Repelita-II. Integration and "regional development" constituted the new emphasis in transmigration, which according to the second development programme could contribute to "regional development" by supplying labour which is scarce in the Outer Islands, and increasing agricultural production. The new orientation of the transmigration programme aimed basically at transforming settlements into "growth centres" able to increase a spontaneous migratory flow (Hardjono, 1977, pp. 93-94).[1] In order to carry out this new programme, the Body for the Expansion of Development in Transmigration Areas was created by Presidential Decree No. 29 of 1974. Its main objective was the co-ordination, programming, implementation, and supervision of development in transmigration areas. It was expected that effective integration and centralisation of activities dealing with transmigration would be achieved.[2]

During the "New Order", and especially under Repelita-II, transmigration acquired a new political dimension. Since 1968, Kopkamtib (the Operational Command for the Restoration of Security and Order) has

---

1   In the next section we shall analyse the instruments that have been proposed for achieving this goal.

2   In addition, international agencies, such as USAID, UNDP, the World Bank, and the Asian Development Bank, as well as government experts (especially from the Federal Republic of Germany, the Netherlands, and the United Kingdom), assist the Indonesian Government in the programming and financing of transmigration.

viewed transmigration as the solution to the security problems posed by political prisoners.[1] This need has become more marked since 1976, when the government, under pressure of international opinion, announced its intention of releasing all prisoners under category B.[2] For this purpose transmigration camps have already been opened in Central and East Kalimantan. New camps are being constructed in North Sumatra and Sulawesi. In many cases the government has made the release of prisoners effectively conditional upon transmigration. Among the several criteria used for a prisoner to obtain release was the requirement that a job must be available for him. Given the fact that the majority of prisoners were originally from Java, where job opportunities are very limited, transmigration appeared as the only way to obtain a release.

The programmed number of migrants and their areas of destination in Repelita-II are shown in table 12. At a more detailed level only a few areas have been given priority during the period to which the table refers (Hardjono, 1977, pp. 46 ff). In Lampung, the northern area has been chosen because of its lower population density, especially the area close to the town of Menggala where the majority of migrants transferred to this province are expected to be settled. In South Sumatra, the selected area is the southern one, in the Pematang Panggang area, where dry farming projects are to be established. Transmigration in the province of Bengkulu is to be mainly focused on the extension of the successful Bukit Peninjauan project established in Repelita-I. In Jambi, transmigration is intended to be concentrated primarily on the development of tidal projects.

In West Kalimantan it is planned to settle migrants in existing projects (Sei Rasau and Kelang) as well as in new ones (Anjungan). Finally, the Luwu area, especially Mamuju and the north-west of South Sulawesi, has been selected in Sulawesi.

Towards the end of 1976, the objective of transmigrating 250,000 families during Repelita-II was reduced to 108,000 families in view of the poor results achieved in the first three years, namely 4,464 families for 1974-75,

---

[1] In view of the important political role given to transmigration by the Indonesian Government itself, it is somewhat odd that recent studies of transmigration have conspicuously overlooked this phenomenon.

[2] This includes people whom the Indonesian Government suspected of being "indirectly" involved in the 1965 events.

Table 12: Number of planned migrants by area
of destination, 1974-75 to 1978-79

Area	Families	%
Kalimantan	42,500	17.0
Sulawesi	57,000	22.9
Sumatra	146,000	58.4
Lampung	(36,000)	(14.4)
South Sumatra	(30,000)	(12.0)
Jambi	(54,500)	(21.8)
Rest of Sumatra	(25,500)	(10.2)
Other islands	4,500	1.8
Total	250,000	100.0

Source: Suratman and Guiness, op. cit., p. 87.

12,109 families for 1975-76 and 13,910 families for 1976-77
(Suratman and Guiness, 1977, p. 88).[1]   Moreover, old
problems persist and hinder the successful development of
settlements.   Thus, Suratman and Guiness have pointed
out three main deficiencies in the present operation of
transmigration.   First, superficial pre-settlement surveys
lead to a bad selection of sites;   second, selection of
migrants is not rigorous, and they often lack the skills
necessary for the development of the settlements;   third,
the state does not provide enough guidelines and support
in the initial phase of the settlements (ibid., pp. 90 ff).
But these authors have identified as the major source of
the failure of transmigration policies during the first
years of Repelita-II the lack of co-ordination between the
three levels on which the Body for the Expansion of
Development in Transmigration Areas operates (ibid., p.
88).   As can be seen, transmigration policies continue to
be a failure.

---

[1] It is unfortunate that the figures were not given
in terms of the total number of transmigrants in 1976-77.
Although there was a big increase in that year the
number was still far short of the target figure.

Summary and Conclusions

Transmigration was originally defined as a welfare policy to cope with the potential social dangers of the tremendous impoverishment of the landless peasantry under the impact of colonial rule. The relative success of its implementation in some fields was on the whole due to the benefits which accrued to colonial capital. It was only in the 1930s, with the crisis in the plantations in the Outer Islands, that transmigration could fulfil the function of supplying a relative surplus population.

In the first post-colonial period, especially during the period of "Guided Democracy", the interests of the landless were reflected to a certain extent. But for the Javanese landless peasantry (the main class involved in the transmigration process), the struggle was not focused on transmigration but on agrarian reform. Moreover, during Sukarno's period transmigration acquired a heavy ideological connotation. The national view of Sukarno, and the inclusion of "security" and "national unity" as goals to be achieved, made transmigration a confusing issue during this period. Owing to the absence of pressure by the landless, intervention by the state through transmigration lacked the force necessary to enable it to carry out an effective policy, as has been noted.

The quantity of labour absorbed by accumulation in Indonesia has always been limited. Our analysis of labour absorption for the current period, where accumulation has been relatively high, has shown these limits. The geographical distribution of population within the Indonesian archipelago has not significantly changed. In 1920, 72.8 per cent of a total population of 49.3 million were located in Java, Madura, and Bali. In 1971, the total population had risen to 119.2 million, of whom 64.2 per cent were still located in these three islands.[1] Migration in general, and transmigration specifically from Java, Madura and Bali to the rest of the archipelago, has therefore not resulted in a balanced geographical distribution of population.[2]

---

[1] The result has been an increase of population densities. Thus in 1920 Java and Madura had a density of 264 inhabitants per square kilometre. In 1971, this figure amounted to 574, exceeding 1,000 in some areas. For Bali the increase was from 161 in 1920 to 361 in 1971.

[2] Moreover, this migratory flow has been partially neutralised by the reverse flow, i.e. migration from the Outer Islands to Java, and by the return of migrants.

Official acceptance of this obvious failure has led to a reconsideration of transmigration in recent years. The new orientation of transmigration aims at making it a part of "regional development". This approach is still, however, largely theoretical. Present state intervention is basically similar to that of previous periods. The persistence of old problems and the subsequent failure of transmigration policies during the first years of Repelita-II have been mentioned above. As Arndt and Sundrum point out:

> "...although there has been a notable increase in the scale of the official transmigration programme in recent years, and some improvement in its administration, the pattern of transmigration has remained fundamentally unchanged. Integration of transmigration into regional development has largely remained an abstract aspiration" (Arndt and Sundrum, 1977, p. 75).

Nevertheless, several important features of the new orientation are worth noting. In the first place, it seems that the transmigration authorities are tending to abolish the distinction between officially sponsored migrants and the partly sponsored migrants. In this context, Suratman and Guiness emphasise the importance of giving more support to spontaneous migrants, whose performance has in fact proved more successful than that of official migrants (Suratman and Guiness, 1977, pp. 99-101). Second, the new orientation aims at developing settlement areas as "growth centres", able to attract a permanent spontaneous migratory flow. In order to achieve such a goal several measures have been suggested.

First, development areas should group about 5,000 families distributed among 10 village units. This would result in economies of scale in such areas as land clearing, road construction, transport services, and processing of agricultural products (Hardjono, 1977, p. 94). Second, each settlement should be administratively integrated into a local district. This would reduce tensions between migrants and local population (ibid., p. 94). As a consequence of these measures, transmigration

According to the 1971 population census, 1.96 million persons born in Java were resident in the Outer Islands while 0.65 million persons born in the Outer Islands were resident in Java (Arndt and Sundrum, 1977, p. 78).

would have more economic impact on the local economy. Actually "the intention", as Hardjono says, "is that the development of the area will be encouraged, for the agriculture-oriented transmigration projects will be able to provide foodstuffs required in non-farming undertakings" (ibid., pp. 94-95). The switch to non-subsistence agriculture requires two additional measures. On the one hand there must be a change in favour of dry crops, for which the Outer Islands are more suitable. This does not mean the abandonment of irrigated rice production, however, but this should mainly be restricted to tidal projects. Suratman and Guiness advocate the adoption of the Bimas programme, which favours dry-crop farming and the establishment of processing industries (Suratman and Guiness, 1977, p. 95).

This way of conceiving the new orientation of the transmigration programme has been criticised by Arndt and Sundrum. For these authors, transmigration as a land settlement programme would amount only to "providing a better livelihood for a few thousand impoverished Javanese farm families each year" (Arndt and Sundrum, 1977, p. 76). While transmigration can indeed be a means of providing labour and thus contributing to "regional development", the use of such labour should not be for agricultural development alone but also for developing infrastructure. According to Arndt and Sundrum the development of an adequate infrastructure is the key to any successful "regional development" in Indonesia. In this sense they propose that the "the employment opportunities offered to transmigrants should be wage employment on public works projects in the provinces of the Outer Islands" (ibid., p. 86).

However, in both these strategies "regional development" is considered to be a key element. But "regional development" means basically an attempt to extend and to foster accumulation in the Outer Islands.

From this point of view, transmigration in the first case (the official view supported by Hardjono and Suratman and Guiness) would mean mobilisation of supernumerary population from Java as labour for agricultural production in the Outer Islands. As regards the nature of the production, two solutions seem possible. Under the first solution settlements would be annexed to the existing primary export sectors. Transmigration projects could then perform a twofold function. On the one hand, transmigrants could provide foodstuffs in order to ensure the adequate supply of labour in the primary export sectors. This would imply the selling of these foodstuffs at the lowest possible price in order to keep wages as low as possible. Transmigrants would then be placed at a disadvantage in the market and their position as petty producers would therefore remain very weak and unstable. A second solution mentioned by Hardjono would imply the settlement of transmigrants as petty producers of rubber, oil palm, and coconut palm. Projects would be located adjacent to estates, as has been proposed for southern Sumatra. According to Hardjono, "the estate would provide not just processing facilities but also extension services and marketing facilities, as well as general management" (Hardjono, 1977, pp. 95-96). But estates are not charity institutions. Two processes might occur in this kind of situation. On the one hand, settled transmigrants might be exploited if they were not able to develop as petty producers by themselves. On the other hand, transmigrants might be able to become pettty producers, but still depend on the estates for the supply of inputs, services, processing, marketing, etc. In other words, the control of capital would remain external.

In the case of the alternative proposed by Arndt and Sundrum it is quite easy to understand the function of transmigration vis-à-vis accumulation. Migrants might remain economically weak initially but would not be controlled directly by private capital. The state would employ labour to create the general conditions for a broader accumulation than at present exists in the Outer Islands.

The first strategy implies the reinforcement of the existing accumulation process (i.e. primary export) in the Outer Islands, while the second pursues a more self-centred process. For Arndt and Sundrum industrialisation can take place in the Outer Islands only if the general conditions for accumulation are fulfilled. This would create more possibilities of labour absorption, although it is doubtful that transmigration could be the appropriate means for supplying the required labour.

Chapter 7

POPULATION DISTRIBUTION POLICIES AND
PLANNED RESETTLEMENT IN NEPAL

By V.B.S. Kansakar*

Introduction

Nepal can be ecologically divided into three regions:
(a) the Himalayan or the mountainous region; (b) the
sub-Himalayan or the hill region; and (c) the Terai
region. The mountainous region lies between 4,800 and
8,800 metres above sea level. It has an alpine-type
climate and is sparsely populated. The main economic
activity in this region is livestock production with limited
agriculture. The hill region lies between 1,800 and
4,800 metres above sea level, and has a temperate climate.
There are some fertile river valleys in this region such as
Kathmandu and Pokhara. The area is densely populated
per unit of cropped land, and farming is carried out by
terracing the slopes of the hills. The Terai region
covers the vast east-west stretch of low-level fertile
Gangetic plains. It has a subtropical climate. Thus the
three regions have distinct climatic and resource endow-
ment attributes, influencing the types of economic activity
and consequently the levels of living of the people. The
hills and the mountain areas are relatively weak economically as compared to the Terai. On account of the
intensive nature of farming in the hills, continued over-
exploitation has resulted in declining marginal
productivity and wide-scale ecological damage to the
environment.

Population pressure in the hills has continued to
increase, although the growth rate has been declining.
In the past, the hills have exported their population both
seasonally and permanently to the Terai as well as to
India. The distribution of the population by geographic
region for the census years 1952-54, 1961, and 1971 is
shown in table 1. The data show that the mountain and
hill regions, which cover about 71 per cent of the total
land area, contained about 53 per cent of the total population of the country in 1971. The proportion of the

    * Centre for Economic Development and Adminis-
tration, Tribhuvan University, Kathmandu.

Table 1: Population distribution by geographic region, 1952-54, 1961 and 1971

Region	% of total area	% of population		
		1952-54	1961	1971
Mountain and hill	71.4	60.3	58.7	53.4
Western	29.5	18.4	18.0	15.9
Central	23.7	21.2	20.7	19.9
Eastern	18.1	20.7	20.0	17.6
Kathmandu valley	0.5	5.0	4.9	5.4
Inner Terai	9.8	5.8	5.7	7.3
Western	1.6	1.1	1.0	1.5
Central	4.7	2.4	2.6	3.6
Eastern	3.5	2.3	2.1	2.2
Terai	18.3	28.9	30.7	33.9
Western	5.6	2.8	2.9	3.7
Central	2.4	4.2	4.3	4.5
Eastern	10.3	21.9	23.5	25.7
All	100.0	100.0	100.0	100.0
Rural		97.1	96.4	96.0
Urban		2.9	3.6	4.0

Source: Central Bureau of Statistics, reports of the censuses for 1952-54, 1961 and 1971.

population living in these regions, however, had recorded a steady decline from 60.3 per cent in 1952-54 to 58.7 and 53.4 per cent in 1961 and 1971 respectively. The Kathmandu valley, which is actually part of the mountain and hill regions, has in all census years contained about 5 per cent of the total population in less than 1 per cent of the total land area.

The inner Terai covers about 10 per cent of the total land area, but in 1971 sustained only 7.3 per cent of the total population, compared to 5.8 per cent in 1952-54. The Terai region consists of only 18.3 per cent of the total land area, but the population of the region as a proportion of the total population has recorded a steady increase from 28.9 per cent in 1952-54 to 30.7 per cent in 1961 and 33.9 per cent in 1971.

The inter-regional differences in population distribution are interesting. This pattern has been associated with the rainfall pattern and consequently with the fertility of the soil. Besides the geographic reasons, the tempo and scale of developmental activities have also shaped the pattern of population distribution. In the past, development activities were concentrated mostly in the central and eastern Terai, not in the western Terai or in the mountains and hills (except the Kathmandu valley). Further, the eradication of malaria in the Terai has led to the massive internal migration of the hill people to this region. In addition, the influx of foreign nationals into the Terai areas has also increased in the wake of growing economic activity in the central and eastern Terai towns and the hinterlands.

Table 1 also shows that the proportion of urban population to the total population has increased from 2.9 per cent in 1952-54 to 3.6 per cent in 1961 and 4 per cent in 1971. The problems of urbanisation in Nepal are not so serious as in most other developing countries, however. The level of urbanisation in Nepal is very low because, being a predominantly agricultural economy, the country lacks the basic resources, infrastructure, and technology needed for industrialisation and consequent urbanisation. Besides, the movement of people from the mountains and hills to the Terai has always been in search of amenable land rather than employment in the urban areas.

The massive movement of population from the hills to the Terai has been characterised by large-scale forest encroachment and resulting deforestation. Concern over reckless deforestation prompted the government to start planned resettlement projects in different parts of the country, with the expectation that this would to some extent solve the problem of settling landless farmers, and help protect the valuable forests from illicit felling.

The purpose of this study is threefold. First, to examine the policies and programmes which have influenced population movements in Nepal. Second, to assess the performance and impact of planned resettlement projects. And third, to suggest measures for regulating the flows of internal migration.

Land Development and Population Movements prior to 1951

During the second half of the eighteenth century and the early nineteenth century, the movement of population in Nepal was conditioned by the prevalence of malaria in the areas up to the altitude of 1,200 metres above sea level and the constant fear of invasion resulting from the ever-increasing dominance of the British East India Company in the Indian sub-continent. As the area up to 1,200 metres above sea level was malarious, more than three-quarters of the population was concentrated in the hill areas, constituting more than four-fifths of the country's total area. The low-lying parts of the country, i.e. the Terai and the inner Terai, were sparsely populated, inhabited by the malaria-immune indigenous ethnic groups such as the Tharu, Dhimal, Kumhal, and Rajbanshi, who had pocket settlements amidst dense forests. The ever-increasing population of the hills thus had no recourse other than to move along the hill areas in search of cultivable land. However, as the hill areas were inhabited by different tribal ethnic groups, each having dominance in their own area, the movement of the hill people along the hills was restricted. They had either to reclaim and cultivate the higher slopes of the hills, or to emigrate to India in search of better economic opportunities. The former led to an ecological imbalance which resulted in soil erosion, floods and land-slides, and the latter to a large-scale drain of the more productive labour force, which resulted in the deterioration of agriculture in the hills (Kansakar, 1980, p. 1).

When the government perceived the threat of invasions resulting from the ever increasing dominance of the British East India Company in the Indian sub-continent, it discouraged the reclamation of the low-lying areas in the south. In order to supplement the food requirement of the densely populated Kathmandu valley, a large part of the inner Terai forest, adjoining the Kathmandu valley, was reclaimed for cultivation by people from the hills, who used to work in the fields during the day and return to the malaria-immune hill slopes in the evening. After the Anglo-Nepalese war of 1814, however, the area was allowed to revert to natural forest for strategic reasons, since it provided a strong line of defence against any invasion from the south (Kirkpatrick, 1811, p. 17). The government adopted a policy that all land belonged to the state and any change in its use could only be made with the government's approval. This ban on alienation and reclamation affected labour mobility and hampered progress in opening up new areas for reclamation and settlement to alleviate the deteriorating economic conditions of the hill people.

The large-scale recruitment of the hill people for the task of territorial expansion resulted in the reduction of agricultural output. Moreover, the expanding size of the kingdom and the increase in military activity necessitated the introduction of the jhara system (compulsory or unpaid labour for the transportation of military and other supplies over long distances, and for the construction, repair and maintenance of roads and bridges). This in turn adversely affected agricultural productivity in the hills and resulted in a further loss of revenue.

In order to increase the revenue from land to meet the increasing military expenditure, the government introduced kut rent, according to which the cultivator had to pay a fixed quantity of farm output, or a fixed sum of cash, to the landlord, irrespective of his actual output. In order to maintain its revenue at the required level, the government raised the kut rent exorbitantly (Regmi, 1971, p. 88). Moreover, landlords were empowered to evict tenants refusing to pay higher rents. Higher rents, tenurial insecurity, mass rural indebtedness, and the jhara system made agriculture less attractive and encouraged many hill people to emigrate to India in search of better economic opportunities.

The modification of the Anglo-Nepalese peace treaty of 1816 empowered the British Government to raise three regiments of the Nepalese hill people for its army (Morris, 1928, p. 50). This provided a further impetus for hill people to emigrate to India for recruitment in the British army. Though the Nepal Government was in principle against the recruitment of its people into a foreign army, it could not check the emigration of the Nepalese from the hills even with such strict measures as the confiscation of property. Foreseeing the difficulties of getting the Nepalese hill people for its army, the British Government established Gurkha settlements in the hill areas of India, such as Dharmashala, Bakloh, Dehradun, Darjeeling and Shillong, to make recruitment easier (United Kingdom, HMSO, 1965, p. 61). After 1886, Nepal relaxed some of the measures taken earlier and the British Government discouraged Nepalese settlements in India. But subsequently, the reclamation of the forest areas of Assam for cultivation and the practice of granting free rice plots to the plantation workers on the tea estates have considerably encouraged Nepalese hill people to emigrate to Assam (Davis, 1951, p. 117).

As the main source of revenue for the government was land, the government could not maintain the restriction on reclamation of the Terai and the inner Terai lands. It therefore adopted several measures such as forced labour, remission of rents, etc., to bring large areas of the Terai under cultivation to meet the financial requirements of the state and of the royal family. But this sort of land development policy met with little success because of the problems of adaptation experienced by the hill people in the Terai and the absence of land ownership and tenancy rights.

In 1846, the Rana family came to power by coup d'état. To help ensure its survival, the regime adopted measures to confiscate the birta lands (where land ownership was alienated from the state in favour of private individuals). In recognition of the assistance rendered by Nepal in quelling the 1857 Mutiny in India by supplying a 12,000 strong army, the British Government returned to Nepal the Qudh Terai ceded to India in the Anglo-Nepalese war of 1814. Prime Minister Jung Bahadur, the first Rana Prime Minister, wanted to reclaim the new area to appropriate income for his family and supporters, and for the state. However, realising the difficulties of reclaiming and cultivating the land in the Terai, he made provision in the first legal code of the country entitling alienation of land through sale or purchase to the foreign nationals residing in Nepal (Government of Nepal, Ministry of Law and Justice, p. 35). Thus the reclamation of the Terai forests for cultivation started, resulting in immigration of Indians in large numbers as well as the purchase of land by Indians living across the India-Nepal border. However, the new measures had no impact on the redistribution of the hill people in the Terai. They continued to emigrate to India for recruitment in the British army, since the recruitment policy favoured Gurkhas coming from the Nepalese hill areas as compared with those from the Gurkha settlements in India. The reclamation in the Terai, however, was mainly confined to the contiguous parts of India, which were opened up from the Indian side, while those lying north of the Indian forests could not be reclaimed owing to the high incidence of malaria (Kansakar, 1974, p. 129).

Nepal had to face a problem of manpower drain during the First World War when 200,000 Nepalese, representing 20 per cent of the eligible male population, actively took part in the war (Bishop, 1952, p. 101). The large-scale emigration of able-bodied males resulted in low agricultural production and a shortage of food. The attempt by the government to call back Nepalese released from the army met with little success because a large number of them preferred to stay in India (United Kingdom, HMSO, 1965, p. 131).

After the First World War, the need to redistribute the population by reclamation of the forest areas of the Terai was realised, partly to solve the problem of population pressure in the hills and partly to check the emigration of surplus landless manpower to India (Collier, 1928, p. 251). Accordingly, the first attempts to reclaim the Terai and the inner Terai forest areas for cultivation and resettlement were made in the districts of Morang, Mahottari, Sarlahi, Chitwan, Surkhet, Kailali and Kanchanpur (Landon, 1928, p. 161). Because of the difficult conditions in the Terai, the hill people did not dare to resettle there, so it only benefited the Indian forest contractors, who procured the cheap sal tree (shorea rebusta) needed for railway sleepers in India, and Indian immigrants in the districts of Mahottari and Sarlahi.

In 1936, Nepal initiated the development of organised industries in the Morang district, and the Second World War provided a considerable boost to these industries. As the Nepalese people lacked the appropriate skills to run such organised industries, the required labour, including management, was provided by immigrants from India. Even today Indians constitute the bulk of the labour force in Nepalese industries, particularly in the Terai. Thus all attempts towards industrialisation actually benefited Indians rather than Nepalese.

During the Second World War, the Japanese invasion of Burma led a large number of Nepalese living in Burma to flee towards Nepal. The British Government established camps in Motihari (Bihar State) for their temporary rehabilitation (United Kingdom, HMSO, op. cit., p. 31). Some of the Nepalese, however, entered Nepal and settled permanently in Dharan and Butawal in the Terai, but most of them returned to Burma after the war.

Thus, prior to the institution of a democratic government in 1951, a clear-cut and effective policy on population redistribution within the country was lacking. The major interest of the government in land development in the Terai and the inner Terai was primarily its importance as a major source of revenue rather than the alleviation of population pressure in the hills. In the absence of employment opportunities outside agriculture, an overwhelming majority of migrants went to India (Kansakar, 1978).

Land Development and Population
Movements after 1951

With the institution of democracy in 1951, a large number of Nepalese exiled in India during the Rana regime, as well as other Nepalese domiciled there, came back to Nepal, full of hopes for a better future. The government adopted two strategies to deal with the problem of population redistribution: the planned settlement of people in the new frontier areas, and a change in the land tenure system.

(a) Planned resettlement programme

The monsoon flood havoc of 1954 and the resulting landslides in the hills made it urgently necessary for the government to rehabilitate the victims, and to redistribute the landless population in the new areas. At the beginning of the First Five-Year Plan in 1956, the Rapti Valley Development Programme was launched in Chitwan district with the aim of relieving the pressure of population in some neighbouring areas, rehabilitating the landless peasants, and partially solving the food problem of the Kathmandu valley (Government of Nepal, 1956, pp. 70-71). But the full implementation of the programme had to wait until 1958, when the malaria eradication programme was launched in the Chitwan valley.

The Rapti Valley Development Programme was the first systematic attempt at land development in Nepal. By the end of the Five-Year Plan (1960), the project had distributed 27,759 hectares of land among 5,233 families. Of this only 37 per cent was cultivated.

Only Nepalese citizens were entitled to purchase land in the project. The order of priority when selling the land was as follows:

1 wage labourers with experience in agriculture and working in the development region, or peasants made landless by floods;

2 diligent persons of good character and health with experience in agriculture;

3 diligent persons of good character and health with education in agriculture;

4 government employees, whether in service or retired.

The eradication of malaria in the Rapti valley and subsequently in other parts of the country led to the large-scale migration of the hill people to the Terai and the inner Terai in quest of cultivable land for resettlement (table 2). The result was reckless deforestation and encroachment in the Terai and inner Terai forests. Migration from the hills to the Terai and the inner Terai, once considered to be the solution to the ever-increasing population problem of the hills, turned out to be a serious problem threatening the conservation of the valuable forest wealth of the country.

Table 2: Population growth of Nepal by regions, 1961-71

Region	Population		Growth rate
	1961	1971	
Eastern Hills	1,880,535	2,061,471	0.92
Western Hills	1,946,502	2,277,831	1.58
Far Western Hills	1,698,083	1,867,586	0.96
Hill (total)	5,525,120	6,206,888	1.17
Eastern Terai	2,213,282	2,948,918	2.91
Western Terai	400,357	595,110	4.04
Far western Terai	271,551	425,242	4.58
Terai (total)	2,885,190	3,969,271	4.05
Eastern inner Terai	193,666	260,031	2.99
Central inner Terai	250,423	393,732	4.63
Western inner Terai	98,607	153,472	4.52
Inner Terai (total)	542,696	807,235	4.05
Kathmandu valley	459,990	572,589	2.21
Nepal	9,412,996	11,555,983	2.07

Source: Central Bureau of Statististics: Population Census of Nepal, 1961 and 1971.

The Rapti Valley Development Project was also marked by malpractices in the distribution of land. As a result landless peasants and flood victims could not get land in the project. Moreover, the same plot of land was often allotted in the name of several persons, which resulted in disputes over land ownership rights.

To control the alarming devastation and destruction of the Terai and the inner Terai, and to rehabilitate the landless peasants of the hills, the government decided to create an autonomous body to run the rehabilitation programme as a joint stock company. Thus the Nepal Punarvas Company (Nepal Resettlement Company) was established in 1964. Among the major objectives of the resettlement programme of the company were:

1 to bring fallow and uneconomic forest land under cultivation through resettlement;

2 to reduce the pressure of population on cultivated land in the hills;

3 to remove the forest encroachers from protected forest areas and resettle them elsewhere in an organised way;

4 to distribute the excess land available through the implementation of the land reform programme.

The first planned resettlement project was launched in Nawalpur to the west of Chitawan. The provision of land at a nominal price and the availability of social and economic infrastructure such as schools, drinking water, roads, agricultural extension services, and credit facilities all within the project area became an important allurement for the hill people (Kansakar, 1979, pp. 36-37). They began to migrate to the resettlement project in large numbers, and the project could not keep pace with the demand for land through forest clearing. Those who had come to Nawalpur in the hope of acquiring land encroached on forests in and around the project areas, and the project had in turn to involve itself in resettling these encroachers. In order to cope with this forest encroachment, the Resettlement Company started its second project in Khajura in Banke district in 1966-67. However, this project could not solve the encroachment problem either.

At the beginning of 1969, His Majesty's Government established the Resettlement Department with the objective of organising land resettlement on a massive scale, and the Resettlement Company was put under it. Initially, the department was attached to the Ministry of Food and Agriculture, but at the end of 1977 it was transferred to the Ministry of Forestry. Though the main task of the Resettlement Department was to deal with the co-ordination and policy of the resettlement programme, it was also involved in small resettlement projects mainly concerned with resettling political sufferers.

However, the programme implemented by the Department was largely ineffective in meeting the objectives of resettling landless peasants and controlling forest encroachment. As it was realised that there was nevertheless an immediate need for controlling and regulating disorganised resettlement, and for resettling genuine landless peasants, in 1973 the government came forward with a new resettlement programme. The main features of the new programme were:

1 resettlement projects would be executed on the basis of the experiences and results of the resettlement programme run by the Resettlement Company;

2 the land distributed under the programme must be cultivated by the owner or his family;

3 the land allotted to the settler should not be transferable through sale, donation, etc., for a specified period of time;

4 no new land should be allotted to a family which had previously received land;

5 co-ordination committees would be set up to ensure co-operation in every sphere of the resettlement programme;

6 the use of improved agricultural techniques would be encouraged through the district agricultural offices;

7 the definition of the household would include a family consisting of at least two members above 16 years of age;

8 settlers would have to pay land revenue after five years from the period of allotment of land;

9 the price of land (Rs. 300 per bigha; 1 bigha = 0.7 hectares) would be payable in instalments after four years from the period of allotment;

10 a land ownership certificate would be issued for easy identification.

So as to control disorganised settlement, each encroacher family was only entitled to 1.5 bighas of land, as against 3 bighas for the settlers under the Resettlement Programme, and the price of the land was Rs. 600 as against Rs. 300. Moreover, the encroachers had to pay the price of the land from the second year, and land revenue from the third year of resettlement, as against the fourth and fifth years respectively in the case of settlers under the Resettlement Programme.

(i) Selection of resettlers

When the Resettlement Company started its first project in Nawalpur, the project manager was empowered to select the resettlers. When scrutinising the authenticity of the landless persons, the project officials usually relied on the information provided by the applicants themselves. With the Resettlement Department projects neither the Department nor the resettlement officials were empowered to select the settlers. Instead resettlement of political sufferers was carried out on the basis of the list of political sufferers provided by the Home Ministry.

Since 1973, the power of the project managers to select settlers has been curtailed. The Company has now adopted a policy of resettling those applicants who have been duly certified and recommended by the concerned Chief District Officer (CDO) as eligible candidates for resettlement. According to the new policy, the application of the settler has to pass through several stages, including the District Land Revenue Office, to ascertain whether the applicant has any landholding registered in his name.

(ii) Size of the allotted plot of land

In the first resettlement project in Nawalpur, each settler family was given 4 bighas of land, and the same was the case with the Department projects. In 1971, the allotment of land to the resettlers was reduced to 3 bighas. Later on it was further reduced to 1.5 bighas for families consisting of more than five members and 1 bigha for families consisting of less than five members. However, in a recent resettlement project to be implemented in Kanchanpur with a loan from the International Development Agency (IDA), the size of the plot of land allotted to settlers has been fixed at 2.25 bighas.

The size of the plot allotted to the forest encroachers resettled by the department went down from 4 bighas in the beginning to 3 bighas in 1972. In 1973, it was reduced to 1.5 bighas for encroacher families. However, on protest from politicians as well as from encroachers, the government then declared that an encroacher family would get land to the extent to which it had encroached, providing it did not exceed more than 3 bighas. This policy benefited those who had encroached on large areas. Realising the wide disparities in the distribution of land under this policy, however, the government later reverted to the policy of allotting 1.5 bighas of land to each encroacher family, irrespective of the amount of land reclaimed through forest encroachment. More recently, the allotment of land to forest encroachers has been reduced to 1 bigha in the case of families consisting of less than five members.

(iii) Price of land

To begin with, the price of land in Company projects was fixed at Rs. 250 a bigha. In July 1973, this was raised to Rs. 300 a bigha. The price was to be paid in instalments within 10 years, beginning from the fourth year of resettlement. Settlers were exempted from land tax (land revenue) for four years.

The price of land in Department projects in the initial stages was Rs. 100 a bigha for all types of settlers. In 1973, it was raised to Rs. 600 per bigha for forest encroachers, and Rs. 300 per bigha for other settlers. The payment had to be completed in instalments within six years from the time of resettlement, starting from the fourth year. In 1973, this period was extended to 10 years. Though the period of full repayment was also 10 years for forest encroachers, they had to start paying instalments from the second year of their resettlement. Regarding land tax, the exemption period was four years for settlers other than forest encroachers, but only two years for the latter.

(iv) Land ownership, alienation, and fragmentation of allotted land

In Company projects, land ownership certificates are conferred after 10 years. During this period, alienation of land ownership and fragmentation are prohibited. In the event of the death of the owner of the land, the land ownership title is transferred to the senior member of the household or to the person referred to in the will of the deceased as the heir apparent. A settler is not entitled to an ownership certificate until he has paid the price of the land, land revenue, and any loan taken from the co-operatives and agricultural development bank.

In Department projects, settlers are given a land ownership certificate and a plot of land immediately. Initially, alienation and fragmentation of land were prohibited for five years, and even after five years a settler was not entitled to alienate or fragment land so long as he had not repaid its price. Since 1973, all types of settlers have been debarred from alienating and fragmenting land for 10 years.

(v) Effectiveness of the resettlement programme

The planned resettlement programme to settle land-less families has not been effectively implemented since its inception (Kansakar, 1979, pp. 249-280). It is widely recognised that there has been malfeasance in the distribution of land under the resettlement programme, and that the majority of landless households have been deprived of the opportunities for resettlement in the Company projects. In the completed project of Nawalpur nearly 50 per cent of the original grantees of land under the project have sold their land and gone elsewhere. Of the remaining grantees a large number have already sold a portion of their land. It shows clearly that the programme has benefited the unscrupulous elements rather than the genuine landless peasants.

The spatial location of both the Company and Department projects has a direct bearing on the effectiveness of the programme. Because of their locationally disadvantageous position, the programme has not been able to cultivate a sense of sentimental attachment to the allotted land among settlers in the projects.

The geographic location of the Company projects along the India-Nepal border has posed several problems, such as the frequent encounters of the settlers with bandits and wild animals. Traditionally, the areas along both sides of the India-Nepal border are noted for banditry, and neither Nepal nor India has been able to solve this problem. The forests on the Indian side have become safe hideouts for the bandits, and resettlement projects located in such areas are therefore more prone to banditry. Moreover, the wild animals from the Indian forests usually invade the resettlement farms and destroy standing crops. In such an insecure situation it is hard to expect that settlers will stay permanently in the resettlement projects.

Most of the resettlement projects (both Company and Department) are surrounded by old settlements of the indigenous people (usually the aboriginal Tharu, Kumhal, Dhimal and Rajbansi). Topographically, the former are located at a higher elevation than the latter. As such most of the resettlement sites are beyond the reach of canal irrigation and thus unsuitable for cultivation. Besides the lack of irrigation facilities, the problem of drinking water is also acute in the settlement areas.

Apart from the Nawalpur and Banke projects, all the Company projects are located in inaccessible areas. Good approach roads to and from the resettlement sites are usually lacking. The difficulty of access to important market centres and townships has posed two problems. First, the settlers have not been able to get reasonable prices for their farm products. Second, during the rainy season it is very difficult for them to obtain their daily necessities.

The resettlement programme from its very inception seriously lacked well-defined criteria for the selection of settlers. In the absence of well-established selection criteria, there were cases of distribution of land by the project officials to their families, relatives, and favourites. The adoption of a new policy by the Company in 1973 of resettling only those applicants who have been duly certified and recommended by the concerned Chief District Officer (CDO) as eligible candidates for resettlement has also been ineffective in selecting genuine landless and needy peasants.

When a cadastral survey was recently conducted in the completed project of Nawalpur to confer land ownership certificates on the resettlers, a large number of claimants, both settlers and non-settlers, emerged. It indicated that there had been considerable alienation of project land through sale or purchase, although this was not supposed to be permissible within 10 years or before receiving the land ownership certificates. Of the 50 per cent of original settlers still residing in the project area, very few families have 4 bighas of land, most of them already having sold a portion of their land.

One of the main objectives of the planned resettlement programme was to increase agricultural production in the resettlement projects through improved agricultural techniques. For this purpose, the projects were provided with agricultural extension services to enable the resettlers to adopt such techniques. Despite these facilities, agricultural development in the Company projects is not remarkable as compared to the surrounding older areas of cultivation. Several factors have been responsible for the failure in achieving increased agricultural production:

1 As most of the resettlement projects are located on ground higher than the surrounding old cultivation areas, irrigation through canals from the rivers is not feasible. The intensity of cultivation in the resettlement projects is therefore very low compared to the surrounding areas.

2 The quality of land in the resettlement projects is not good compared to the surrounding low lands.

3 The settlers do not get adequate loans and credit in time. In such a situation, they have to take

recourse to borrowing from moneylenders at exorbitantly high rates of interest.

4   The inaccessibility of the projects, coupled with the absence of marketing facilities, have been the main constraints on the settlers' securing reasonable prices for their farm produce. Usually they have to sell their produce at low prices to the moneylenders or the local grain traders. Low income from the farm produce adversely affects their ability to make further improvements on the land and consequently results in low productivity.

As agriculture is characterised by slack seasons, the settlers are unemployed or underemployed for a large part of the year. The resettlement programme has not been able to provide alternative employment opportunities outside agriculture during the slack seasons to generate additional income for the settlers. Moreover, with the gradual increase in the size of their families, the allotted land in the resettlement projects is not enough for families to maintain a livelihood. Fragmentation of land in the resettlement projects is likely to lead to the emergence of landless families or families with inadequate land within the settlement areas. The programme completely lacks a plan of action to deal with second-generation problems.

Thus the programme has not been able either to emerge as an example of agricultural development or to raise the standard of living of the settlers. The apathy on the part of the settlers in carrying out any agricultural development, and the discouraging environmental conditions of the resettlement projects, indicate that the settlers are just waiting to acquire land ownership certificates in order to sell the allotted land and go elsewhere.

(b) Land Reform Programme

With a view to ensuring the equitable distribution of cultivated land, Nepal introduced the Land Reform Programme in 1964. The Land Act of 1964 fixed the ceilings on landholdings in different regions, as shown in table 3.

Land in excess of the ceiling was acquired by the government on payment of compensation at prescribed rates. The Act also imposed ceilings on tenancy holdings: 2.7 hectares in the Terai and the inner Terai, 0.5 hectares in the Kathmandu valley, and 1 hectare in the hills. The acquired land was allotted on a priority basis to:

(i) sitting tenants;

(ii) farmers of the adjoining land;
(iii) other tillers of the area; and

(iv) the rest of the citizens of Nepal, in that order.

Table 3: Ceiling on landholdings in different regions (in hectares)

| Region | Agricultural land | Homestead | |
		Urban	Rural
Terai and inner Terai	16.4	0.67	2.01
Kathmandu valley	2.7	0.25	0.4
Hills	4.1	0.50	0.8

Source: Zaman (1974).

The Act abolished the jimindari system (the system of assigning the responsibility for land tax collection at the village level in the Terai) and set up government revenue offices. The land attached to the jimindars (revenue collecting agents) was converted to raikar land (state-owned land, but cultivated by the peasant in the capacity of a tenant). Tenancy rights were accorded to the actual cultivators and the rights of intermediaries between landlord and tenant were abolished through legal action on the grounds of reduction in the value or productivity of land, default in the payment of rent, or discontinued cultivation for one year. Tenancy rights were made inheritable, but not transferable or subdivisible.

The Act also provided for a fixed rent to be payable by the tenant to the landlord, which could never exceed 50 per cent of the gross annual product in the Terai, inner Terai and the hills, and about one-third in the Kathmandu valley. However, in 1968 the rent for all land, excluding the Kathmandu valley was reduced to half of the main crop, the quantity of which was also fixed depending on the quality of land.

The imposition of ceilings on landholdings broke down the hegemony of big landowners on land. It also did away with the unlimited acquisition of land through monetary investment. Land reform also accorded greater security of tenure to tenants as well as provision for sharing the major portion of the produce. However, the Land Reform Programme was largely ineffective in changing the agrarian structure (Regmi, 1976, pp. 197-223). It could not achieve its objective of ensuring an equitable distribution of cultivable land. As land reform was implemented in the absence of land records, the government had to depend on whatever information was provided by the landowners themselves. The landowners therefore took advantage of the situation. Moreover, since the land reform was enforced throughout the country in stages, landlords took anticipatory measures such as redistribution of land among their own family members and relatives, and registering themselves as cultivators by evicting tenants. The government could not therefore redeem the amount of surplus land it had expected. The land acquired was only 62,672 hectares, which was hardly sufficient to solve the problem of the landless peasants. The reform encouraged landowners to acquire land for personal cultivation and resulted in the progressive displacement of small farmers. Moreover, the legal provisions aimed at protecting tenancy rights were never effectively implemented.

A recent cadastral survey of the Terai and inner Terai districts revealed that, whereas about 88 per cent of the farming families have nearly 45 per cent of the total cultivated land (table 4), 3.2 per cent of the families account for nearly 30 per cent of the land.

Table 4: Distribution of farming families by the size of landholdings (in Terai and inner Terai)

Size of holdings (bighas)	No. of families	%	Area of landholding (bighas)	%	Average size of holdings (bighas)
0-4	676,661	88.10	719,951.01	44.96	1.06
4-10	66,996	8.66	408,954.29	25.56	6.15
10-15	13,288	1.73	170,955.69	10.68	12.87
15-20	9,778	1.27	192,094.22	12.00	19.65
20 and above	1,878	0.24	108,798.18	6.80	57.93

Source: Department of Land Reform.

The data show clearly that the objective of redistributing excess land made available through the implementation of land reform, and thereby redistributing population from the hill areas with a high labour-land ratio to the Terai and the inner Terai, with a low labour-land ratio, has simply not been achieved. The Land Reform Programme also envisaged the diverting of inactive capital and manpower from land to other sectors of the economy in order to accelerate the pace of national development. Accordingly, the Land Act prescribed that both tenants and landlords should make compulsory savings in kind from the major crops with a view to supplying agricultural credits and thus financing industrial and other enterprises. However, the scheme was suspended in 1969 because of large-scale defalcation. The Land Reform Programme thus could not change the overwhelming dependency of the population on agriculture.

Fifth Five-Year Plan (1976-80) and the
Population Distribution Policy

For the first time in the history of development planning in Nepal, population policy was included in the Fifth Plan. An explicit formulation of population policy was necessitated by three factors:

(a)   the rapid growth of population;

(b)   the uncontrolled migration from the hills to the Terai resulting in destruction and encroachment of forest land; and

(c)   the immigration of Indians in the Terai and their large-scale penetration in industry and trade, which made it difficult for the Nepalese to compete with them.

Of the five major elements of the population policy one was related to population control through family planning, but the remaining four were related to population mobility. The policies related to migration were:

1   to control immigration so as to minimise its role in the growth of population;

2   to regulate internal migration from the hills to the Terai and from rural to urban areas in a planned way;

3 to redistribute population within the Terai for optimum utilisation of resources; and

4 to establish small towns for gradual urbanisation in selected areas.

The policy concerning immigration was explicitly related to controlling the immigration of Indians, because Indian immigrants, according to the census of 1971, constituted 94.4 per cent of all foreign nationals, and 95.6 per cent of them were concentrated in the Terai alone. Because of the open border between Nepal and India, any attempt at providing employment opportunities for the Nepalese has in fact benefited Indian immigrants, who by virtue of their skill, capital, entrepreneurial ability, and adaptability have dominated employment and investment opportunities in the Terai. In the meantime their domination is gradually extending to other parts of the country as well, while it has become very difficult for the unskilled and semi-skilled Nepalese to compete with them. Thus, the only opportunity available for unskilled Nepalese hill people is to emigrate to India for recruitment in the army and police services, or to work as watchmen or household servants.

As regards internal migration, the lack of effective machinery and mechanisms have remained major constraints on the implementation of population distribution policies and programmes. Though the need to enhance employment opportunities outside the agricultural sector in order to absorb surplus manpower has been emphasised since the First Five-Year Plan, so far no concrete steps have been taken in this respect. In the absence of employment opportunities outside agriculture, land is seen as the only source of employment and income.

The large-scale migration of the hill people to the Terai inhabited by malaria-immune indigenous ethnic groups has resulted in hostility between the hill people and these groups. Several cases of displacement of the shy and simple-minded indigenous ethnic groups by the shrewd hill people have been reported.

The policy regarding regulation of migration from rural to urban areas has also been largely ineffective. Owing to the predominantly agricultural base of the urban centres in Nepal, they have not been able to generate adequate employment opportunities outside agriculture to attract population from the rural areas. Even where employment opportunities are available in the non-agricultural sectors, the immigration of skilled Indian labour has deterred the entry of the unskilled Nepalese rural population.

The policy of establishing the small towns needed for urbanisation so as to achieve regional development has remained stillborn. The growth of urban centres in Nepal is confined to the most accessible Terai belts while inaccessibility has deterred their growth in the hills and mountains. The growth of industry and trade has to some extent assisted in the development of urban centres in the Terai.

In view of the failure of the population policy to achieve its objectives, the Sixth Plan (1971-85) contains no explicit policy regarding migration. It only emphasises the need for the continuation of the resettlement programme while conserving adequate forest land for future use and ecological balance.

Summary and Conclusions

Prior to 1951, the hill people were compelled to emigrate to India in search of better economic opportunities. Several push factors and policies, including the prospects of joining the British army, encouraged this type of migration. There was no effective clear-cut policy on population redistribution in Nepal.

After 1951, with the institution of democracy, the government adopted a policy of settling the population in the frontier area and changed the land tenure system to accommodate the surplus agricultural labour force.

After the monsoon flood havoc of 1954, which caused severe landslides, the government had to rehabilitate the victims and redistribute the landless population in new areas. With malaria eradication in the Rapti valley in Chitawan district in 1958, large-scale migration of hill people to Chitawan took place.

On the basis of a survey of the Terai and the inner Terai for the location of possible resettlement areas, the Nepal Punarvas Company (Nepal Resettlement Company) was established in 1964, and the first resettlement project was launched in Nawalpur to the west of Chitawan. This project could not keep pace with the demand for land by the hill people, however.

In 1964, Nepal implemented a Land Reform Programme and fixed ceilings on landholdings in the Terai, inner Terai, Kathmandu valley, and hill regions. However, the excess land available for redistribution was not sufficient to solve the problem of landless peasants.

The launching of the second resettlement project in Khajina in Banke district in 1966-67 to cope with forest encroachment did not solve the problem either. In 1969, therefore, the government established a Resettlement Department to tackle the problem on a national scale. However, the scale of migration from the hills to the

Terai became so great that spontaneous migration over-shadowed the government's planned resettlement programme and forest encroachment became rampant.

In the Fifth Five-Year Plan period (1976-80) specific attention was given to population policy, including the problem of uncontrolled migration from the hills to the Terai areas.

Lack of effective machinery has been a major constraint on the implementation of internal migration policies in Nepal. Despite considerable investment, the land settlement programme has not been able to solve population distribution problems or to raise the standard of living of the settlers. The present indications are that the settlers are just waiting to acquire land owner-ship certificates before they sell their land and go elsewhere. If attempts are not made immediately to improve conditions in the settlement areas, the whole programme may emerge as a failure.

However, in view of the virtual non-existence of reclaimable land owing to the need for conserving forest resources, the prospects for redistributing population through land resettlement programmes are bleak. The solution to the growing population and unemployment in the hills has to be sought in situ, and within the agricul-tural sector. Improvements in the agrarian structure and rural economic conditions should be sought through changes in land tenure and landholding policies, a land consolidation programme, control of land fragmentation, provision of irrigation, introduction of co-operative farming, and development of cottage and small-scale industries.

One of the major constraints on agricultural develop-ment in Nepal, particularly in the hills, is the lack of accessibility to markets. Efforts should be made to improve agricultural marketing, either by developing marketing institutions or by providing incentives to the indigenous traders. Considering the inaccessibility of much of the hill areas, there is an urgent need for permanent link roads with important highways, towns, and settlements.

Chapter 8

SOCIO-ECONOMIC DEVELOPMENT AND RURAL-URBAN MIGRATION IN POLAND

By I. Frenkel*

Introduction

In Poland, during the past 35 years, the shift from agricultural to non-agricultural activities and the movement of people from rural to urban areas have been unprecedented. Although the main force behind these movements was rapid industrialisation, they were also influenced by the new political and socio-economic system created and developed after the Second World War.

The present study analyses migration within a macro-dynamic framework, focusing on the role of migration in the transformation of the Polish economy. In Poland, the shift from agricultural to non-agricultural activities often does not involve migration from rural to urban areas; these processes are therefore dealt with separately. The study is divided into three parts. The first part outlines the background and the main features of the post-war developmental strategy. Particular attention is given to the evolution of industrialisation, urbanisation, and agricultural policies which were largely responsible for massive population movements in Poland during this period. The second part discusses the effects of specific policies on the rate and pattern of migration. The final part deals with problems of migration policy and highlights inconsistencies between population distribution policies and other aspects of socio-economic development.

Migration and Socio-economic Background

(a) Post-war reconstruction and basic socio-economic reforms

The occupational structure of the population in pre-war Poland was typical of less developed countries with low rates of economic development. According to

---

* Institute of Rural and Agricultural Development, Polish Academy of Sciences, Warsaw.

the 1931 General Census, almost 61 per cent of the population derived their livelihood mainly from agriculture and only 13 per cent from industry. About 73 per cent of the population lived in villages, of which almost 81 per cent was dependent on agriculture. A similar situation prevailed at the time of the Second World War.

The economic backwardness of pre-war Poland resulted not only in a delayed - in relation to the majority of other European countries - industrialisation, but also in a slower rate of economic growth. The Polish economy between the First and Second World Wars made no progress. In fact, there was a slight decline in industrial activity. For example, gross and per capita industrial output in 1938 amounted to only 95 per cent and 82 per cent respectively of the 1913 level (Kuzinski, 1976, p. 10). On the other hand, the growth rate of the labour force in this period was relatively high.

During the period 1921-39, the population aged 15-64 increased by 5.5 million. Moreover, there existed substantial labour reserves in the form of open and disguised unemployment in both the rural and the urban areas. In 1938 the number of registered jobseekers amounted to almost 17 per cent of the total labour force (Józefowicz, 1962, p. 47). Table 1 also shows that in 1936 the surplus population in rural areas in the age group 15-59 constituted roughly one-quarter of the total peasant population in this age group. Among males aged less than 30, this proportion varied from one-third to one-half.

Table 1: Surplus population as a percentage of total peasant population by age and sex, 1936

Age (in years)	Males	Females
15-17	40.9	33.3
18-19	55.2	43.1
20-22	54.7	39.9
23-24	49.4	28.7
25-29	35.4	15.4
30-39	23.8	6.5
40-49	13.5	2.8
50-59	5.7	2.3
All	29.9	15.8

Source: Wieś w liczbach (1954), p. 97.

The huge population and material losses which Poland sustained during the Second World War, and the subsequent territorial adjustments, generated several important changes in the relationship between land and labour. In 1939 Poland's population was estimated at 35.1 million, while in 1946 it was only 23.8 million. Since the country's total territory was somewhat reduced, from 388,600 square kilometres to 312,700 square kilometres, the population density declined from about 90 persons per square kilometre to 76 persons per square kilometre. The reduction in Poland's population was mainly a result of wartime losses and Nazi extermination policies. It not only reduced the absolute size of the labour force but also adversely affected its quality. It is estimated that as an outcome of the war, about 590,000 people, mainly of working age, were disabled. A significant proportion of them had technical skills.

Besides population losses, Poland suffered enormous material losses. Thirty-eight per cent of national fixed capital was completely destroyed during the war. However, in spite of these losses, the war had an effect on the country's productive potential, mainly on industrial growth. After the Second World War economic infrastructure, although greatly impaired, was confronted with a reduced labour force. This partly corrected the disequilibrium between labour demand and labour supply which had been typical of the pre-war period.

The process of reconstruction, recognised by the country's political leadership as one of the most important and urgent tasks of the time, was implemented with great success. A substantial investment fund was earmarked for the purpose. Already in 1946 the total volume of these funds exceeded that for 1938, which had been considered a record year in this respect (Karpinski, 1965). In 1949 investment was three times higher and industrial output 64 per cent higher than in 1938.

One of the most urgent tasks in agriculture was to eliminate fallow land, which in 1945 covered 7.9 million hectares, i.e. 48 per cent of all arable land. By the end of the 1940s almost all this land had been brought under cultivation. Agricultural output per unit of land in 1949 was 15 per cent higher than the pre-war level.

One of the basic factors behind rapid and successful implementation of post-war economic reconstruction was nationalisation of industry and the banks. The Three-Year Plan covering the period 1947-49 was the first medium-term and comprehensive plan. Its main tasks were reconstruction of the economy, consolidation of a new socio-economic system, linking the western and northern territories with the rest of the country, and achieving a substantial increase in national income and consumption as compared with the pre-war level. As a result, per capita income in 1949 was 75 per cent higher and consumption 42 per cent higher than in 1938.

The agricultural system of pre-war Poland was characterised by the existence, on the one hand, of a small number of large estates, and, on the other hand, of millions of small agricultural holdings. The main aim of agricultural reform was the elimination of semi-feudal land ownership and capitalist exploitation in agriculture and the redistribution of land in favour of the poor rural population. The state took over 652,000 farms which exceeded 50 hectares in the old territories and 100 hectares in the western and northern territories, as well as smaller farms whose owners had emigrated from the country or abandoned the farms for other reasons. The total land area taken over by the state amounted to 13.8 million hectares. Almost half of that land was distributed among agricultural workers and peasants on very easy terms (Wieś w liczbach, 1954, pp. 11 and 18).

State farms were established on the remaining land suitable for cultivation. These farms accounted for 9.6 per cent of the total area of agricultural land in 1950, whereas private farms accounted for 89.6 per cent. The remaining 0.8 per cent belonged to co-operative farms.

The far-reaching socio-economic transformations in rural and urban areas resulted in an ever-growing demand for labour. The number of persons employed in industry increased from 1.20 million in 1946 to 1.73 million in 1949 (Rocznik Statystyczny, 1957, pp. 4 and 9). In the non-agricultural sectors as a whole, the number of employed persons grew from 2.51 million to 4.35 million during the same period. Although these data probably overestimate the amount of employment increase, they do suggest that the growth of labour demand outside agriculture was very high during this period. On the other hand, the analysis of labour supply indicates that urban labour reserves were highly inadequate and that the increase in demand could only be satisfied by way of a substantial inflow of labour from the rural areas.

The year 1949 closes the stage of the country's reconstruction from war damage. It does not mean, however, that all damage was fully repaired. Despite huge efforts, the traces of this damage were still to be seen for many years to come. The level of reconstruction was, however, so advanced that the authorities decided to start implementation of the basic, long-term task of the country's industrialisation.

(b) Industrialisation and development
    of non-agricultural sectors

The shift of surplus agricultural labour to work in
more efficient sectors of the economy was a prerequisite
for the modernisation of the agriculture itself, and the
consequent raising of productivity. Without further
industrialisation achievement of this would have been
impossible in Polish conditions.[1]

(i) Development of industry

The movement towards industrialisation started at the
turn of the 1940s and gained momentum during the 1950s.
The share of capital accumulation in national income grew
from 16 per cent during the period 1946-49 to 24 per cent
during the period 1950-55. During the same period the
share of industry in investment outlays increased from
23.6 per cent to 44.8 per cent and that of agriculture
declined from 24.8 per cent to 10 per cent. A substantial reduction was also noted in the share of outlays
devoted to community and housing services as well as
those for transport and communications.

The reconstruction of old industrial plants and
concentration of investment in new projects led to a very
high rate of growth of industrial output during the period
1950-55, averaging 13.3 per cent per annum. Table 2
shows that the rates of growth of capital goods and
consumer goods industry were 14.9 per cent and 11.5 per
cent respectively.

Particularly rapid industrialisation took place in the
first four years of the Six-Year Plan for the period
1950-55. The share of capital accumulation in national
income increased from 21 per cent in 1950 to 28 per cent
in 1953, and the absolute volume of investment outlays

---

[1] This aspect of industrialisation was appropriately
expressed by one of the leading Polish agricultural
economists, Styś, who wrote in 1948 that any idea about
modernization of our agriculture will remain empty words
so long as our country is so over-populated. Neither by
land reform nor by co-operative action will agriculture
radically overcome its weaknesses. It is not in a position
to cure itself. To reconstruct our agriculture, our
whole national economy has to be remodelled. One of the
reconstruction plan targets must be a shift of the surplus
population from agriculture to other occupations, mainly
industrial ones. Without industrialisation of the country
one cannot speak about improvements in agriculture
(Józefowicz, 1962, p. 88).

Table 2: Average annual growth rate of industrial output, 1950-76

| | Total | Socialised industry | | | | |
		Total	Capital goods	Consumer goods	Mining	Manufacturing
1950-55	13.3	13.9	14.9	11.5	6.8	13.7
1950-53	14.9	15.0	16.3	12.1	6.8	14.9
1954-55	11.4	11.4	12.3	10.5	6.6	11.8
1956-60	9.9	9.7	10.1	8.7	4.2	10.1
1961-65	8.4	8.6	9.8	6.6	3.8	8.9
1966-70	8.3	8.4	9.4	6.6	6.3	8.5
1971-75	10.4	10.5	10.6	10.4	5.8	10.8
1976-78	6.9	6.9	6.9	6.9	3.2	7.1

Sources: Rocznik Statystyczny Przemslu, 1945-1965, pp. 132-133, p. 138; idem, 1972, p. 80; idem, 1976, p. 42; Maly Rocznik Statystyczny, 1979, pp. 87-88.

grew at a record rate of 48 per cent per annum in this period. The rate of growth of industrial output was also very high - on average 14.9 per cent per annum.

Such an enormous industrialisation effort, substantially exceeding the original expectations of the Six-Year Plan, led, however, to several economic difficulties and social tensions. Among the most important were the deterioration of the agricultural situation and the slow growth of residential construction. As a result, several changes in the allocation of investment outlays were introduced in the last years of the Six-Year Plan. The share of industry was reduced, whereas relatively more funds were earmarked for agriculture and residential construction.

After a temporary slackening of the pace of industrialisation in the second half of the 1950s (and strictly speaking during 1954-58), the 1960s were marked by a renewed increase in the industrialisation effort. The share of capital accumulation in national income increased from an average of 23 per cent in 1956-60 to 26 per cent in 1961-65, and 28 per cent in 1966-70. Together with expansion of the raw material base, much attention was focused on the development of manufacturing industry. As compared to the earlier years, the 1960s were characterised by a slower rate of growth of industrial output - about 8.4 per cent per annum.

The period from 1950 to 1970 can be considered as the first stage of Poland's socialist industrialisation. The 1970s can then be regarded as the beginning of a new phase in which the existing industrial base was further developed and modernised. The first phase of a new stage of industrialisation falls in the period 1971-75. With a general increase in the share of capital accumulation in national income to the record level of 34 per cent, the share of outlays for industry grew to about 44 per cent of total investment outlays. Industrial output went up at an average rate of 10.5 per cent per annum.

This investment boom, accompanied by the rapid rise in the living standards of the population, had its adverse effects on the economy. Due to many internal and external factors, investment costs in 1971-75 significantly exceeded the planned figures for this period. On the other hand, general economic performance was lower than expected, and difficulties were encountered concerning exports to the Western countries, largely due to the prolonged economic recession in the West.

All this had adverse effects on the economic situation, leading to cuts in investment and changes in investment patterns. On average, the share of capital accumulation in national income amounted to 32 per cent during 1976-78. However, certain shifts in investment in favour of agriculture and housing were once again carried out. More deeper changes in this direction have taken place since 1979, and are foreseen in the plans for the country's socio-economic development in the near future.

The rapid development of industry during the post-war period in Poland was accompanied by substantial changes in its location. The policy of reducing the inequality in development of different parts of the country was given very high priority, and exerted a substantial impact on the spatial concentration of industry. According to the estimates made by Dziewoński and Malisz, the Gini coefficient of concentration of 0.606 in 1946 declined to 0.574 in 1949, and to 0.428 in 1970.[1] The decentralisation of industry was reflected clearly in the changes in the share of particular regions in total output and employment in industry. The share of three voivodships (Katowice, Wroclaw and Lódź), for example, declined from 60 per cent in 1950 to 36.4 per cent in 1970.

The implementation of the policy of equal industrial distribution was not uniform over the whole post-war period. Up to 1970 the policy was considered the main tool for equalising living standards in different regions, for preventing the over-concentration of industry and population, and for contributing to the better utilisation of labour resources. It was also believed that moving industry to places where labour was available was both economically and socially more rational. Although this policy brought many positive results some of its assumptions turned out to be unjustified or, in the course of time, outdated. In particular, the belief that more equitable industrial distribution leads to the better utilisation of labour and reduced inter-regional differences in living standards did not prove to be true. Consequently, the policy of more equal industrial distribution, though not abandoned in the 1970s, differed substantially from what it had been a decade earlier. In particular, more attention was given to such factors as the economic effects of alternative locations of new plants; the specialisation of various regions; and the need for environmental protection.

Whatever the differences before and after 1970, however, the main result of the long-term policy of more equal industrial distribution has been that at present

---

[1] The concentration coefficients were estimated on the basis of Lorenz's curve, using data on the distribution of industrial employment by voivodships (Dziewonski and Malisz, 1978, p. 31).

there is practically no region in Poland which is beyond
the reach of industrial centres (Dziewoński and Malisz,
op. cit., p. 33).

(ii) Non-agricultural demand
for agricultural labour

One of the most important features of industrialisation in Poland was its high labour absorption. The
data in table 3 on the role of employment in increases in
output show that, on average, almost 40 per cent of the
increase in industrial output during the period 1950-78
was achieved due to increased employment. Several
factors were responsible for this. Among them were the
adoption of labour-intensive technologies, and the use of
investment outlays for creating new productive capacities.

As a result of the high labour absorption in industry
as well as in the services sector, the rate of employment
growth in the non-agricultural sector as a whole was very
high. On average, it was 3.7 per cent per annum
during 1950-58. The highest growth in employment took
place during the period of the Six-Year Plan - 7 per cent
per annum. It was even higher in the first four years
of this period, whereas in the last two years it declined
considerably.

The high rate of employment increase outside agriculture produced a strong demand for labour from the
agricultural sector. During the period 1951-75, on
average, agriculture had to supply almost half the labour
needed by the non-agricultural sectors. In the initial
phase of industrialisation this demand was even higher.
There were also significant differences between the
demand for male and female agricultural labour. Both in
the 1950s and in the 1960s the former was significantly
higher than the latter. During the 1970s, however, the
rapid growth of job opportunities for women, due to the
expansion of services and general shortage of male
labour, intensified the need for female migration from
agriculture. During the period 1971-75, this outflow
constituted almost half the employment increase outside
agriculture, as against one-third in the case of males.

(iii) Rate of industrialisation versus
rate of urbanisation

The rapid growth of industry located mainly in
urban areas provided a strong stimulus to the country's
urbanisation process, but the rate of the country's industrialisation considerably exceeded the rate of urbanisation.
Measuring the former by the rate of employment growth
outside agriculture and the latter by the rate of urban

Table 3: Net output, employment, and productivity outside agriculture, 1950-78

Period	Net output		Economically active population outside agriculture		Labour productivity		Share of employment in output increase	
	Total	Industry	Total	Industry	Total	Industry	Total	Industry
	Average annual growth rate (%)						(%)	
1950-55	13.4	13.2	7.2	6.8	5.8	6.0	53.7	51.5
1950-53	14.0	15.2	9.5	8.0	4.1	6.6	67.9	52.6
1954-55	12.5	9.8	3.0	4.4	9.2	4.8	24.0	44.9
1956-60	8.0	8.2	2.6	2.3	5.2	5.6	32.5	28.0
1961-66	7.3	8.9	2.7	3.4	4.2	5.4	37.0	38.2
1966-70	7.7	7.7	3.7	3.5	3.6	4.1	48.1	45.0
1971-75	11.3	10.8	3.2	2.7	7.9	7.9	28.3	27.8
1976-78	-	6.6	0.6	0.6	-	6.0	-	9.1

Sources: Rocznik Statystyczny Dochodu Narodowego, 1971, p. 17; idem, 1976, p. 86; Rocznik Statystyczny Przemysłu, 1976, p. 54; Rocznik Statystyczny Pracy, 1945-1968, pp. 16-17; Mały Rocznik Statystyczny, 1979, pp. 38 and 51, as well as author's own calculations.

population growth, the data in table 4 show that the rates of industrialisation and urbanisation during the period 1950-77 were 3.8 per cent and 2.9 per cent respectively.[1]   In the 1960s the rate of urban population increase was considerably lower than the rate of employment increase outside agriculture.   In the 1950s and 1970s, however, these differences were smaller.   And during 1956-60 and 1976-77, the rate of urbanisation was actually higher than that of industrialisation.

Table 4:   Average annual growth of employment outside agriculture and urban population, 1950-77

| | Employment outside agriculture | | Urban population | | | |
| | | | Total | | Working age population[a] | |
	000s	%	000s	%	000s	%
1950-55	332	6.8	525	5.1	312[b]	4.8[b]
1956-60	161	2.5	467	3.5	208	2.7
1961-65	240	3.2	256	1.7	157	1.9
1966-70	346	3.9	236	1.7	225	2.3
1971-75	335	3.4	388	2.2	359	3.4
1976-77	110	1.0	479	2.5	352	2.9
1971-77	282	2.6	414	2.3	357	3.2
1950-77	270	3.8	414	2.9	258[c]	3.0[c]

[a]   Males aged 18-64, females aged 18-59.

[b]   1951-55.

[c]   1951-77.

Sources: Rocznik Demograficzny, 1945-1965, p. 55; idem, 1978, pp. 2 and 11, as well as author's own calculation.

---

[1]   Adjusting for definitional and boundary changes, the rate of urban population increase during the period 1950-77 works out to 2.9 per cent per annum.

The slow pace of urbanisation as compared with industrialisation acted as a strong limiting factor on migration from rural to urban areas. In fact, this was one of the major reasons for the rapid increase in the number of non-agricultural workers commuting to work in urban areas.

(c) Agricultural policy and development

During the post-war period, there have been two major elements in agricultural policy: the fast growth of agricultural output and the socialist transformation of agriculture. The fast growth of agricultural output in Poland has been of necessity largely due to a relatively low - in European terms - level of food consumption, very high income elasticity of demand for food, rapid population growth, and the need to export agricultural products, mainly because of the huge demand for imports of capital goods.

The increase in agricultural output in Poland could not be achieved through extension of the land area under cultivation, since reserves of cultivable land had already been exhausted. Nor could it be achieved through an increase in the number of people employed in agriculture, since labour was needed for the non-agricultural sectors. In such circumstances, the only way to increase agricultural output was by a more intensive utilisation of land and labour resources, as well as an increase in capital outlays.

The socialist transformation of agriculture was achieved through expansion and strengthening of state, co-operative and other forms of collective ownership; elimination of capitalist tendencies; state monitoring of output, prices, and other associated processes; and co-operation between the socialised and non-socialised sectors.

Agriculture in Poland has been subjected to many changes during the post-war period. Taking into account the most important changes, agricultural policy and the main trends of Polish agricultural development can be divided into three basic stages: the first was more or less the period of the Six-Year Plan; the second covered the years 1956-70; and the third started at the beginning of the 1970s.

The transition to intensive industrialisation at the beginning of the 1950s entailed a decline in the share of agriculture in total investment outlays from 25 per cent in 1947-49 to 10 per cent in 1950-53. With the aim of mobilising resources for industrial development as well as improving the availability of food for a rapidly increasing urban population, the system of compulsory deliveries was introduced. This made it obligatory for all farms to sell a specified quantity of four basic agricultural products (cereals, potatoes, meat, and milk) to the state authorities. Prices were fixed at the level of free-market prices at that time. However, due to the strong upward tendency of the latter, the prices paid by the state went down relatively quickly, and by the end of 1953 amounted to only half the free-market prices. This brought about a considerable change in the character of compulsory deliveries, which began to play a supplementary function in financial accumulation for industrialisation requirements.

The reduced level of investment in agriculture adversely affected the growth of agricultural output. During the period 1950-53 the rate of growth of agricultural output amounted to only 1 per cent per annum, although this was partly due to unfavourable weather conditions in these years.

The turn of 1953-54 brought about several changes in agricultural policy. There was a certain revival in production and investment activities on the farms, which together with an improvement in weather conditions contributed to the growth of agricultural output during 1954-55. This improved the over-all growth rate of output for the Six-Year Plan period (2.1 per cent per annum), as shown in table 5.

Table 5:   Average annual growth rate of agricultural output, 1946-78

Period	%
1947-49	2.5
1950-55	2.1
1956-60	3.7
1961-65	2.4
1966-70	1.9
1971-75	3.7
1976-78	1.5

Sources: Rocznik Statystyczny, 1978, p. XL; Rocznik Statystyczny Rolnictwa i Gospodarki Zywnościowej, 1970, p. 155; Maly Rocznik Statystyczny, 1979, p. XXIX.

There were also favourable changes in living conditions in the rural areas during this period. Education opportunities for rural juveniles were immensely increased. The percentage of farms having electricity grew from 2.2 per cent in 1945 to 19 per cent in 1950, and 33.6 per cent in 1955. In addition, about 400 state machine centres were established, rendering mechanisation services, mainly for co-operative farms.

The appraisal of agricultural policy in the Six-Year Plan period led to the formulation of a new agricultural policy, which emphasised:

(a) the increase of investment outlays for agriculture;

(b) a gradual departure from the policy of compulsory deliveries towards the development of a voluntary contracting system between farms and the state;

(c) an improvement in the profitability of agricultural output through cheap credit and changes in prices in favour of agricultural products;

(d) voluntary or free entry into co-operative farms and the creation of a conducive political climate to stimulate the output of private farms;

(e) reactivation of different types of rural co-operatives; and

(f) strengthening of the state sector in agriculture.

Apart from the reduction in compulsory deliveries, there were also changes in their role in accumulation: from financing industrialisation to agricultural financing. This was realised through the establishment of the Agricultural Development Fund in 1959. The size of this fund was determined by the difference between free-market prices and those paid to farmers for compulsory deliveries. This fund was put at the disposal of agricultural associations and earmarked for collective investments in peasant agriculture, mainly for the purchase of machinery and development of mechanisation services for private farms. All these changes led to a high and relatively stable rate of growth of agricultural output. Leaving aside the bad harvest of 1959, agricultural output grew in 1956-60 by 3-7 per cent annually; over the whole five-year period growth averaged 3.7 per cent annually, compared to 2.1 per cent in the Six-Year Plan period.

The agricultural policy followed in the 1960s was more or less a continuation of the policy formulated in the second half of the 1950s. However, both the volume of direct and indirect agricultural investments and profit-ability were uneven in particular years during this period. The decline in agricultural profitability and investment were particularly noticeable in the second half of the 1960s. Whereas in 1961-65 agricultural output increased by 2.8 per cent annually, the rate of growth of output was only 1.9 per cent during the second five-year period.

The 1960s also saw the beginning of the state social security system. The first step in this direction concerned disability and old-age pensions. This gave farmers the opportunity to receive a state pension or retirement benefits provided they handed over their land to the state. It is estimated that during the period 1968-70 the state took over about 200,000 hectares of farm land on this basis, putting it mainly at the disposal of the state agricultural farms.

During the 1970s the emphasis shifted to the modern-isation of agriculture and the development of the existing socio-economic and institutional structures. This change brought about many new decisions, among which the most important were the following:

(a) The abolition of compulsory deliveries and strength-ening of the contracting system. At present, about 80 per cent of marketed output is purchased by the state through a contracting system.

(b) A significant raising of purchase prices.

(c) The enhancement of pensions and retirement pay-ments to farmers who handed over their farms to the state. In 1971-78 more than 200,000 farms were taken over by the state, with a total area of almost 1.3 million hectares.

(d) Formulation of the laws on the general pension system and other social benefits which equalised, in principle, social benefits as between the socialised and non-socialised sectors.

(e) The large-scale mechanisation of agriculture. The number of tractors during 1971-78 grew, on average, by 36,000 per annum.

(f) Continued expansion of the socialised sector. The proportion of agricultural land in this sector increased from about 25 per cent in 1976 to more than 31 per cent in 1978, largely due to private farmers handing over their land to the state in exchange for a pension.

The 1970s also emphasised specialisation in the peasant economy and co-operation between private and socialised farms, particularly the state farms. Most frequently the co-operation was based on a short- or long-term contract between farms in these sectors concerning joint production and investment activities, mainly in vegetable production and animal raising. This co-operation contributes to better utilisation of labour, promotes specialisation in the private farms, lowers the costs of production, and is considered as a form of socialist transformation of peasant agriculture.

Another important element of agricultural policy in the 1970s was the improvement of land structure on private farms. Although small farms are still producing more per unit of land than the large farms, the rate of growth of output of the former is much slower. Moreover, the larger farms are more susceptible to modernisation and, as experience shows, they conform much more easily to state guidelines than the small farms. With this in mind, several tax concessions and other incentives have been introduced to induce farmers to expand the areas of their farms.

A substantial improvement in the rate of growth of agricultural output took place in the 1970s. This growth was very uneven, however. After rapid growth in 1971-74, there was stagnation and even a temporary slowdown, caused to a large extent by unfavourable weather conditions.

On the whole, the 1970s can be seen as the period in which Polish agriculture was put on the road towards social and economic transformation. Despite this progress, however, the level of modernity achieved, particularly in terms of technology and agrarian structure, still remains far behind other European countries and is still inadequate to meet the level of industrialisation and food requirements of the country, as well as the aspirations of the agricultural population, particularly the younger generations of farmers.

(d) Income disparity and differences in living conditions between rural and urban areas

Three groups of factors exert a decisive impact on differences in living conditions as between the agricultural and non-agricultural population and between the rural and urban population in Poland. These are income and consumption patterns, level of social security, and housing conditions.

(i) Income

The data on growth of and disparity between incomes from agricultural and non-agricultural activities for the first decade after the war are very scanty. However, they do suggest that there was a narrowing of the income gap between agricultural and non-agricultural activities as compared with the pre-war period (Pohorille, 1966, p. 209). From 1955 onwards, the data are available to compare the real wages of persons employed in the socialised economy with the real income of private farmers from agricultural production.[1] The latter can be measured in terms of the agricultural consumption fund per fully employed person in agriculture.[2] The comparison is shown in table 6. These data indicate three main tendencies. First, there has been a considerable growth in income for both population groups. Second, the rate of growth of incomes from agricultural and non-agricultural activities has not been much different. Third, agricultural incomes are, on average, 15-20 per cent lower than non-agricultural incomes.

The Polish experience indicates that the farmer's propensity to remain and to invest in agriculture strongly depends on the income disparity between agricultural and non-agricultural activities. If agricultural incomes fall below a given level relative to non-agricultural incomes, the propensity is reduced, and vice versa. This turning point is known as the "threshold income disparity" in

---

[1] The average level of wages in the socialised economy is very close to the average level of wages in the whole economy outside agriculture. This is due to the fact that employees of the socialised sector constitute almost 97 per cent of the total number of persons employed outside agriculture, and taking the socialised sector as 100, those employed outside agriculture constitute 94 per cent (1974 micro census).

[2] The agricultural consumption fund is defined here as total income from farming minus all expenditures connected with agricultural production such as capital outlays for current needs and investments, taxes, assurances, interest payments, wages, etc. In other words this is the part of the farmer's agricultural income which he spends on the consumption needs of his family. Thus, it is fairly comparable with the earnings of non-agricultural workers. The number of fully employed persons in agriculture is the total number of persons working in this sector on a full or part-time basis converted into full-time units.

Table 6: Annual consumption fund in non-socialised agricultural sector and net earnings in socialised economy per employed person, 1955-78 (at constant 1971 prices)

	Non-socialised sector in agriculture	Socialised economy	Income disparity
	In thous. zl. per employed person		Socialised economy = 100
1955	15.1	18.7	80.7
1960	19.3	24.2	79.8
1965	22.0	26.1	84.3
1970	23.3	28.9	80.6
1971	25.7	30.6	83.7
1972	28.4	37.8	86.5
1973	29.6	35.4	83.6
1974	29.2	37.7	77.5
1975	29.8	41.9	71.1
1976	32.8	43.9	74.7
1977	34.5	44.8	77.0
1978	33.7	43.6	77.2
	Average annual growth rate (%)		
1956-60	5.1	5.2	–
1961-65	2.7	1.5	–
1966-70	1.2	2.1	–
1971-78	4.8	5.3	–
1956-78	2.9	3.1	–

Source: Grochowski and Woś (1979), p. 169.

Polish economic literature. On the basis of empirical research conducted by the Institute of Agricultural Economics, it was established that "threshold income disparity" amounted to approximately 80 per cent. In periods when farmers' incomes were substantially above this figure their expenditure on inputs and investments was visibly higher than in periods when they fell considerably below this level (Grochowski and Woś, 1979, pp. 168-170).

The income of peasant families in Poland is derived from three sources: farming, work outside agriculture, and social benefits such as pensions, retirement payments, family allowances, etc. A major role is played by income from agricultural production. However, its share in the total consumption fund has shown a strong downward trend. According to some estimates this share declined from 81 per cent in 1960 to 69 per cent in 1970, and 65 per cent in 1976 (Gorzelak and Grochowski, 1971, cited in Ostrowski, 1978, p. 80). The main reason for this decline was a very rapid increase in the number of persons working outside the farm.

As far as income from social benefits is concerned, it plays a different role depending on the type of farm. In the family budget surveys conducted by the Central Statistical Office (CSO), and in many similar investigations, all peasant households are divided into two main groups:

1 agricultural households, those consisting of persons dependent exclusively on their farm;

2 peasant-worker households, which have at least one family member working permanently outside the farm. In some studies these households are subdivided into the following groups: (a) those where the head of the household works outside the farm; and (b) those where only other family members work outside the farm.

The data in table 7 show that the peasant households derive a smaller proportion of their income from social benefits (1.7 per cent) than peasant-worker households. These differences stem mainly from the fact that during the reference period, dependent members of families of persons working outside agriculture were authorised to participate in the state social security system, whereas families depending exclusively on their own farms were deprived of these benefits. This situation has been corrected since 1977. However, it is interesting to observe that all categories of peasant households derive a

Table 7: Percentage distribution of average annual income by type of household and source of income, 1976

Source of income	Type of household				
	Wage/salary-earners	Peasants	Peasant-worker		Wage/salary-earners on state farms
			With family head working outside the farm	With other family members working outside the farm	
Farming	–	92.3	30.4	52.2	–
Gainful employment	85.0	4.2	60.6	42.2	78.4
Social benefits	10.5	1.7	7.8	4.8	10.8
Other	4.5	1.8	1.2	0.8	10.8
All	100.0	100.0	100.0	100.0	100.0

Source: Ostrowski (1978), p. 81.

smaller proportion of their income from social benefits than wage-earner households.

Taking into account all income sources, the data in table 8 show that wage-earner households have the highest per capita income. In 1976 the per capita income of peasant households amounted to about 83 per cent of this. The data on the distribution of income also indicate that whereas only 2.3 per cent of wage-earner households have a per capita income of less than 12,000 zloties, the percentage of peasant households earning less than 12,000 zloties per capita income is 12.4 per cent.

The level of income from agricultural production varies among peasant families. A certain part is played by farm area: the larger the farm, the higher the income per person. However, the scale of income differences is relatively small. In 1976, farms of 0.5-3 hectares had 18 per cent lower incomes than the over-all average, while farms of 10-15 hectares and those above 15 hectares had 12 and 32 per cent, respectively, higher incomes. In peasant-worker households the area differences play an equally small role. The lower income from agricultural production on small farms is partly compensated by higher income from earnings outside the farm.

Table 9 compares the level of income of wage-earners in socialised agriculture with the level of income of employees working in the socialised non-agricultural sector. The data show that up to 1975 the average wage of persons employed in socialised agriculture has been lower than that of those employed outside agriculture, particularly in industry and construction. However, the size of this gap has declined systematically, and in 1978 the average wage in socialised agriculture was equal to that in industry and much higher than in the non-agricultural sector over-all. The agricultural wage was still somewhat lower than that in construction, however, this being one of the best paid sectors of the economy.

(ii) Social security

In the post-war period up to 1970 progress in extending social security to the whole agricultural population was sluggish. Only those employed in state and co-operative farms had the same social benefits as those enjoyed by people employed in the socialised economy outside agriculture.

The turning point in the field of social security for the peasant population came with the approval in 1971 of the law on free medical treatment for the whole agricultural population and the 1977 law on pensionary and other benefits for farmers.

Table 8: Average number of persons and income by type of household, 1976

Type of household	Average number of persons per household	Annual per capita income	
		In zloties	% of wage/ salary- earners
Wage/salary-earners	3.45	27,197	100.0
Peasants	3.50	22,557	82.9
Peasant-worker:			
with family head working outside the farm;	4.54	20,805	76.5
with other family members working outside the farm	5.16	23,546	86.6
Wage/salary-earners on state farms	4.59	20,472	75.3

Source: Ostrowski (1978), pp. 72 and 230.

Table 9: Average monthly wage in socialised agriculture as percentage of wage in socialised non-agriculture, 1955-78

Year	All	Industry	Construction
1955	76.5	69.9	63.0
1960	81.2	74.2	69.2
1965	79.1	74.1	68.8
1970	83.5	78.1	69.8
1975	88.7	84.7	74.3
1975*	99.1	94.2	83.1
1976	103.1	97.2	88.7
1977	102.1	96.3	89.0
1978	106.1	100.6	93.8

* Based on new classification of industries and wages.

Sources: Rocznik Statystyczny, 1967, p. 547; idem, 1974, p. 166; idem, 1978, p. 86; Maly Rocznik Statystyczny, 1979, p. 64.

By virtue of the Decree of the Ministry of Health and Social Welfare on 14 December 1971, all farm operators and members of their families were entitled to free medical treatment from 1 January 1972. This paved the way for equalising benefits for farm operators with those received by persons working in the socialised economy.

A decisive move in this direction was the law of 27 October 1977 on pensionary and other benefits for farmers. By virtue of this law, each farmer has the right to an old-age pension if he or she:

1 reaches the pension age (65 for males and 60 for females, and in certain circumstances five years earlier);

2 has sold agricultural products of a yearly value of not less than 15,000 zloties to the state over a period of at least 25 years (20 years for females), including the last five years on a continuous basis, before handing over the farm to the successor or to the state;

- 273 -

3 pays a premium to the pension fund;

4 hands over the farm to the successor or to the state without payment.

Moreover, the law entitles farmers to receive a disability pension in case of disability of the first or second degree, a family pension for children in case of the death of both parents, a pension in case of occupational disease or injuries at work, etc. It also entitles farmers to several other allowances (e.g. child delivery allowance, allowance for handicapped children, workmen's compensation insurance) which had previously been granted only to wage-earner households.

The amount of retirement pay and disability pension are determined by the average annual value of the agricultural produce sold to the state during the last five years before the farm is handed over to the successor or to the state. The law anticipates that retirement pay can range from 1,500 zloties to 6,500 zloties monthly.

Granting these benefits constitutes a milestone in reducing social and income inequalities between the agricultural and non-agricultural populations, but there is still much to be done in this field. For example, individual farmers are still not eligible for some social benefits granted to wage-earners, such as family allowances and paid maternity leave.

(iii) Housing conditions

The differences in housing conditions between urban and rural areas are more of a qualitative than a quantitative nature. The quality of housing in the rural areas in the pre-war period was very poor. In the first 20 years after the war there were some improvements but on the whole progress was very slow. In 1970 the standard of the majority of farm buildings was still not much higher than in the pre-war period. It is only in the last 10 years that there has been an intensive development of housing in the rural areas, both in quantitative and in qualitative terms.

Up to 1970 the average usable floor space of dwelling per inhabitant was somewhat lower in rural than in urban areas. Since 1970 the situation has been reversed. The same is true of the number of rooms per dwelling, which is at present substantially higher in rural than in urban areas, as shown in table 10. However, due to larger family sizes in rural areas, the number of persons per room, although declining, is still higher in rural than in urban areas. The differences are, however, much smaller than in 1950.

Table 10: Size of dwelling in urban and rural areas, 1950-74

		Urban areas	Rural areas	Urban areas = 100
Number of rooms per flat	1950	2.43	2.26	93
	1960	2.50	2.42	97
	1970	2.77	3.00	108
	1974	2.86	3.14	110
Usable floor space per person in sq. m.	1970	46.9	55.7	119
	1974	47.2	57.2	122
Number of persons per room	1950	1.55	1.95	126
	1960	1.53	1.80	118
	1970	1.32	1.44	109
	1974	1.23	1.36	111
	1978	1.10	1.25	114

Sources: Rocznik Statystyczny, 1967, p. 401; idem, 1977, p. 340; Wiadomości Statystyczne, 1979, No. 3, p. 1.

As regards facilities in dwellings, there are still very marked differences between rural and urban areas. The data in table 11 show that in 1974 only one-fifth of rural dwellings were equipped with a water supply system as compared with four-fifths in urban areas. The data also show that a much smaller percentage of rural dwellings had a gas supply.

An accelerated development and improvement in housing construction standards has taken place in the last decade, both in the socialised and in the non-socialised sectors. Housing conditions are, however, generally better in the former than in the latter, especially as far as modern facilities are concerned.

In the absence of detailed empirical research it is difficult to present a systematic appraisal of the changes in living standards which have taken place in the post-war period in both the rural and the urban areas.

However, there is some evidence that living standards in the rural areas are now much closer to living standards in the urban areas than they were previously. This refers, in different degrees, to general income level, housing conditions, and social benefits.

Table 11: Percentage of dwellings with selected
facilities in urban and rural areas,
1950-74

Year	Type of facility					
	Water supply		Lavatory		Gas	
	Urban	Rural	Urban	Rural	Urban	Rural
1950	42.3	–	25.7	–	26.2	–
1960	55.4	3.6	35.6	1.7	33.7	0.4
1970	74.8	11.8	54.6	5.0	47.9	0.8
1974	80.2	19.7	62.8	9.5	52.6	1.3

Sources: Rocznik Statystyczny, 1967, p. 403; idem,
1978, p. 341.

Inter-sectoral and Spatial Mobility

(a) Mobility of labour from agricultural to non-agricultural sectors

The mobility of labour from agriculture, as discussed in this section, covers people who change their main source of living from agricultural to non-agricultural activities.

(i) Rate and patterns of labour mobility

The process of labour mobility from agriculture in Poland occurs in two basic forms: a complete abandonment of agriculture as a source of income, and partial abandonment when a person undertaking an off-farm job carries on working on the farm. Mobility from agriculture is therefore not necessarily linked with migration from rural to urban areas or with any other type of spatial mobility.

Until the end of the First World War mobility from agricultural to non-agricultural sectors was very low. In the inter-war period there was some increase in inter-sectoral mobility. During the period 1921-39, whereas the total population of Poland increased by about 29 per cent, the increase in the agricultural population was 17

per cent.   Net movement from agriculture thus amounted
to 0.5 per cent annually.   This constituted less than
half of the natural increase in the agricultural population.
    In the post-war period there was a rapid increase in
the net movement from agriculture.   The data in table 12
show that during the period 1951-78 net movement from
agriculture amounted to almost 6.7 million persons (or
more than 23 persons per 1,000 agricultural population in
a year).   The average annual shift during this period
was approximately twice as high as the rate of natural
increase of the agricultural population and four times
higher than that of the shift in the inter-war period.
The data also show that the over-all shift was much
higher in the 1970s than in the 1960s.   Movement from
agriculture can be divided into three groups:

Table 12:   Estimated net movement from agriculture
             by sex, 1951-78

| Sex | Period | No. of persons (000s) | | Average annual rate |
		Whole period	Annual average	
Total	1951-78	6,693	239	2.31
	1951-60	2,225	223	1.93
	1961-70	2,428	243	2.30
	1971-78	2,040	255	2.86
Males	1951-78	3,276	117	2.49
	1951-60	1,238	124	2.34
	1961-70	1,238	124	2.60
	1971-78	800	100	2.49
Females	1951-78	3,417	122	2.16
	1951-61	987	99	1.58
	1961-70	1,190	119	2.05
	1971-78*	1,240	155	3.17

*   Preliminary figures.

Source: Latuch (1978), p. 60 as well as author's own
calculations.

1   persons for whom a shift from agriculture involves abandonment of the farm and changing their place of residence from a rural to an urban area;

2   persons who in spite of changing their main source of livelihood from agriculture to non-agriculture have remained on the farm and work in agriculture for a supplementary income;

3   persons who in spite of taking a job outside agriculture still live on the farm but are not generally involved in agricultural work.

An estimate of the relative share of each type of movement is available only for the period 1960-70. The data indicate that movement linked with abandonment of the farm (type 1) amounted to about 40 per cent of net movement, change to dual employment (type 2) about 28 per cent, and change of occupation without leaving the farm (type 3) about 32 per cent.

The data in table 13 show that movement from agriculture in Poland is highly selective with respect to age. The highest rate is among the agricultural population aged 15-29, especially at the age when young people generally finish their schooling. It is also interesting to observe that among older age groups, the tendency to leave agriculture declines steadily up to the age group 55-59, whereafter it increases, mainly among pension-earners. The same pattern was observed in the 1960s and 1970s, although in the 1970s movement of persons in the older age groups was much higher than in previous periods.

In the whole post-war period the movement was, on average, higher among males than among females, i.e. 25 and 22 persons per 1,000 agricultural population respectively. This male predominance was, however, smaller in the 1960s than in the 1950s and in the first half of the 1970s the movement among females was actually higher than that among males. The male predominance was, in general, stronger among lower age groups.

Substantial differences, not only in respect of the rate but also in respect of the direction of movement, existed between the private and socialised agricultural sectors. A higher than average net outflow in the former sector was followed by a net inflow in the latter. This was largely due to the expansion in the land area and development of state and co-operative enterprises rendering services to the private farms. An especially strong inflow to the socialised economy took place in the 1970s. Within the non-socialised sector mobility was higher among small farmers than among large farmers.

Table 13: Net movement from agriculture as percentage of agricultural population by age and sex, 1951-60 and 1961-70

Age at end of each period	Total		Males		Females	
	1951-1960	1961-1970	1951-1960	1961-1970	1951-1960	1961-1970
10-14	4.3	9.5	3.9	8.3	4.7	10.1
15-19	24.7	18.6	27.9	19.7	21.4	17.3
20-24	50.4	51.4	52.1	49.9	48.6	53.0
25-29	43.6	47.4	50.6	52.2	36.9	43.0
30-34	19.5	16.5	29.9	28.8	10.4	4.9
35-39	6.0	2.2	14.6	9.1	0.0	0.0
40-44	3.3	3.0	8.7	8.4	0.0	0.0
45-49	2.3	3.4	5.3	7.2	0.0	1.1
50-54	1.8	4.5	3.0	7.1	0.8	2.8
55-59	1.9	5.9	1.1	6.5	2.6	5.6
60-64	3.9	7.4	0.7	5.1	6.3	9.1
65 and more	10.4	10.6	8.7	7.1	11.6	12.9

Source: Frenkel (1974), table 6.

Moreover, among small farmers mobility largely took the form of commuting to work or taking up a non-agricultural job in the village itself, whereas among large farmers it mainly involved spatial mobility.

Mobility from agriculture in Poland is strongly and positively correlated with the level of education. This is true both of persons moving to the urban areas and of those working outside agriculture but remaining on the farm. Table 14 shows the percentage distribution of economically active farm population in rural areas by age, education and place of work. The data indicate that education selectivity is stronger among persons who have completely severed their links with agriculture.

(ii) Impact of inter-sectoral mobility on agriculture

As shown in table 15, the outflow of people from agriculture during the post-war period has resulted in a substantial reduction of both the absolute number of the agricultural population and its share in the total

Table 14: Percentage distribution of economically active farm population in rural areas by age, education and place of work, 1974

Age group		Level of education						
		Higher	Secondary	Basic vocational	Primary	Primary incompleted	Not specified	All
Total[a]	A	0.1	1.5	4.7	49.4	43.8	0.5	100
	B	0.9	9.9	18.6	55.6	14.8	0.3	100
	C	1.4	18.5	33.9	40.9	5.0	0.4	100
Working age[b]	A	0.1	1.7	5.9	56.2	35.8	0.3	100
	B	0.8	10.0	18.7	55.9	14.4	0.3	100
	C	1.4	18.9	33.9	40.6	4.8	0.4	100
Younger	A	0.1	2.6	10.2	67.3	19.5	0.3	100
	B	0.7	12.5	24.9	54.8	6.7	0.3	100
	C	1.3	20.4	37.7	37.6	2.7	0.4	100
Older	A	0.0	0.8	1.4	44.5	52.9	0.4	100
	B	1.0	5.5	7.7	57.8	27.8	0.2	100
	C	1.8	10.3	11.9	58.4	17.1	0.4	100
Post-working age	A	0.0	0.9	0.7	25.2	72.3	0.9	100
	B	3.3	5.0	4.4	37.3	49.6	0.4	100
	C	2.2	7.0	6.8	43.9	40.3	0.7	100

a A – working exclusively on their own farm; B – working mainly outside the farm, part-time on the farm; C – working exclusively outside the farm.

b Working age: males 18-64, females 18-59; younger: males 18-44, females 18-44; older: males 45-64, females 45-59.

Post-working age: males 65 and more, females 60 and more.

Source: Frenkel (1976), p. 49.

Table 15: Agricultural population, 1921-78

Year	Agricultural population (000s)	Agricultural population as percentage of total population	Average annual rate of change (%)	
			Agricultural population	Share of agricultural population in total population
1921[a]	17,900	66.6	–	–
1931	19,350	60.6	+0.8	-0.6
1946	12,100	51.8	–	–
1950	11,598	47.1	-1.0	-1.2
1960	11,244	38.2	-0.3	-0.9
1970	9,732	29.8	-1.4	-0.8
1978[b]	8,085	23.1	-2.2	-0.8

a The data for 1921 and 1931, particularly the absolute figures, are not strictly comparable with post-war data because of significant changes in boundaries.

b Preliminary figures.

Sources: Rocznik Demograficzny, 1945-1966, p. 95; Rocznik Statystyczny, 1976, p. 41; Wiadomości Statystyczne, 1979, No. 3, p. 1; as well as author's own calculations. Apart from the data for 1946 which are estimates, all other data are taken from censuses.

population. The share of the agricultural population in the total population declined from about 52 per cent in 1946 to 23 per cent in 1978. In the same period, the absolute number of the agricultural population went down from about 12.1 million to about 8.1 million, or from 59 persons to 43 persons per 100 hectares of agricultural land. The rate of decline of the share of the agricultural population in the total population did not show much change in particular subperiods, whereas the rate of decline in absolute numbers increased from about 0.3 per cent annually in the 1950s to about 2.2 per cent in the 1970s.

As already mentioned, mobility from agriculture in Poland took place, to a large extent, without a change in place of residence from rural to urban areas. This led to a significant increase in the proportion of the non-agricultural population living in rural areas: from abut 27 per cent in 1950 to about 51 per cent in 1978. The results of the 1974 micro-census indicate that for only 26 per cent of rural households was their source of income totally outside agriculture, whereas about 37 per cent of households were exclusively dependent on it. The remaining households drew their sustenance both from agricultural and from non-agricultural sources. Farming constituted the main source of living in the case of about 53 per cent of households (table 16).

Table 16: Percentage distribution of rural households by source of living in 1974

Type of household	Households		Average number of persons per household
	No.	%	
All	4,017	100.0	3.81
Not linked with agriculture	1,044	26.0	3.13
Linked with agriculture	2,973	74.0	4.05
exclusively agricultural	1,463	36.6	3.68
mainly agricultural	793	19.7	4.69
mainly non-agricultural	712	17.7	4.69

Source: Frenkel: Wies i roluietwo, No. 3, 1976, p. 8.

Available data, although not presented here, indicate that the degree of attachment to agriculture is substantially lower among younger than among older age groups. The percentage of persons with a non-agricultural source of livelihood is much higher among the former than among the latter. The analysis also shows that in recent years the majority of persons migrating from rural to urban areas are from the non-agricultural population.

As mentioned earlier, there were substantial labour reserves in Polish agriculture at the time of the launching of post-war industrialisation. The concept of "labour reserves in agriculture" is used to describe both current and potential reserves. "Current reserves" occur when the labour supply in agriculture actually exceeds what is required under a given agrarian structure and technological conditions to ensure a given level and growth of agricultural production. "Potential reserves", on the other hand, refer to the situation where the labour supply in agriculture exceeds the requirements of agriculture under changing institutional and technological conditions.

Current labour reserves in Poland appear to exist mainly in two forms. First, there are "surplus" persons, whose departure is unlikely to affect agricultural production adversely. This form of reserve we will refer to as "free reserves". The second form of "current reserves" includes people whose presence on the farm, under a given agrarian structure and technological conditions, is essential in the sense that they cannot leave the farm without adversely affecting production but who at the same time are not fully employed in agriculture. This kind of underemployment we shall refer to as "tied-up reserves".

One of the most important consequences of the post-war shift from agriculture is the elimination of "surplus" population in the rural areas. By and large, with the present agrarian structure and level of mechanisation, there are few possibilities of transferring any substantial number of workers, particularly males, from agricultural to non-agricultural occupations. According to the census data, the economically active population in agriculture went down from about 7.1 million in 1950 to 5.2 million in 1978.[1] These data do not cover the first post-war quinquennium, since the 1946 census did not take into account the occupational characteristics of the population. This was, however, undoubtedly a period of rapid decline in the economically active population in agriculture, by an estimated 500,000-900,000 persons.

---

1 Preliminary figures.

In the whole post-war period, therefore, the economically active population in agriculture declined by at least 2.4 million persons. In terms of per 100 hectares of agricultural land, it declined from at least 37 persons in 1946 to 35 in 1970 and 27 in 1978. The rate of decline was substantially slower in the 1950s and 1960s than in the 1940s and 1970s. The rate of decline was particularly high among the active population in the working age groups. It was also higher among males than among females.

During the first few years after the Second World War, the problem of free labour reserves (surplus persons) appeared to be most acute on the small farms. In 1950 the labour-land ratio, in terms of male workers up to 60 years of age per 100 hectares of agricultural land, was four times higher on farms below 2 hectares than on farms of 15 hectares and more. However, the movement of persons from agriculture during the post-war period was negatively correlated with farm size. By 1970, therefore, the difference had been considerably reduced, and in comparison with medium-sized farms (5-15 hectares) it had completely disappeared. The virtual elimination of surplus labour is also confirmed by the study carried out by the Institute of Agricultural Economics in 1972. The results of this study show that only 4 per cent of the farmers interviewed stated that some members of their families could leave the farm without impairing production. A similar study conducted in 1935 had found that 38 per cent of farms had surplus persons.

Simultaneously with the elimination of free labour reserves there has been a substantial reduction in under-employment, largely due to migration, rapid development of dual employment among the farm population, and a considerable growth in production on small and medium-sized farms. This is not to say, however, that the problem of tied-up reserves has been completely solved.

While for the majority of farms the shrinkage in the labour force has been reflected in their growing ability to balance labour supply and labour demand, for many others it has almost amounted to a new disequilibrium. As has been shown by various studies, a large number of farms suffer from labour shortages. In many cases these shortages are of a seasonal nature, being most severe at harvest and potato lifting seasons. Such periodic shortages of labour, however, do not result in major losses in agricultural production, because they are usually offset by longer working hours, additional help from family members (working mainly outside agriculture), help from neighbours, and mechanisation.

Several recent studies have shown that the level of production on farms run by elderly farmers varies. Some of these farmers still function quite efficiently, but most of them barely cope with the farm work, and the result has been a continuous decline in output. The data show that the older the holder of the farm, the lower its productivity. Apart from the aging of the agricultural population, there has been a decline in the quality of agricultural labour because of the low levels of education of the farmers, especially in the private sector. According to estimates based on the 1974 micro-census data, the education gap between agricultural and non-agricultural sectors measured by average number of years of schooling per person employed amounted to 3.4 years; the average years of schooling per person employed outside agriculture was about 9 years, as against 5.6 years on private farms.

The aging of the farm population and the prolonged existence of the educational gap between the agricultural and non-agricultural populations were to some extent unavoidable because of the strong age and educational selectivity of migration. Their negative consequences would not have been so acute, however, had the process of modernisation in rural areas been better adjusted to the changing manpower situation in agriculture.

(b) Rural-urban migration

The data on rural-urban migration in Poland are covered by the current demographic statistics, derived from population records. Three types of registration are distinguished according to the planned length of stay in a given locality:

1 permanent residence;

2 temporary stay lasting more than two months; and

3 temporary stay of less than two months.

Spatial mobility in Poland is therefore classified into two basic types: permanent and temporary migration. Registration for a stay of less than two months is not included in migration statistics.

The notion of "permanent migration" used in general censuses does not correspond to that used in current statistics. Permanent migration in censuses is usually defined as a permanent change in domicile (in the respondent's view) irrespective of whether this is connected with registration for a permanent or temporary stay. In view of the more detailed information on

rural-urban migration in current statistics, the analysis
in this paper is largely based on current statistics and
refers to permanent migration only.

(i)   Causes and flows of migration

One of the most characteristic features of the
migration process in Poland is that the rate of rural-
urban migration is considerably lower than that of
movement from agriculture.

The data in table 17 show that net migration from
rural areas during the post-war period was two to three
times lower than net movement from agriculture and that
these differences were larger before 1970.

Table 17:   Rates of rural-urban migration and of
movement from agriculture, 1946-78

Period	Net movement from agriculture		Net rural-urban migration	
	Number of persons (000s)	Number of persons per 1,000 agricultural population	Number of persons (000s)	Number of persons per 1,000 rural population
	Annual average			
1946-50			202	12.8
1951-60	223	19.3	96	6.2
1961-70	243	23.0	120	8.4
1971-78	255	28.6	200	13.1
1951-78	239	23.1	134	8.9

Source: Latuch (1978), p. 60; Rocznik Demograficzny,
1979, p. 24, as well as author's own calculations.

Although modest in relation to movement from agriculture, the volume of migration from rural to urban
areas was, nevertheless, quite large.   During the years
1946-78, net rural-urban migration was almost 4.8 million
persons;   in fact, it may have been higher by half a
million persons, mainly due to the absence of records and
incomplete registration in some years of the 1950s and

1960s (Stpiczyński, 1971, p. 10). This means that, on average, net rural-urban migration amounted to at least 150,000 persons annually during the post-war period. Table 18 contains data on the size of population movements between rural and urban areas. It shows three main features. First, in the whole post-war period there was no single year in which the net rural-urban migration was not negative for the rural areas and positive for the urban areas. Second, both the absolute size of the migration flows and net rural out-migration show substantial differences in particular years. We can distinguish three main periods, two with a relatively high and one with a relatively low migration rate. The first period of high net migration is approximately 1946-53, when net migration amounted to about 174,000 persons annually, and the second period was after 1970 when the net migration was about 178,000 persons annually. In the period 1954-70, net annual rural-urban migration amounted to about 104,000 persons on average. Third, the extent of urban-rural migration was initially very high but since the second half of the 1950s it has shown a strong downward tendency.

In the first decade after the war the high out-migration from rural to urban areas was connected mainly with the needs of economic reconstruction. Labour resources in urban areas were insufficient for this purpose, particularly as population losses resulting from the war were much higher in urban than in rural areas. Moreover, at the beginning of the 1950s there was a rapid increase in non-agricultural demand for agricultural labour due to industrial expansion. Since the process of reconstruction and industrial expansion took place during this period within existing urban centres often located far from the regions where agricultural labour surpluses were concentrated, their use outside agriculture required a substantial population shift from rural to urban areas.

Although the non-agricultural demand for rural labour was very high throughout the first decade after the war, the role of agricultural policy was very different in the first and second half of this period. As discussed earlier, one of the major elements of agricultural policy after the war was land reform. This, therefore, had an impact on reducing movement out of agriculture. First, the distribution of land among smallholders and agricultural workers improved their economic situation and increased the over-all labour absorption capacity of the agricultural sector. Second, the change of social status of those who received the land (from agricultural workers to farm operators) increased the proportion of the agricultural population with a relatively low propensity to migrate.

Table 18: Rural-urban migration, 1947-78

| Year | From rural to urban areas | | From urban to rural areas | | Net rural-urban migration | | |
	(000s)	Per 1,000 rural population	(000s)	Per 1,000 rural population	(000s)	Per 1,000 population Rural	Urban
1946	-	-	-	-	-320.0	-20.0	+41.3
1947	-	-	-	-	-180.0	-11.5	+22.4
1948	-	-	-	-	-150.0	-9.6	+17.8
1949	-	-	-	-	-170.0	-10.9	+19.4
1950	-	-	-	-	-190.0	-12.1	+20.9
1951	-	-	-	-	-136.2	-8.9	+13.7
1952	385.2	24.8	252.2	16.2	-133.0	-8.6	+12.8
1953	356.3	23.0	247.5	15.9	-168.8	-7.1	+10.3
1954	370.6	23.7	268.6	17.2	-102.0	-6.5	+9.4
1955	340.5	22.1	285.1	18.5	-55.4	-3.6	+4.7
1956	323.2	21.0	277.3	18.0	-45.9	-3.0	+3.7
1957	300.3	19.4	229.1	14.8	-71.2	-4.6	+5.6
1958	326.0	21.1	217.0	14.1	-109.0	-7.0	+8.2
1959	353.2	22.8	234.4	15.1	-118.8	-7.7	+8.7

1960	307.7	20.1	232.9	15.1	-74.8	-5.0	+5.2
1961	283.9	18.3	212.8	13.7	-71.1	-4.6	+5.0
1962	263.7	16.9	168.4	10.8	-95.3	-6.1	+6.5
1963	255.4	16.3	153.0	9.8	-102.4	-6.5	+6.8
1964	249.9	15.8	135.5	8.5	-114.4	-7.3	+7.5
1965	250.9	15.8	131.2	8.2	-119.7	-7.6	+7.7
1966	234.1	14.7	112.7	7.1	-121.4	-7.6	+7.7
1967	243.7	15.3	108.4	6.7	-135.3	-8.6	+8.4
1968	249.3	18.5	115.0	7.3	-134.3	-8.5	+8.1
1969	265.0	16.7	119.8	7.6	-145.2	-9.1	+8.7
1970	273.3	17.6	111.8	7.2	-161.5	-10.4	+9.5
1971	277.6	17.8	106.2	6.8	-171.4	-11.0	+9.9
1972	282.1	18.1	117.3	7.6	-164.8	-10.5	+9.4
1973	275.6	17.9	107.6	7.0	-168.0	-10.9	+9.3
1974	278.0	18.1	95.1	6.2	-182.9	-11.9	+9.9
1975	342.4	22.5	91.3	6.0	-251.1	-16.5	+13.4
1976	360.2	23.8	118.7	7.8	-241.5	-16.0	+12.5
1977	321.3	21.3	114.8	7.7	-206.5	-13.9	+10.4
1978	346.4	23.3	129.7	8.7	-216.7	-14.6	+10.8

Sources: Ruch wedrówkowy ludności w Polsce w latach, 1960-1967 (Warsaw, 1969, GUS), p. 17; Rocznik Demograficzny, 1977, pp. XVI-XIX and 160-161; Maly Rocznik Statystyczny, 1979, p. 24.

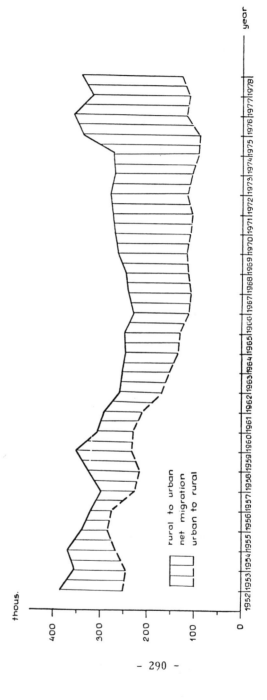

Figure 1: Rural-urban migration in Poland, 1952-78

But agricultural policy changed sharply on the threshold of the 1950s. The share of agriculture in capital outlays had fallen dramatically, an onerous system of compulsory deliveries of the main agricultural products was introduced, and a policy of rapid collectivisation was promoted, often against the will of the peasants. All these measures adversely affected the economic and political climate which had prevailed in the countryside during the first few years after the war, and stimulated the outflow of agricultural population.

During the years 1955-70, however, three sets of factors were responsible for lowering rural-urban migration. First, a slowdown of the industrialisation process and the accentuation of more rational utilisation of labour resources reduced the growth of employment outside agriculture. Second, the number of village residents commuting to work in the cities increased systematically. And, third, more emphasis was laid on the location of new industrial plants in less urbanised regions with agricultural labour surpluses.

The New Agricultural Policy introduced in 1957 was another important factor in lowering the rate of rural-urban migration, particularly in the late 1950s and 1960s. Since technological change in agriculture was rather slow, the increase in agricultural output had to be achieved mainly by using labour-intensive techniques. This weakened the push factors in the rural areas.

The renewed increase in the rate of rural-urban migration in the 1970s should be attributed to several factors. First, there was a rapid growth of production and employment in the non-agricultural sectors during this period. Second, the modernisation of agriculture led to a net decrease in the demand for agricultural labour. Third, the 1970s was the period when the bulk of the post-war "baby boom" entered the labour force. This substantially increased the volume of migration, even though the age-specific migration rates remained unchanged. Fourth, there was increased migration of older women, who moved to towns to help their working daughters at home. Fifth, there was increased mobility among farmers who had handed over their land to the state in return for a pension. Finally, the acceleration of housing development and the removal of administrative restrictions on migration led to increased rural-urban migration. Thus, both the "pull" and the "push" factors, as well as the peculiar demographic situation in the 1970s, stimulated the outflow of people from agriculture.

(ii) Role of migration in rural and
urban population change

In the whole post-war period, the percentage of
rural population in the total population declined systematically, whereas its absolute size was more or less stable
except for the first few years after the war and in more
recent years, when there has been some actual decline in
the rural population (table 19).

Table 19: Distribution of population by rural and
urban areas, 1946-78

Year	Population (000s)			% of population	
	Total	Urban	Rural	Urban	Rural
1946	23,930[a]	7,517	16,109	31.8	68.2
1950	25,008[b]	9,605	15,009	39.0	61.0
1960	29,776[c]	14,219	15,187	48.4	51.6
1970	32,642	17,064	15,578	52.3	47.7
1974	33,636	18,213	15,423	54.1	45.9
1978[d]	35,023	20,129	14,894	57.5	42.5

Breakdown into rural and urban areas excludes:
(a) 304,000; (b) 394,000; (c) 370,000; d = preliminary results.

Sources: Rocznik Demograficzny, 1978, p. 2; Wiadomości
Statystyczne, 1979, No. 3, p. 1.

Changes in the size of the rural population resulted
from four factors: natural increase, rural-urban
migration, external migration, and administrative changes.
In the post-war period, the size of the rural population
was largely influenced by natural increase and by net
movement from agriculture, but the remaining factors
played an important role in particular subperiods. The
impact of external migration was strong only in the first
few years after the war, mainly due to the emigration of
German minorities which was only partially compensated
for by the repatriation of the Polish population. As far
as administrative changes are concerned, their greatest

impact was in the 1950s. At that time they influenced the size of the rural population more strongly than net movement from agriculture. In the 1970s there were also many administrative changes, but they played a considerably smaller role.

As mentioned above, the growth of the rural population was largely dependent on the relationship between natural increase and net rural out-migration. During 1946-77, on average, net migration amounted to 61 per cent of natural population growth in the rural areas. This percentage was, however, different in particular years, ranging from 15 to 142 per cent.

In contrast to small changes in the absolute size of the rural population, the size of the urban population showed a very high growth rate. In the period 1946-78 the urban population - according to census data - went up by 12.6 million persons, which means that it grew at an average rate of 3 per cent per annum. The important factors which influenced this growth were: natural increase; migration from rural to urban areas; and administrative changes, in that order. Up to 1950 and after 1965, however, the main factor in urban population growth was migration from rural to urban areas, whereas in the years 1950-65 the urban population grew mainly under the impact of its own natural growth.

(iii) Age and sex of migrants

Like movement of people from agricultural to non-agricultural activities, rural-urban migration is selective with respect to age, although in the case of the latter the selectivity is relatively weaker. The data in table 20 show that juveniles and young people aged below 30 had a relatively higher propensity to migrate. This refers both to gross migration flows and to net migration between rural and urban areas. However, within this general pattern there were certain changes in age selectivity in the post-war years which are worth noting.

First, throughout the whole post-war period the age at migration of juveniles has increased systematically. At the beginning of the 1950s juveniles started moving to the cities at the age of 14-15, while their largest outflow usually occurred at the age of 18-19. But since the second half of the 1970s rapid juvenile migration starts at the age of 18-19, reaching a peak at the age of 23-24. As a result the migration rate for juveniles aged 14-17 is now hardly 9 per 1,000, almost seven times lower than that among the youth aged 18-24, whereas in 1952-53 the rate was 43 per 1,000 and was only one-third lower than that among older youth. One of the main reasons for this change was the rapid expansion of education,

Table 20: Rural-urban migration rate by age and sex, 1952-78
(per 1,000 rural population)

Age/sex	1952–1953	1955–1956	1960–1961	1965–1966	1970–1971	1975–1976	1977–1978
	Migration from rural to urban areas						
Total	23.9	21.4	19.2	15.3	17.7	23.2	22.5
0-13	13.4	11.9	11.7	10.7	13.5	19.5	20.0
14-17	43.2	34.5	25.2	9.8	8.7	8.5	8.5
18-24	65.8	62.5	67.6	49.9	47.8	56.8	48.8
25-29	42.7	41.8	40.7	41.4	49.9	69.9	67.4
30-44	16.2	15.5	14.2	11.6	14.2	18.8	20.4
45-59	8.6	8.0	7.4	6.0	4.8	7.2	6.8
60+	10.1	9.3	11.2	10.1	10.7	10.7	10.2
Males	24.1	22.6	19.6	14.5	16.6	21.5	21.1
Females	23.7	20.3	18.8	16.0	18.7	24.9	23.8
	Migration from urban to rural areas						
Total	16.1	18.1	14.5	7.7	7.0	6.9	8.2
0-13	9.8	10.2	7.9	4.8	4.8	5.2	6.3
14-17	16.9	21.0	18.2	3.8	2.7	1.7	1.9
18-24	44.6	55.2	55.7	26.5	20.5	18.1	20.4
25-29	31.4	36.0	30.8	20.5	18.8	19.5	23.5
30-44	13.0	15.0	11.5	6.4	5.7	5.5	6.6
45-59	6.3	6.8	5.2	3.2	2.0	2.4	2.7
60+	6.5	7.1	6.7	5.3	4.6	4.2	5.0
Males	17.6	20.9	16.7	8.0	7.0	6.9	8.0
Females	14.0	15.5	12.4	7.3	7.0	7.0	8.4
	Net rural out-migration						
Total	7.8	3.3	4.7	7.6	10.7	16.3	14.3
0-13	3.6	1.7	3.8	5.9	8.7	14.3	13.7
14-17	26.3	13.5	7.0	6.0	6.0	6.8	6.6
18-24	21.2	7.3	11.9	23.4	27.3	38.7	28.4
25-29	11.3	5.8	9.9	20.9	31.1	50.4	43.9
30-44	3.1	0.5	2.7	5.2	8.5	13.3	13.8
45-59	2.3	1.2	2.2	2.8	2.8	4.8	4.1
60+	3.6	2.2	4.5	4.8	6.1	6.5	5.2
Males	6.5	1.7	2.9	6.5	9.6	14.6	13.1
Females	9.1	4.8	6.4	8.7	11.7	17.9	15.4

Source: Migration data published by the Central Statistical Office, Warsaw.

especially the increase from seven to eight years of obligatory schooling.

The increase in age at migration is linked with another change, namely increase in the share of family migration. In the 1950s and 1960s this did not exceed 10-20 per cent of the total migration from rural to urban areas, whereas in the 1970s this share was more than 30 per cent.

The data in table 20 also indicate an upward trend in the net migration rate among older people. This is largely due to their lower urban-rural migration rate. However, in connection with the aging process of Polish society, the percentage of persons aged 60 and over in total migration from rural to urban areas has shown an upward tendency and is now more than twice as high as it was in the 1950s.

Unlike movement from agriculture, in which males were predominant except in the 1970s, rural-urban migration is dominated by females. This refers mainly to net migration. In the whole post-war period there was no single year in which the net migration rate was not higher among females than among males. With reference to gross migration flows the situation was, however, somewhat different. Higher migration rates among females from rural to urban areas date from roughly the second half of the 1960s. As far as urban-rural migration is concerned, the data in table 21 show that the predominance of females is quite a new phenomenon.

However, it is interesting to observe that both in rural-urban and in urban-rural migration there is a predominance of males in the age group 25-44.

It is worth mentioning that in spite of the growing share of females in migration in both directions, their share in net migration shows a decline from about 63 per cent in the 1950s to 55 per cent in the 1970s. This apparent contradiction is largely due to the differences in the sex ratio in the rural-to-urban and urban-to-rural migration flows as well as the decreasing share of the latter in the total migration between rural and urban areas.

(iv) Education of migrants

Migrants from rural to urban areas in Poland generally have a better education than the remaining rural population. The data in table 22 show that the percentage of rural-urban migrants having post-primary and higher education is more than two and a half and four times higher, respectively, than that among the population who remained in the rural areas. As far as the level of education of migrants from urban to rural

Table 21:   Percentage females in rural-urban
            migration, by age, 1952-78

	1952-1953	1955-1956	1960-1961	1965-1966	1970-1971	1975-1976	1977-1978
Migration from rural to urban areas							
Total	51.1	48.7	50.3	53.4	53.7	54.2	53.1
0-13	50.1	49.0	49.3	49.3	49.4	48.9	19.9
14-17	53.2	51.8	55.0	56.4	56.0	57.0	56.5
18-24	53.1	49.3	52.1	61.0	61.4	65.0	64.2
25-29	43.0	40.0	33.4	40.1	41.4	45.3	45.1
30-44	46.6	44.8	44.2	43.8	41.4	41.1	41.2
45-59	56.0	54.8	59.9	64.1	62.5	57.5	56.8
60+	68.9	69.6	69.0	71.9	69.9	67.8	67.7
Migration from urban to rural areas							
Total	46.9	43.9	44.0	48.7	50.5	50.7	51.2
0-13	47.8	48.5	47.6	47.5	48.2	48.5	48.2
14-17	49.5	48.1	47.2	51.9	51.4	50.0	52.5
18-24	46.7	42.1	42.9	51.4	55.4	56.0	57.6
25-29	41.9	36.4	34.7	36.3	37.9	40.5	42.0
30-44	44.2	40.6	39.6	39.7	37.0	37.4	38.0
45-59	49.7	48.7	49.6	59.7	57.4	52.5	53.7
60+	66.5	67.4	68.1	72.0	72.5	73.1	74.6

Source: Migration data published by the Central
Statistical Office, Warwaw.

areas is concerned, it is close to or even somewhat higher
than that of rural-urban migrants.

A detailed scrutiny of the data indicates that the
selectivity of education results in favourable changes
among the non-agricultural rural population and the
population linked with socialised agriculture, whereas
adverse changes are observed among the population linked
with the private economy (Rosner, 1977, pp. 63-64).

(v)   Labour force participation and employ-
      ment status of migrants in urban areas

Table 23 presents data on labour force participation
rates by age, sex, and migrant status.   The data show
that among male migrants aged 15-34 the labour force

- 296 -

Table 22: Percentage distribution of in-migrants[1] and population aged 15 and above by level of education, 1970

Population group	Level of education				
	Post-secondary	Secondary and basic vocational	Primary	Less than primary	All
Total					
Urban population	8.0	35.4	43.8	12.8	100
Rural population	1.4	14.1	46.1	38.4	100
Migrants from rural to urban areas	5.7	34.3	50.0	10.0	100
Migrants from urban to rural areas	9.8	36.7	41.4	12.1	100
Aged 15-19					
Urban population	0.2	31.5	59.6	8.7	100
Rural population	0.1	20.7	63.7	15.5	100
Migrants from rural to urban areas	0.2	29.0	66.1	4.1	100
Migrants from urban to rural areas	0.2	31.3	53.9	14.6	100
Aged 20-24					
Urban population	12.0	62.8	24.2	1.0	100
Rural population	3.1	42.6	50.1	4.2	100
Migrants from rural to urban areas	9.5	56.6	33.1	0.8	100
Migrants from urban to rural areas	13.1	56.7	28.5	1.7	100
Aged 25-39					
Urban population	12.6	42.1	41.1	4.2	100
Rural population	3.0	17.4	58.4	21.2	100
Migrants from rural to urban areas	8.2	35.0	52.3	4.5	100
Migrants from urban to rural areas	12.0	36.9	44.4	6.1	100
Aged 40 and above					
Urban population	6.4	24.4	25.9	23.3	100
Rural population	0.6	4.2	34.6	60.6	100
Migrants from rural to urban areas	3.5	13.1	43.8	39.3	100
Migrants from urban to rural areas	6.1	20.8	42.0	31.3	100

[1] In-migrants to the present place of residence in intercensal period 1960-70.

Source: Calculations based on the 1970 General Census.

Table 23: Labour force participation rates of total urban population and migrants from rural to urban areas, 1974

Age	Males		Females		Labour force participation rate of migrants as a percentage of participation rate of total urban population	
	Total	Migrants from rural areas	Total	Migrants from rural areas	Males	Females
15-19	20.9	34.4	16.5	33.9	165	205
20-24	79.6	91.7	69.8	70.3	115	101
25-29	96.4	97.6	80.4	72.3	101	90
30-34	97.3	97.2	78.7	67.1	100	85
35-39	96.6	95.9	80.1	63.5	99	79
40-44	95.2	93.8	77.2	59.9	99	78
45-49	92.0	89.3	71.5	49.8	97	70
50-54	88.3	83.7	63.1	39.7	95	63
55-59	81.0	73.1	48.3	27.7	90	57
60-64	63.2	52.2	18.2	14.6	83	80
65-69	25.8	22.8	10.0	8.9	68	89
70+	13.9	13.0	5.4	5.5	94	102
15+	72.8	84.0	53.0	54.3	115	101

Source: 1974 Micro Census of Population and Housing; Roeznik Demograficzny, 1975, pp. 258-259.

participation rate is equal or in some cases even higher than that of the total urban population, whereas in the age group 35-49 it is only slightly lower. Since migrants aged 15-44 constitute almost 86 per cent of total male migration from rural to urban areas, employment opportunities for migrants in the urban areas are, in general, the same as for the urban population as a whole. Only among males aged 45 and above is the labour force participation rate 10-20 per cent lower than in the urban population as a whole.

A study conducted by the Central Statistical Office shows that in 1974, 27 per cent of males aged 45 and above who moved to the urban areas were looking for professional work. It seems, therefore, that the slightly lower labour force participation rate among older male migrants from rural to urban areas is linked more with specific job requirements than with difficulties in finding job opportunities in urban areas.

In respect of females, the data show that the labour force participation rates of migrants are lower than those of the total urban population, except in the case of juveniles and females in the oldest age group. One of the reasons for these differences are, undoubtedly, the difficulties of finding jobs in urban areas, especially if one takes into account the fact that a substantial part of migration from the rural areas is directed towards smaller cities and rapidly developing centres of heavy industry which offer relatively fewer job opportunities for females. Moreover, there are difficulties in combining work outside the home with the duties of running the house. A number of females migrate from rural to urban areas mainly to look after the children of their daughters or daughters-in-law, thus making it possible for them to take up jobs. There is, therefore, a certain feedback between the high labour force participation rate of indigenous females in the urban areas and the lower rate for female migrants from rural areas.

Table 24 contains data on the occupational structure of migrants and the total urban population. The data show that, among migrants from rural areas, the predominance of workers is much higher than among the indigenous population, whereas the proportion of wage-earners and self-employed persons is relatively lower. Over-all, however, the occupational distribution among in-migrants does not appear to be much different from that among the total urban population. This conclusion is, perhaps, valid for the whole post-war period, although in the first half of this period there was less competition for migrants in the urban labour market than in more recent years, mainly due to the fact that their

Table 24: Percentage distribution of total economically active population in urban areas in 1970 and migrants from rural areas during 1961–70 by occupational status

	All		Males		Females	
	All	Migrants from rural areas	All	Migrants from rural areas	All	Migrants from rural areas
Non-agricultural occupations	95.3	95.8	96.7	96.8	93.4	94.5
Workers[a]	54.1	65.7	61.6	74.0	44.8	54.2
Qualified	45.3	54.2	55.4	65.5	32.6	38.6
Unqualified	7.0	8.2	4.2	5.1	10.5	12.5
Not specified	1.8	3.3	1.9	3.4	1.7	3.1
Wage/salary-earners[b]	37.5	27.8	31.8	21.2	44.4	36.9
Managerial staff	3.2	1.9	4.8	2.7	1.2	0.8
Experts	12.9	10.2	11.6	7.2	14.4	14.3
Technical professions	5.6	3.5	7.7	4.6	3.0	2.1
Non-technical professions	7.3	6.7	3.9	2.6	11.5	12.2
Working in administration, offices and services	17.5	11.7	10.2	5.8	26.6	19.9
Not specified	3.9	4.0	5.2	5.5	2.2	1.9
Home-workers[b]	0.9	0.9	0.2	0.1	1.8	1.8
Self-employed[b]	2.8	1.5	3.1	1.5	2.4	1.5

Agricultural and forestry occupations						
Workers	4.6	4.0	3.2	3.1	6.5	5.3
	0.6	1.2	0.7	1.3	0.5	1.1
Wage/salary-earners	0.3	0.7	0.5	0.9	0.2	0.4
Farmers	3.5	2.0	1.9	0.8	5.6	3.7
Other[b]	0.2	0.1	0.1	0.1	0.2	0.1
All	100.0	100.0	100.0	100.0	100.0	100.0

a   Including members of labour and farm co-operatives.

b   Including those employed on the basis of agency contracts.

Source: Population and Housing Census, 30 March 1974, table 6.

educational level at that time was significantly lower than the educational level of the indigenous urban population.

Migration Policy and its Consequences

During the post-war period, there has been no explicitly stated migration policy in Poland. Nevertheless, some elements of such a policy are implicitly incorporated into national and regional development policies and plans. With regard to population redistribution between the agricultural and non-agricultural sectors and between the rural and urban areas, one can distinguish three main periods of migration policy. The first, covering the first decade after the war, was a period of rapid shift from agriculture as well as migration from rural to urban areas. In the first half of this period this was mainly the result of the increased demand for labour in the urban areas to repair war losses, while in the second half it was due to the rapid growth of labour demand outside agriculture resulting from intensive industrialisation.

The second period, covering the years 1955-70, was a period of slower movement from agriculture as well as from rural to urban areas. This change was brought about by several factors. First, the transition to more balanced economic growth and the increased emphasis on rational use of labour reduced the demand of industry for agricultural labour. Second, free labour reserves in agriculture seemed to be smaller than expected. It was therefore considered that outflow from agriculture should not, in principle, exceed the natural increase of agricultural labour. Third, there was a change in the industrial location policy, putting more emphasis on the construction of new projects in regions with surplus labour.

The third period starts after 1970. In this period there was a reversal of the policy of restricting migration from rural to urban areas. This change in policy occurred largely because urbanisation was lagging considerably behind the process of industrialisation. Besides, the policy of rapid development required generally higher labour mobility, in particular between rural and urban areas. As far as the policy towards movements from agriculture was concerned, in the 1970s more emphasis was put on changing the composition of these movements, with the aim of encouraging the least productive farmers to abandon farming and restraining the outflow of those who were actually or potentially more efficient. This change in emphasis was obviously a reaction to the worsening composition of the agricultural labour force, and the negative economic and social effects of this.

- 302 -

As mentioned earlier, migration policy in Poland still lacks a clear identity. This is reflected not only in the absence of any precise formulation, but also in the lack of any coherent system for its implementation. Nevertheless, the planned character of the Polish economy provides the state with a wide range of instruments for influencing migration flows and directing them in ways considered socially desirable. With regard to movement from agriculture and from rural to urban areas, the basic instruments of indirect control, which play a decisive role, include the following:

1 Planned investment and employment in the socialised sector outside agriculture - in a given demographic situation this practically determines the volume of non-agricultural demand for agricultural labour.

2 Planned enrolment in post-primary schools - this influences, to a large extent, the volume of juvenile outflow from agriculture.

3 Planned allocation of investment outlays outside agriculture into productive investments and those earmarked for housing construction and other urban facilities. This affects very strongly the size of the shift from agriculture and migration from rural to urban areas, as well as the level of commuting and dual employment in rural areas.

4 Planned territorial distribution of the size and composition of non-agricultural investments. This determines the inter-regional flows of migration.

5 Planned supply of investment goods to the agricultural sector and other measures taken to influence the choice of techniques in agriculture (whether labour-intensive or capital-intensive), and changes in the agrarian structure (e.g. changes in proportions between the socialised and non-socialised sector as well as the land structure of peasants' farms). All these exert a strong impact on the demand for labour in agriculture.

6 Measures taken to influence incomes in peasant and socialised agriculture on the one hand, and in the non-agricultural sector, on the other.

7 Measures taken to influence living standards in urban and rural areas, particularly in the fields of education, public health and old-age security.

Among the indirect instruments for directing the movement of people from agriculture and from rural to urban areas, an important role is also played by the planned labour balance, which constitutes an integral part of the socio-economic plans for the country as a whole as well as for the different regions. This balance, determined on the basis of an evaluation of the need for employment growth outside agriculture, and an assessment of labour supply and labour demand in agriculture, indicates the desirable flows of labour between the agricultural and non-agricultural sectors as well as between the rural and urban areas. Regional labour balances take into account the expected volume of inter-regional movements of labour. This is partly determined on the basis of regional labour resources, particularly in agriculture, and partly on the plans for spatial development of the country. However, it should be pointed out that the volume and direction of migration flows used for deriving labour balances are purely indicative in character, and constitute only the starting point for determining appropriate incentives and disincentives to achieve the given targets.

There have also been attempts at more direct intervention to change migration flows. The first, and perhaps the more important one, was the organisation of population movements from the south-east and central part of Poland to the western and northern territories connected with the post-war changes of state borders. Although these movements were in part spontaneous, they were to a large extent organised by the state. This refers mainly to movements linked with land redistribution within the framework of land reform. The settlement operation - as the organisation of these transfers used to be called in Poland - was, in principle, completed by the end of the 1950s. It played a basic role in the economic integration of the western and northern territories with the rest of Poland as well as constituting an example of active and direct participation by the state in the direction of mass territorial population movements.[1]

Other forms of direct control of labour mobility are exercised through labour recruitment and labour clearing systems. The former covers mainly recruitment of wage-earners from rural areas and small towns, while the latter acts as an inter-regional employment agency for salary-earners. During 1950-55, i.e. the period of implementation of the first phase of the country's industrialisation, recruitment activities played a very essential

---

1   Organised agricultural and forestry settlement took place in later years, but on a small scale.

role in securing the needs of the non-agricultural labour market as well as in transferring labour from rural to urban areas.

Labour recruitment was regulated in 1951 by the Resolution of Government Presidium. According to the provisions of this Resolution, recruitment was to be carried out in compliance with an annual plan of labour distribution worked out by the State Commission of Economic Planning and approved by the Council of Ministers. The first such plan was worked out in 1952.

There were two main reasons for the great importance attached to recruitment activities during this period. First, in view of the rapid increase in the demand for labour outside agriculture it was expected that traditional forms of regulating the labour market through employment agencies would be insufficient. A special organisation was therefore needed to regulate the flow of labour to work outside agriculture. Second, putting an emphasis on recruitment activities and treating them as an element of a central plan was a reflection of the tendency towards stronger centralised planning in general and regulation of the labour market in particular.

From the second half of the 1950s, the role of planned recruitment declined considerably. There were several reasons for this. First, there was a substantial slackening in the process of industrialisation and a slower growth of employment outside agriculture. Second, large-scale migration from rural to urban areas had substantially reduced the size of free labour reserves in agriculture. Third, the rapid development of the education system at the post-primary level narrowed the base for recruitment activities. Finally, the end of the 1950s and especially the 1960s were marked by the location of new plants in less developed, labour-abundant regions which limited the need for permanent movements from rural to urban areas and stimulated the development of commuting migration.

In view of the changed situation in 1959, a new resolution was passed on workers' recruitment, revoking the Resolution of 1951. The new regulations to a large extent decentralised the planning and management of recruitment activities. In order to reduce intervoivodship movements of labour, it was recommended that recruitment activities should be carried out within the voivodship. The implementation of this recommendation encountered several obstacles, however, particularly where voivodships did not have sufficient labour reserves, and recruitment activities continued to constitute an important instrument of labour distribution, particularly in new industrial regions. A survey carried out in 1968 among the workers of a copper combine in a rapidly developing industrial region, for example, showed that about 22 per cent of them had come to the factory as a result of the recruitment activities of the combine itself (Izyk, 1975, p. 44).

As compared to the 1950s, recruitment carried out in the later years differs not only quantitatively but also qualitatively. Whereas in the period of the Six-Year Plan recruitment activities were mainly concerned with the transfer of unqualified agricultural labour to work outside agriculture, in the later years their role was to redistribute labour within the non-agricultural sector. This was not necessarily restricted to unqualified workers.

A third group of activities which can be included among direct methods of migration control is an attempt at urban and industrial decentralisation. In Poland a distinction is made between active and passive decentralisation. The former means restrictions on the construction of new plants and expansion of existing plants in large cities, as well as restrictions on migration from outside. The latter implies relocation of certain industrial plants and institutions outside large cities.

Restrictions on settlement in large cities by inmigrants were first introduced in 1954. Initially they applied only to the capital of Poland, Warsaw, which had experienced the greatest migration pressure. Later on, similar restrictions were introduced in other large cities.[1] Although the restrictions reduced migration to the cities themselves, they increased the flow of population to towns located in suburban areas. Due to the fear of excessive and chaotic proliferation of these satellite towns, the inflow of population to some of these towns was also restricted later.

The policy of decentralised urbanisation was rigorously pursued in the 1960s. In the 1970s active decentralisation was more or less renounced and the scope of passive decentralisation was substantially reduced. Under the Registration Resolution, effective from 1 January 1975, migration restrictions on permanent residence in all previously closed cities were lifted, except in Warsaw, where they were partly retained.

It seems that this departure from the policy of administrative restrictions on migration to larger cities resulted partly from the adverse economic and

---

[1] It should be kept in mind that these restrictions referred to permanent migration and did not cover persons coming for other purposes, e.g. education. Besides, there were various exemptions from the general rule, particularly for some groups of professionals, close family members, etc.

demographic effects of this policy. Since in most of these cities the natural growth of population is very low, they are not self-sufficient as far as labour is concerned and often experience labour shortages (Ciechocińska, 1978, p. 170). Moreover, the aging of the population in these cities is proceeding much faster than in other parts of the country.

The negative demographic consequences of the "closure" of the large cities could become even worse in the future. Latuch argues that if one assumes that from 1970 the population of Warsaw would grow exclusively through natural increase, then the number of people living in the capital would go down almost by half in the next 50 years, to about 0.8 million persons, while the share of post-working age population in the total population (males aged 65 and above and females aged 60 and above) would increase from 16 to 43 per cent. The author, therefore, underlines the positive role of migration in development of the capital.

Conclusions

The mass flow of population from rural to urban areas and to non-agricultural occupations constituted an integral part of the development strategy implemented in the post-war period. An accelerated rate of industrial-isation, the creation of new industrial regions, and the rapid development of other non-agricultural sectors all contributed to the fast growth of employment and necessitated considerable intersectoral and spatial mobility of labour. Moreover, this mobility, especially the outflow of surplus or underemployed agricultural labour to work in more efficient non-agricultural sectors, was a very essential factor in accelerating the rate of economic growth and improving living standards.

These basic advantages of the rapid shift of population from agriculture should not obscure the fact that it also created many problems. One of the most important was the problem of adjusting agricultural development to the changing manpower situation in agriculture. During the whole post-war period outflow from agriculture was causing not only relative but also absolute decline of the agricultural labour force. As long as the decline resulted mainly from the outflow of surplus farm labour, its influence on the growth rate of agricultural output was neutral, because the lost labour could be replaced by fuller labour utilisation of those remaining on the farm. This situation did not last long, however. In the early 1960s Polish agriculture entered the stage where any further increase in agricultural output became more and more dependent on capital outlays and structural changes in agriculture. Not enough was done to meet these new demands. The analysis shows that the amount of money earmarked for agriculture and rural infrastructure was not adequate to meet the requirements.

Likewise, too little was done to adjust the migration flows to labour requirements in agriculture. The aims and instruments of agricultural policy did not pay much attention to its impact on migration - in particular, on limiting the outflow from the more productive farms and groups of agricultural labour. The same was true of employment policy, which for a long time was directed mainly at meeting the demands of the non-agricultural labour market while neglecting the needs of the agricultural sector.

With regard to the effectiveness of migration-related policies, an analysis of the migration flows envisaged in the development plans and those actually occurring shows that they were only partly effective. The rate of success was higher on the national than on the regional level. The policy directing migration from rural to urban areas seems to have been more effective than that influencing the outflow of people from agriculture. As far as the shift from agriculture is concerned, the outflow of people was throughout the whole post-war period rather greater than that assumed by the planners.

The differences between envisaged and real migration trends are partly unavoidable. Even if the planning procedure is a perfect one - and it is far from that - it can hardly determine accurately a process such as migration which is by its nature largely stochastic. Nevertheless, the gap between the planned and actual flows could have been reduced if the plans had clearly defined the targets and instruments of implementation, and had taken into account the causes and consequences of various population movements.

Migration in Poland is assessed within the framework of manpower planning. There is no doubt that the situation in the labour market is one of the most important determinants of migration; the "employment bias" of migration planning and policy is therefore largely justified. However, it should not lead to the neglect of other factors which influence population mobility.

Among the deficiencies of migration planning and policies in Poland one may also mention that quite often they are devised under pressure of current circumstances without paying due attention to their long-term consequences and negative side-effects. Such an approach leads to over-reaction. The rapid shift from agriculture, for example, led to a substantial aging of the farm population which in turn lowered productivity and farm output. Some measures were taken to correct this situation but only with a time lag of 10 to 15 years.

As far as the relative importance of direct and indirect methods of directing migration is concerned, there is no doubt that the former, as a rule, have played only a secondary role. The most important methods have been those affecting the size and allocation of non-agricultural labour demand, housing and infrastructure development, stability of private farming and its equality with the socialised sector, the type and pace of modernisation processes in agriculture, and inter-sectoral and inter-regional differentials in living standards. The effectiveness of both direct and indirect methods depends largely on the target population. Young farmers in the non-socialised sector of agriculture and those employed on state farms react differently to the same set of incentives. The time factor is also important. What was effective 10 or 20 years ago is not necessarily of the same importance now.

Among the direct migration policy instruments those based on economic and social incentives generally proved more effective than the administrative regulations. Though the latter may bring quick results in the short-term, their efficiency in the long run is rather poor and they often tend to create more problems than they solve.

There are grounds for believing that the rate of decrease of the agricultural labour force will be even faster in the future than in the past. This means that the problem of mutual adjustment between movement from agriculture and development of the whole agricultural economy will gain added importance. Moreover, the adjustment measures will be more costly, for at least three reasons: first, the new generations of farmers are no longer prepared to accept lower levels of income and living standards than those in non-agricultural occupations; second, the scope of mechanisation will have to be extended to cover almost all the main branches of agricultural production; third, the level of rural infrastructure will have to be raised to that in urban areas. Although the shift towards more capital-intensive agriculture is absolutely necessary, it would be premature to give up all labour-intensive techniques and small-scale production. On the contrary, wherever possible they should be promoted. This is particularly important with regard to the vast peasant sector which plays a very important role in supplying agricultural products. At the present stage of socio-economic development, and with the present demographic and socio-economic structure of the farm population in Poland, a combination of capital-intensive and labour-intensive techniques, large-scale and small-scale production, together with equalisation of the working and living conditions between rural and urban areas, seem to be the necessary conditions for harmonising the needs for further outflow of people from agriculture with the need to maintain a high rate of growth of agricultural output.

BIBLIOGRAPHY

Abercrombie, K.C. (1972): "Agricultural mechanisation and employment in Latin America", in International Labour Review (Geneva), July, pp. 11-45.

Abhayaratne, G.M. (1972): Economic aspects of some peasant colonisation in Ceylon, unpublished Ph.D. thesis (Oxford University).

Abhayaratne, O.E.R. and Jayawardene, C.H.S. (1965): "Internal migration in Ceylon", in Ceylon Journal of Historical and Social Studies (Colombo), Vol. 8, Nos. 1 and 2.

Arndt, H.W. (1966): "Survey of recent developments", in Bulletin of Indonesian Economic Studies (Canberra), Nov., pp. 1-24.

Arndt, H.W. and Sundrum, R.M. (1977): "Transmigration: Land settlement or regional development?", in Bulletin of Indonesian Economic Studies (Canberra), Nov., pp. 72-90.

Bahrin, T.S. (1979a): "Development planning: Land settlement - Policies and practices in South-East Asia", in R.J. Pryor (ed.): Migration and development in South-East Asia: A demographic perspective (Kuala Lumpur, Oxford University Press).

--- (1979b): Review and evaluation of attempts to direct migrants to frontier areas via land colonization schemes, paper presented at UN/UNFPA Workshop on Population Distribution Policies in Development Planning, Bangkok, 4-13 September.

Barraclough, S. (1970): "Agrarian policy and land reform", in Journal of Political Economy (Chicago, Illinois), No. 78.

Bilsborrow, R.E. (1979): Population pressure and agricultural development in developing countries: A conceptual framework and recent evidence, paper presented at the Annual Meeting of the Population Association of America, Philadelphia.

Birks, J.S. and Sinclair, C.A. (1980): International migration and development in the Arab region (Geneva, ILO).

Biro Pusat Statistik (1970): <u>Statistik industri, 1970</u> (Jakarta).

--- (1976): <u>Statistik Indonesia, 1975</u> (Jakarta).

Bishop, R.N.W. (1952): <u>Unknown Nepal</u> (London, Luzac).

Böhning, W.R. (1981): <u>Black migration to South Africa: Selection of policy-oriented research</u> (Geneva, ILO).

Bose, A. (1980): <u>India's urbanization, 1901-2001</u> (New Delhi, Tata McGraw-Hill).

Boserup, E. (1965): <u>The conditions of agricultural growth: The economics of agrarian change under population pressure</u> (London, Allen and Unwin).

Brahme, S. (1977): "The role of Bombay in the economic development of Maharashtra", in A.G. Noble and A.K. Dutt (eds.): <u>India's urbanization and planning: Vehicles of modernization</u> (New Delhi, Tata McGraw-Hill).

Brigg, P. (1973): <u>Some economic interpretations of case studies of urban migration in developing countries,</u> World Bank Staff Working Paper No. 151 (Washington, DC, Mar.).

Caldwell, J.C. (1963): "The demographic background", in T.J. Silcock and E.K. Fisk (eds.): <u>The political economy of independent Malaya</u> (Canberra, Australian National University).

Caldwell, M. (1968): <u>Indonesia</u> (Oxford, Oxford University Press).

Castles, L. (1965): "Socialism and the private business: The latest phase", in <u>Bulletin of Indonesian Economic Studies</u> (Canberra), June.

Central Bank of Ceylon (1974): <u>Bulletin No. 5</u> (Colombo), May.

--- (1975): <u>Review of the Economy</u> (Colombo).

--- (1976): <u>Review of the Economy</u> (Colombo).

Central Statistical Office of Poland (1957): <u>Industry statistics, 1945-1955</u> (Warsaw).

Chan, P. (1980): Regional industrial policies and employment shifts in intermediate urban centres in Peninsular Malaysia, Intermediate Cities in Asia Conference (Honolulu, Hawaii, East-West Center).

--- (1981a): Case study of migrant settlers in three land schemes in Peninsular Malaysia, report on ASEAN migration in relation to rural development (Kuala Lumpur, University of Malaya).

--- (1981b): The political economy of urban squatting in metropolitan Kuala Lumpur (Kuala Lumpur, University of Malaya).

--- (1982a): Preliminary findings of survey on out-migration in West Johor region (Kuala Lumpur, University of Malaya).

--- (ed.) (1982b): Malay female migrant workers (Kuala Lumpur, University of Malaya).

Chander, R. (1972): Urban conurbations: Population and households in the gazetted towns and their adjoining built-up areas (Kuala Lumpur, Department of Statistics).

--- (1973): Age distribution (Kuala Lumpur, Department of Statistics).

Cheong, K.C. (1979): Regional development in Malaysia (Tokyo, Institute of Developing Economies).

Ciechocińska, M. (1978): "Polityka migracyjna Polski Ludowej w latach 1945-1974", in Problemy migracji wewnetrznych w Polsce i ZSRR (Warsaw, Państwowe Wydawnictwo Ekonomiczne).

City Hall, Kuala Lumpur (1981): Report on squatters.

City and Industrial Development Corporation of Maharashtra (CIDCO), (1973): New Bombay - Draft development plan (Bombay).

Collier, J.V. (1928): "Forestry in Nepal", in P. Landon: Nepal (London, Constable), Vol. II, Ch. IX.

Dasgupta, P. (1979): "Perspective of Dandakaranya", in Desh (Calcutta), 17 Feb.

Davis, K. (1951): The population of India and Pakistan (Princeton, New Jersey, Princeton University Press).

de Jong, J.A. (1976): De industrialisatie in Nederland tussen 1850 en 1914 (Nijmegen, Sun).

de Witt, J.B. (1973): "The Kabupaten programme", in Bulletin of Indonesian Economic Studies, Vol. IX, No. 1.

Dias, H.D. (1977): Dispersal of human settlements: A study of the Sri Lankan experience, paper presented at the Expert Group Meeting on Migration and Human Settlements, ESCAP, Bangkok, 7-13 June.

Dietz, T. (1977): Dutch state monopolistic imperialism with regard to Indonesia a historical and contemporary case study, paper for the Workshop on Imperialism and the Spatial Analysis of Peripheral Capitalism, Amsterdam, May.

--- (1979): "The redevelopment of Dutch imperialism with regard to Indonesia since 1965", in P. Zarembka (ed.): Research in political economy (Greenwich, Connecticut, Jai Press), Vol. 2.

Dobby, E.H.G. (1952): "Resettlement transforms Malaya: A case history of relocating the population of an Asian rural society", in Economic Development and Cultural Change (Chicago, Illinois), Vol. 1, No. 3.

Dziewoński, K. and Malisz, B. (1978): Przeksztalcenia przestrzennogospodarczej struktury kraju (Warsaw, Państwowe Wydawnictwo Naukowe).

Ellman, A.O. et al. (1976): Land settlement in Sri Lanka (Colombo, Agrarian Research and Training Institute).

Esman, M.J. (1978): Landless and near-landlessness in developing countries (Ithaca, New York, Cornell University, Center for International Studies).

Fallenbuchl, Z.M. (1974): "The impact of the development strategy on urbanisation: Poland, 1950-1970", in A. Brown, J. Licari and E. Neuberger (eds.): Urban and social economics in market and planned economies (New York, Praeger), pp. 287-318.

--- (1977): "Internal migration and economic development under socialism: The case of Poland", in A. Brown and E. Neuberger (eds.): Internal migration: A comparative perspective (New York, Academic Press), pp. 305-328.

Farmer, B.H. (1952): "Pioneer colonisation schemes", in Pacific Affairs (Vancouver), 25 Dec.

--- (1957): Pioneer peasant colonisation schemes in Ceylon (London, Oxford University Press).

Findley, S. (1977): Planning for internal migration: A review of issues and policies in developing countries (Washington, DC, United States Department of Commerce, Bureau of the Census).

Frenkel, I. (1974): Tendencje zmian zatrudnienia w rolnictwie polskim w latach 1950-1970 (Warsaw, Instytut Rozwoju Wsi i Rolnictwa PAN).

--- (1976a): Zmiany zatrudnienia w rolnictwie w latach 1970-1974 (Warsaw, Instytut Rozwoju Wsi i Rolnictwa PAN).

--- (1976b): "Ludność wiejska i zatrudnienie w rolnictwie w latach 1946-1974", in Wieś i Rolnictwo (Warsaw), No. 3.

Furnivall, J.S. (1944): Netherlands India (New York, Macmillan).

Ganguli, B.N. (1955): "Institutional implications of a bolder plan with special reference to China's experience", in Planning Commission, India: Papers relating to the formulation of the Second Five-Year Plan (New Delhi).

Gaude, J. (1982): Phénomène migratoire et politiques associées dans le contexte africain (Geneva, ILO).

Geertz, C. (1963): Agricultural involution: The process of ecological change in Indonesia (Berkeley, California, University of California Press).

Glassburner, B. (1962): "Economic policy-making in Indonesia, 1950-57", in Economic Development and Cultural Change (Chicago, Illinois), Vol. X, No. 2.

--- (1971): "Indonesian economic policy after Sukarno", in B. Glassburner (ed.): The economy of Indonesia: Selected readings (Ithaca, New York, Cornell University Press).

Godbole, M.D. (1978): Industrial dispersal policies (Bombay, Himalaya Publishing House).

Gorzelak, E. (1972): Polityka agrarna (Warsaw, Szkola Główna Planowania i Statystyki).

Gorzelak, E. and Grochowski, Z. (1971): "Dochody ludności rolniczej", in Nowe Drogi (Warsaw), Vol. 10, No. 269.

Gosling, L.A.P. (1963): "Migratory agricultural labour in Malayan padi production", in Proceedings, 9th Pacific Science Congress (Anthropology and Social Sciences), No. 3.

Government of Ceylon, National Planning Council (1959): Ten Year Plan (Colombo).

Government of India: (1961): Census of India, 1961, Part III-C(iii): migration tables (New Delhi).

--- (1979): Census of India, 1971, Series 1 - India, Part II-D(i): migration tables (tables D-i to D-iv) (New Delhi).

---, Department of Rehabilitation (1959): Report, 1958-59 (New Delhi).

--- --- (1978): Report, 1977-78 (New Delhi).

--- --- (1979): Letter from Deputy Secretary, DO No. 14/33/79-Desk III, dated 21 November (New Delhi).

---, Estimates Committee (1962): 170th Report on the Ministry of Rehabilitation (New Delhi, Estimates Committee, 1961-62, Second Lok Sabha, Lok Sabha Secretariat).

--- --- (1965): 72nd Report - Dandakaranya Project (New Delhi, Estimates Committee, 1964-65, Third Lok Sabha, Lok Sabha Secretariat).

--- --- (1978): Report, 1977-78 (New Delhi).

--- --- (1979): Dandakaranya Project - Exodus of settlers (1978), 30th Report, presented to Lok Sabha on 9 April (New Delhi, Sixth Lok Sabha, Lok Sabha Secretariat).

---, Ministry of Health (1965): Report of the Committee on Urban Land Policy (New Delhi).

---, Ministry of Works and Housing (1977): Report of the Task Force on Planning and Development of Small and Medium Towns and Cities (New Delhi), Vol. I.

Government of India, Ministry of Works and Housing (1979): "Guidelines for centrally sponsored scheme for integrated development of small and medium towns", letter from the Ministry to Chief Secretaries, dated 20 December (New Delhi).

---, Planning Commission (1952): First Five-Year Plan (New Delhi).

--- --- (1956): Second Five-Year Plan (New Delhi).

--- --- (1969): Fourth Five-Year Plan (New Delhi).

--- --- (1973): Draft Fifth Five-Year Plan (New Delhi), Vol. II.

--- --- (1976): Fifth Five-Year Plan (New Delhi).

--- --- (1978): Draft Five-Year Plan: New Bombay project (1978-79 to 1982-83) (New Delhi).

--- --- (1979): Revised Draft Sixth Plan (1978-83) (New Delhi).

Government of Malaysia (1971): Second Malaysia Plan, 1971-1975 (Kuala Lumpur, Government Press).

--- (1973): Mid-term Review of the Second Malaysia Plan, 1971-1975 (Kuala Lumpur, Government Press).

--- (1976): Third Malaysia Plan, 1976-1980 (Kuala Lumpur, Government Press).

--- (1979): Mid-term Review of the Third Malaysia Plan, 1976-1980 (Kuala Lumpur, Government Press).

Government of Nepal (1956): Brief draft of Five-Year Plan (Kathmandu).

---, Ministry of Law and Justice (1966): Legal code formulated during the reign of King Surendra Bikram Shah (Kathmandu, Kanoon Byabastha Semiti).

Government of Sri Lanka, Department of Census and Statistics (1977): Sri Lanka Yearbook (Colombo).

--- (1978): General report: Census of Population, 1971 (Colombo).

--- Ministry of Industries and Scientific Affairs (1971): Ceylon's industrial policy (Colombo).

Government of Sri Lanka, Ministry of Industries and Scientific Affairs (1976): Preliminary report on the field survey of manufacturing industry in Sri Lanka, 1975-76 (Colombo).

Gray, R.H. (1974): "The decline in mortality in Ceylon and the demographic effects of malaria control", in Population Studies (London), July.

Grenville, S. (1973): "Survey of recent developments", in Bulletin of Indonesian Economic Studies (Canberra), Vol. X, No. 1.

Griffin, K. (1973): "Policy options for rural development", in Oxford Bulletin of Economics and Statistics (Oxford), Nov., pp. 239-274.

--- (1976): Land concentration and rural poverty (London, Macmillan).

Grochowski, Z. and Woś, A. (eds.) (1979): Procesy rozwojowe polskiego rolnictwa (Warsaw, Państwowe Wydawnictwo Rolnicze i Leśne).

Gunasekera, H.A.S. and Godippily, H.M.A. (1971): "Employment creation through regional development: Recent experience in Sri Lanka", in International Labour Review (Geneva), July-Aug., pp. 39-52.

Gunatilleke, G. (1973): The rural urban balance and development: The experience of Sri Lanka (Colombo, Marga Institute), Vol. 2, No. 1.

Gupta, D.B. (1979): Employment implications of cottage industries, working paper (Delhi, Institute of Economic Growth).

Gupta, D.B. and Dasgupta, A.K. (1979): Benefit-cost analysis of rural industrialisation programme, working paper (Delhi, Institute of Economic Growth).

Hamzah-Sendut (1962): "Resettlement villages in Malaya", in Geography (Sheffield), Vol. 47, pp. 41-46.

Hansen, N. (1979): A review and evaluation of attempts to direct migrants to smaller and intermediate-size cities paper presented at UN/UNFPA Workshop on Population Distribution Policies in Development Planning, Bangkok, 4-13 September.

Hardjono, J.M. (1977): Transmigration in Indonesia (Kuala Lumpur, Oxford University Press).

Heeren, H.J. (1967): Transmigratie in Indonesië (Meppel, Drenthe, Boom).

Hickson, J. (1973): "Rural development and class contradictions on Java", in R. Mortimer (ed.): Showcase state: The illusion of Indonesia's "accelerated modernisation" (Sydney, Angus and Robertson).

Indraratna, A.D.V. de S. (1966): "The guaranteed price scheme and marketed agricultural surplus in a peasant economy", in University of Ceylon Review (Colombo), Apr. and Oct., Vol. XXIV, Nos. 1 and 2.

International Labour Organisation (1976): Poverty and landlessness in rural Asia (Geneva).

International Review Group of Social Science Research on Population and Development (IRG) (1979): Final report. Social science research for population policy: Directions for the 1980's (Mexico City, El Colegio de Mexico).

Ishikawa, S. (1978): Labour absorption in Asian agriculture (Bangkok, ILO/ARTEP).

Iżyk, W. (1975): Ruchy migracyjne w rejonie uprzemyslawianym (Warsaw, Państwowe Wydawnictwo Naukowe).

Jayasuriya, J.D. (1977): Educational policies and progress during British rule in Ceylon (Sri Lanka), 1796-1948 (New York, International Publications Service).

Jones, G.W. (1965): "The employment characteristics of small towns in Malaya", in Malayan Economic Review (Singapore), Vol. 10.

Jorgenson, D.W. (1961): "The development of a dual economy", in Economic Journal (London), June.

Joshi, P.C. (1980): Perspectives of planners from above and peoples' perception from below: The problem of bridging the hiatus, paper for seminar on "Development of Backward Areas with Special Reference to Hill Areas", organised by Giri Institute of Development Studies and Government of Uttar Pradesh, Nainital, 21-24 April; mimeographed.

Józafowicz, A. (1962): "Polityka ludnościowa i zatrudnienia w Polsce", in Biuletyn Instytutu Gospodarstwa
Spolecznego (Warsaw), No. 4.

Kamal, S. (1975): "Industrialization strategy, regional
development and the growth centre approach: A case
study of West Malaysia", in Proceedings of the
Seminar on Industrialization Strategies and the Growth
Pole Approach to Regional Planning and Development: The
Asian Experience, Nagoya, 4-13 November (UNCRD).

Kannagara, I. (1954): A demographic study of the city of
Colombo, Monograph No. 2 (Colombo, Department of Census
and Statistics).

Kansakar, V.B.S. (1974): Population change in Nepal: A
study of mobility during 1911-1961, unpublished Ph.D.
thesis (Patna University).

--- (1978): "A review of policy and research on
migration", in M.S.J.B. Rana (ed.): National seminar on
employment and population planning, 14-16 November 1978
(Kathmandu, Centre for Economic Development and Administration, Tribhuvan University).

--- (1979): Effectiveness of planned resettlement programme in Nepal (Kathmandu, Centre for Economic
Development and Administration, Tribhuvan University).

--- (1980): Land resettlement policy as a population distribution strategy in Nepal, paper presented at the
symposium on Development and Population Redistribution
in South Asia, organised by the Commission on Population Geography, International Geographical Union,
Karachi, 4-10 January.

Karpiński, A. (1965): Fazy rozwoju gospodarczego Polski
Ludowej (Warsaw, Ksiażka i Wiedza).

Karunatilake, H.N.S. (1974): "Changes in income distribution in Sri Lanka", in Staff Studies (Colombo,
Central Bank of Ceylon), Apr.

--- (1974): "Changes in income distribution in Sri
Lanka", in Staff Bulletin (Colombo, Central Bank of
Ceylon), Apr.

Kernial, S. (1964): "Emergency resettlement in Malaya",
in Journal of Tropical Geography (Singapore), Vol. 18.

Kirkpatrick, W. (1811): An account of the Kingdom of Nepal (London, Miller).

Kruger, K. (1979): A study of growth centres in Peninsular Malaysia (Kuala Lumpur, University of Malaya; mimeographed).

Kunasingham, A.S. (1972): Economics of new land settlement projects in Ceylon, unpublished Ph.D. thesis (University of Hawaii).

Kuziński, S. (1976): Polska na gospodarczej mapie świata (Warsaw, Państwowe Wydawnictwo Ekonomiczne).

Landon, P. (1928): Nepal (London, Constable), Vol. II, Ch. II.

Laquian, A.A. (1979): Review and evaluation of accommodationist policies in population redistribution, paper presented at UN/UNFPA Workshop on Population Distribution Policies in Development Planning, Bangkok, 4-13 September.

Latuch, K. (1978): "Przeplywy ludności z rolnictwa do pozarolniczych działów gospodarki narodowej w latach 1951-2000", in Wieś i Rolnictwo (Warsaw), No. 1.

Latuch, M. (1973): "Pochodzenie terytorialne mieszkańcow Warszawy", in Kronika Warszawy (Warsaw), No. 3.

Lee Boon Thong (1977): Metropolitan growth in Southeast Asia: The role of small towns in Peninsular Malaysia, paper presented at the Conference on Southeast Asian Studies (Kota Kinabalu, Sabah, Malaysia), November.

Lee, E.S. (1966): "A theory of migration", in Demography (Washington, DC), Vol. 3, No. 1.

Leeden, C.B. van der (1952): Het aspect van landbouwkolonisatie in het bevolkingsprobleem van Java (with a summary in English), Ph.D. thesis (The Hague, University of Leiden, Faculty of Law).

Leiserson, M.W. (1974): "Employment perspectives and policy approaches in Indonesia", in International Labour Review (Geneva), Vol. 109, No. 4.

Leszek, A.K. (1975): "Education and internal migration", in H.V. Muhsam (ed.): Education and population: Mutual impacts (Dolhain, Liège, Ordina).

van Leur, J.C. (1955): _Indonesian trade and society_ (The Hague, van Hoeve).

Lewis, A. (1954): "Economic development with unlimited supplies of labour", in _Manchester School of Economic and Social Studies_ (Manchester), May.

Lewis, J.P. (1962): _Quiet crisis in India_ (Washington, DC, Brookings Institution).

Mabogunje, A.L. (1979): _Arguments for government intervention to influence regional population distribution_, paper presented at UN/UNFPA Workshop on Population Distribution Policies in Development Planning, Bangkok, 4-13 September.

MacAndrews, C. (1977): _Mobility and modernisation: The Federal Land Development Authority and its role in modernising the rural Malay_ (Jakarta, Gadja Meda University Press).

--- (1978): "Transmigration in Indonesia: Prospects and problems", in _Asian Survey_ (Berkeley, California), May, pp. 458-472.

Mackie, J.A.C. (1971): "The Indonesian economy, 1950-1963", in B. Glassburner (ed.): _The economy of Indonesia_ (Ithaca, New York, Cornell University Press).

Maharashtra Economic Development Council (1970): _Twin city for Bombay - Development prospects and problems_, seminar proceedings and papers (Bombay).

Mangkusuwondo, S. (1973): "Dilemmas in Indonesian economic development", in _Bulletin of Indonesian Economic Studies_, Vol. IX, No. 2.

Marga Institute (1976): _Major issues arising from the transfer of technology: A case study of Sri Lanka_, report prepared for UNCTAD (Colombo).

McNicoll, G. (1968): "Internal migration in Indonesia: Descriptive notes", in _Indonesia_ (Jakarta), April.

Meegama, S.A. (1969): "The decline in maternal and infant mortality and its relation to malaria eradication", in _Population Studies_ (London), Vol. XXIII, No. 2.

von der Mehden, F.R. (1973): _Industrialization in Malaysia: A Penang micro-study_ (Houston, Texas, Rice University).

Missen, G.J. (1972): Viewpoint on Indonesia: A geographical study (Melbourne, Nelson).

Mitra, A. (1976): Where do we go from here? The problems of Calcutta metropolitan region, paper for Conference on Calcutta-2000 (Calcutta, Indian Chamber of Commerce; mimeographed working paper).

Morris, C.J. (1928): The Gurkhas (London, John Lane, The Bodley Head).

Mortimer, R. (1973): "Indonesia: Growth or development?", in R. Mortimer (ed.): Showcase state: The illusion of Indonesia's accelerated modernisation (Sydney, Angus and Robertson).

Munro, R. (1977): "The real China: Life in the city is only for the select few", in Globe and Mail (Toronto), 10 Oct. 1977, pp. 1-2, cited in Simmons (1979).

Narayanan, S. (1975): Urban in-migration and urban labour absorption: A study of metropolitan urban Selangor, unpublished M. Econ. thesis (Kuala Lumpur, University of Malaya).

Narayanasamy, C. (1974): New approaches to settlement in Sri Lanka (Peradeniya, Ceylon Studies Seminar).

National Council of Applied Economic Research, India (1963): Development of Dandakaranya (New Delhi).

Nitisastro, W. (1961): "Public policies, land tenure and population movements", in W. Froehlich (ed.): Land tenure, industrialisation and social stability: Experiences and prospects in Asia (Milwaukee, Wisconsin, Marquette University Press).

--- (1970): Population trends in Indonesia (Ithaca, New York, Cornell University Press).

Oberai, A.S. (1979): "Determinants of rural-urban migration and its implications for rural areas with special reference to ILO research", in IUSSP: Economic and Demographic Change: Issues for the 1980's, Proceedings of the Conference, Helsinki, 1978 (Liège, Ordina).

Oberai, A.S. and Manmohan Singh, H.K. (1980): "Migration, remittances and rural development: Findings of a case study in the Indian Punjab", in International Labour Review (Geneva) Mar.-Apr., pp. 229-241.

Oberai, A.S. and Manmohan Singh, H.K. (1983): <u>Causes and consequences of internal migration: A study in the Indian Punjab</u> (New Delhi, Oxford University Press).

Ocampo, R. (1977): "Policies and programs influencing spatial mobility", in <u>Philippine Labor Review</u> (Manila), Vol. 2, No. 3.

Oey, M. and Astika, K.S. (1978): <u>Social and economic implications of transmigration in Indonesia: A policy-oriented review and synopsis of existing research</u> (Jakarta, University of Indonesia).

Ostrowski, L. (1978): <u>Przeobrażenia warunków bytu rodzin chlopskich w procesie socjalistycznej przebudowy rolnictwa w PRL</u> (Warsaw, Wyższa Szkola Nauk Spolecznych przy KC PZPR).

Paauw, D.S. (1963): "From colonial to guided economy", in R.T. McVey (ed.): <u>Indonesia</u> (New Haven, Connecticut, Hraf Press).

Palmer, I. (1977): <u>The new rice in Indonesia</u> (Geneva, UNRISD).

Palmer, I. and Castles, L. (1971): "The textile industry", in B. Glassburner (ed.): <u>The economy of Indonesia</u> (Ithaca, New York, Cornell University Press).

--- (1978): <u>The Indonesian economy since 1965</u> (London, Frank Cass).

Palte, J.G.O. (1976): "De Indonesische vijf-jaren plannen (Repelita)", in <u>Geografisch Tijdschrift</u> (Amsterdam), Vol. I, No. 2.

Palte, J.G.O. and Tempelman, G.J. (1974): <u>Indonesië</u> (Bussum, Holland, Romen).

Peek, P. (1980): <u>Urban poverty, migration and land reform in Ecuador</u>, Occasional Papers No. 79 (The Hague, Institute of Social Studies).

Peek, P. and Standing, G. (1979): "Rural-urban migration and government policies in low-income countries", in <u>International Labour Review</u> (Geneva), Nov.-Dec. pp. 747-762.

--- (1982): <u>State policies and migration: Studies in Latin America and the Caribbean</u> (London, Croom Helm).

Pelzer, K.J. (1945): Pioneer settlement in the Asiatic tropics (New York, Institute of Pacific Relations).

--- (1971): "The agricultural foundation", in B. Glassburner (ed.): The economy of Indonesia (Ithaca, New York, Cornell University Press).

Pérez-Sainz, J.P. (1979): Transmigration and accumulation in Indonesia (Geneva, ILO; mimeographed World Employment Programme research working paper; restricted).

Pluvier, J.M. (1965): Confrontations, a study in Indonesian politics (Oxford, Oxford University Press).

Pohorille, M. (1966): "Rozwiazanie problemu przeludnienia agrarnego w świetle doświadczeń Polski", in A. Müller and A. Woś (eds.): Rolnictwo a wzrost gospodarczy (Warsaw, Państwowe Wydawnictwo Rolnicze i Leśne).

Pryor, R.J. (1971): Internal migration and urbanisation: An introduction and bibliography, Monograph Series No. 2 (Townsville, Queensland, James Cook University, Geography Department).

--- (1972a): Rural-rural migration and frontier settlement schemes: The case of West Malaysia, paper for Commission on Population Geography, Symposium on Internal Migration, 22nd International Geographical Congress, Edmonton (mimeographed).

--- (1972b): The changing urbanisation space of West Malaysia, paper for Urban Geography Section, 22nd International Geographical Congress, Montreal (mimeographed).

--- (1974): Spatial analysis of internal migration: West Malaysia, Monograph Series No. 5 (Townsville, Queensland, James Cook University, Geography Department).

--- (1975): "Population redistribution and development planning in South East Asia", in W. Brockie et al. (ed.): Proceedings of the International Geographical Union Regional Conference and Eighth New Zealand Geography Conference (Hamilton, Auckland Geographical Society).

--- (1976a): Methods of analysing population redistribution policies, paper for Symposium on Problems of Macroscale Research in Population Geography, International Geographical Union, Minsk, USSR.

Pryor, R.J. (1976b): <u>Population redistribution: Policy research</u>, Studies in Migration and Urbanisation No. 2 (Canberra, Australian National University, Department of Demography).

--- (ed.) (1979): <u>Migration and development in South-East Asia: A demographic perspective</u> (Kuala Lumpur, Oxford University Press).

Raj, M. (1978): "Housing strategy till 2001", in C.S. Chandrasekhara and D. Raj (eds.): <u>Urban perspectives - 2001</u> (New Delhi, National Institute of Urban Affairs).

Rama Gowda, K.S. (1977): "Bangalore: Planning in practice", in A.G. Noble and A.K. Dutt (eds.): <u>India's urbanization and planning: Vehicles of modernization</u> (New Delhi, Tata McGraw-Hill).

Rao, V.K.R.V. and Desai, P.B. (1965): <u>Greater Delhi - A study in urbanization: 1940-1957</u> (Bombay, Asia Publishing House).

Regmi, M.C. (1971): <u>A study in Nepali economic history</u> (New Delhi, Manjusri Publishing House).

--- (1976): <u>Landownership in Nepal</u> (Berkeley, California, University of California Press).

Roff, W.R. (1967): <u>The origins of Malay nationalism</u> (Kuala Lumpur, University of Malaya Press).

Romero, L.K. and Flinn, W.L. (1976): "Effects of structural and change variables on the selectivity of migration: The case of a Colombian peasant community", in <u>Inter-American Economic Affairs</u> (Washington, DC), Vol. 29, No. 4, pp. 35-58.

Rosner, A. (1977): <u>Odplyw ludności ze wsi i rolnictwa</u>, unpublished Ph.D. thesis (Warsaw).

Rudner, M. (1976): "The Indonesian military and economic policy", in <u>Modern Asian Studies</u> (London), Vol. 10, Part 2.

Samaraweera, V.K. (1973): "Land policy and peasant colonization, 1914-1948", in K.M. de Silva (ed.): <u>History of Ceylon</u> (Peradenya, University of Ceylon), Vol. III, pp. 446-460.

Senanayake, D.S. (1935): <u>Agriculture and patriotism</u> (Colombo, Associated Newspapers of Ceylon).

Sethuraman, S.V. (1976): Jakarta: Urban development and employment (Geneva, ILO).

Shryock, H.S. and Siegel, J.S. (1973): The methods and materials of demography (Washington, DC, United States Department of Commerce).

Simmons, A.B. (1979): "Slowing metropolitan city growt! in Asia: policies, programs and results", in Population and Development Review (New York), Mar.

Sivaramakrishnan, K.C. (1977): New towns in India: Report on a study of selected new towns in the Eastern region (Calcutta, Indian Institute of Management; mimeographed).

Soebiantoro, R. (1974): "Experiences in the implementation of transmigration in Indonesia", in The role of transmigration in national and regional development, proceedings of the 1971 Transmigration Workshop (Jakarta).

Soehoed, A.R. (1967): "Manufacturing in Indonesia", in Bulletin of Indonesian Economic Studies (Canberra), No. 8.

Standing, G. and Sukdeo, F. (1977): "Labour migration and development in Guyana", in International Labour Review (Geneva), Nov.-Dec., pp. 303-313.

State Council of Ceylon (1932): Hansard (London), 28 Jan.

Stohr, W. (1979): Evaluation of some arguments against government intervention to influence territorial population distribution, paper presented at UN/UNFPA Workshop on Population Distribution Policies in Development Planning, Bangkok, 4-13 September.

Stpiczyński, T. (1971): Wewnetrzny ruch wedrówkowy ludności (Warsaw, Glówny Urzad Statystyczny).

Sundrum, R.M. (1975): "Manufacturing employment", in Bulletin of Indonesian Economic Studies (Canberra), Vol. XI, No. 1.

Suratman, and Guiness, P. (1977): "The changing focus of transmigration", in Bulletin of Indonesian Economic Studies (Canberra), July, pp. 78-101.

Taeuber, I.B. (1949): "Ceylon as a demographic laboratory: Preface to analysis", in Population Index (Princeton, New Jersey), Oct.

Taylor, J. (1974): "The economic strategy of the 'New Order'", in J. Taylor et al.: Repression and exploitation in Indonesia (Nottingham, Spokesman Books).

Thirlwall, A.P. (1972): Growth and development (London, Macmillan).

Thomas, K.D. and Panglaykim, J. (1966): "Indonesian exports: Performance and prospects 1950-1970, Part I", in Bulletin of Indonesian Economic Studies (Canberra), No. 5.

--- (1969). "Indonesia's development cabinet background to current problems and the Five-Year Plan", in Asian Survey (Berkeley, California), Vol. IX, No. 4.

Todaro, M.P. (1976): Internal migration in developing countries (Geneva, ILO).

Townpore, P.M. (1979): "Employment decentralisation: Policy instruments for large cities in less developed countries", in Progress in Planning (London, Pergamon Press), Vol. 10, Part 2.

United Kingdom, Her Majesty's Stationery Office (1965): Nepal and the Gurkhas (London).

United Nations (1970): Methods of measuring internal migration, Manuals on methods of estimating population VI (New York; sales No. 70.XIII.3).

---, Department of Economic and Social Affairs (1980): World population trends and policies: 1979 monitoring report, Vol. I: Population trends, Population Studies No. 70 (New York).

---, Economic and Social Commission for Asia and the Pacific (1975): Comparative study of population growth and agricultural change: Case study of Sri Lanka, Asian Population Studies Series No. 23 (Bangkok).

--- --- (1976): Population of Sri Lanka, Country Monograph Series No. 4 (Bangkok).

--- --- (1977): Report on the Expert Group Meeting on Migration and Human Settlements, Asian Population Studies Series No. 38 proceedings of a meeting held in Bangkok, 7-13 June (Bangkok).

Utrecht, E. (1969): "Land reform in Indonesia", in Bulletin of Indonesian Economic Studies (Canberra), Vol. V, No. 3.

Utrecht, E. (1975): "The military élite", in M. Caldwell et al.: Ten years of military terror in Indonesia (Nottingham, Spokesman Books).

Vamathevan, S. (1960): Internal migration in Ceylon, 1946-1953, Monograph No. 13 (Colombo, Department of Census and Statistics).

Wallerstein, I. (1974): The modern world system (New York, Academic Press).

Weerackody, K.N. (1970): Colonization in Ceylon: A review (Colombo; mimeographed).

Weiner, M. (1973): "Socio-political consequences of interstate migration in India", in W.H. Wriggins and J.F. Guyot (eds.): Population, politics and the future of southern Asia (New York, Columbia University Press).

--- (1975): Sons of the soil: Migration, ethnicity and natives in India (Cambridge, Massachusetts, Center for International Studies, Massachusetts Institute of Technology).

--- (1978): Sons of the soil: Migration and ethnic conflict in India (Bombay, Oxford University Press).

Wertheim, W.F. (1956): Indonesian society in transition (The Hague, van Hoeve).

--- (1964): "Inter-island migration in Indonesia", in East-West Parallels (The Hague, van Hoeve).

--- (1978): Indonesië: van vorstenrijk tot neo-kolonie (Amsterdam, Boom Meppel).

Whering, K. (1976): Squatters in the Federal Territory: Analysis and programme recommendation (Kuala Lumpur, Urban Development Authority).

Wieś w liczbach (1954) (Warsaw, Ksiażka i Wiedza).

Ying, Soon Lee (1977): An analysis of internal migration in Peninsular Malaysia: dimensions, causes and some policy implications, University of the Philippines, Council for Asian Manpower Studies, Discussion Paper Series 77-06, June, quoted in Simmons, op. cit.

Young, M.L. (in progress): Internal migration in Peninsular Malaysia, Ph.D. thesis (Canberra, Australian National University, Department of Demography).

Zaman, M.A. (1974): <u>Evaluation of land reform in Nepal</u> (Kathmandu, His Majesty's Government, Land Reform Department).

AUTHOR INDEX

SUBJECT INDEX

(Note: page numbers underlined indicate tables)

India (continued)

Resettlement (continued)
indigenous population
and 248
infrastructure for 238,
250
lacking 242, 244
land ownership under
241, 243-4, 250
land shortage for 250
locations of, disadvan-
tageous 242, 243
malpractices in land
distribution 237, 242
of migrants 217, 220
of refugees, in Andaman
and Nicobar Islands
174-5, 176, 177, 178
price of holdings 239,
241
size of holdings 239,
240-1, 244
(see also land develop-
ment; land settlement;
settlers)
Rural areas
amenities in 21-2, 25,
264
co-operatives 219, 250,
264
credit facilities 100
improving attractiveness
of 11, 19-20, 25, 64,
128-9
industrialisation in 156,
160, 181-2
cost-benefit analysis
156, 160
infrastructure 308-9
labour recruitment in,
planned 304-6
output in, out-migration
increasing demand for
8-9
poverty in 2-3, 16, 29,
41, 63-4
income support and
21
population of 252, 280-1,
282, 293

resettlement in 12,
14-17, 25-6 (see also
Sri Lanka)
Rural development 11,
15, 18, 19-22, 25;
Malaysia 15-17, 27-9;
Poland 21; Sri Lanka
99-100, 129
integrated 21-2, 25, 50
Malaysia 54, 63-6
urbanisation and 50
(see also land settle-
ment)
Rural-to-rural migration
8; India 139-40, 141,
142, 180; Malaysia 31,
40, 46-7, 50, 64, 65
Rural-urban commuting 8,
18, 22n, 60; Poland 8,
262, 278-9, 291
Rural-urban migration
India 137, 139-40,
141-4, 156, 158,
180-2; Malaysia 27,
32, 39, 54, 64, 65, 66,
69, 70-1, 72-6; Nepal
247; Poland 26,
285-6; Sri Lanka 89,
93, 105, 117, 128
age groups 278, 279,
283, 293, 294, 295,
298, 299
agriculture and 255,
286, 287, 291, 302-3,
307-10
causes of 2-8
Poland 251, 254, 287,
291, 302, 307
consequences of 8-10
control of, by govern-
ment 7, 9-10, 24-30,
39, 60
education and 279,
280, 293, 295-6, 297,
303
flows of 276-8, 286-7,
288-9, 290
reducing 19-24, 66,
105, 117

Rural-urban migration
(continued)
industrialisation and
251, 255, 259, 287,
291, 302-3
male/female 277, 278,
279, 294, 295, 296,
298, 299
population distribution
and 292, 293
restrictions on 12-13,
306-7
state influence on
304-10
within Indian states
138
(see also urban areas;
in-migration)

Satellite towns 19
Schools stimulating out-
migration 6
Settlers
departure from settle-
ment 165, 166,
167-70
incomes of 44
indigenous population
and 137, 180-1,
205-6, 219, 225, 248
living standards 250
loans for 193, 195, 202,
217, 243-4
number of 46, 47, 52-3
second generation
employment problem
49, 76, 244
selection of 94-5, 236,
240, 243 (see also
migrants, selection of)
Slums 147-8, 150, 158
Social benefits in agriculture 269, 271, 274
conditions for 265,
273-4, 291
Social security 265, 271
Social services investments,
urban 6-7
Social welfare 21, 105,
191, 215-16, 255

Socialist countries
causes of rural-urban
migration in 7 (see
also planned
economies)
Socialist transformation,
agricultural 262-6, 291
Spatial distribution of
economic activity 138
(see also industrial
decentralisation; popu-
lation distribution)
Squatter settlements 72-6,
98, 147
Sri Lanka
education in 105-6, 107
foreign investment
incentives 129
hospitals 108, 111, 112,
113
housing 112, 114
industries, distribution
of 133-4
irrigation schemes 16,
95, 96, 129
land reform 100-1
Lorenz curves 135
Mahakandarawa land
settlement 117-21,
118, 120
malaria 106-8, 109-10,
128
population
data 80, 81
distribution 79, 115,
128, 134
growth 91-2, 89, 93
rural development 99-
100
rural-urban migration
89, 93, 105, 117, 128
social welfare 105
squatters in settlement
areas 98
transport 114
urban population growth
89, 92, 93
village councils 89